SPIRITUAL COMPANIONING

A GUIDE TO PROTESTANT THEOLOGY AND PRACTICE

ANGELA H. REED, RICHARD R. OSMER,

AND MARCUS G. SMUCKER

Baker Academic

a division of Baker Publishing Group

Grand Rapids, Michigan

© 2015 by Angela H. Reed, Richard R. Osmer, and Marcus G. Smucker

Published by Baker Academic
a division of Baker Publishing Group
P.O. Box 6287, Grand Rapids, MI 49516–6287
www.bakeracademic.com

Printed in the United States of America

Library of Congress Cataloging-in-Publication Data
Reed, Angela H.
    Spiritual companioning : a guide to Protestant theology and practice / Angela H. Reed,
Richard R. Osmer, and Marcus G. Smucker.
        pages cm
    Includes bibliographical references and index.
    ISBN 978-0-8010-4989-7 (pbk.)
    1. Spiritual formation—Protestant churches. 2. Spiritual direction—Protestant churches.
3. Interpersonal relations—Religious aspects—Christianity. 4. Mentoring—Religious
aspects—Christianity. 5. Protestant churches—Doctrines. I. Title.
BV4511.R435 2015
253.5′3—dc23   2015020885

15   16   17   18   19   20   21   7   6   5   4   3   2   1

To Marcus G. Smucker,
friend, colleague, mentor,
and spiritual guide

Though you crossed over to be with our Lord as this book was completed, it bears witness to your wisdom and is a gift to all who practice spiritual companioning.

Contents

Acknowledgments   ix

Introduction   xi

1. Spiritual Companioning as Presence   1

2. Spiritual Companioning in the Congregation   26

3. Spiritual Companioning in Spiritual Direction   51

4. Spiritual Companioning in Small Groups   77

5. Spiritual Companioning in Everyday Life   101

6. Spiritual Companioning and the Journey of Life   125

7. Spiritual Companioning for Leaders   151

Bibliography   177

Scripture Index   183

Subject Index   185

Acknowledgments

After the completion of this manuscript, Marcus Smucker, one of the primary authors, passed away. We (Angela and Rick) learned a great deal from Marcus over the years, and we cannot imagine this project without his contribution. We dedicate this book to him and are grateful that his final contribution to the field of spiritual companioning comes to expression in this book. It is a tribute to you, Marcus!

A word of special thanks is also due to the persons with whom we have worked at Baker. James Ernest entered into a conversation with us about this project several years ago and has offered guidance and many insights along the way, including thinking through the structure of the book. Arika Theule-Van Dam was our project editor. She was readily available and exceptionally helpful in the final stage of manuscript preparation. We also thank Robert Banning, who served effectively as our copy editor. We are grateful to all of you.

Introduction

Among the smiling faces of those passing through the church doors on Sunday mornings are many who long for deeper, more genuine relationships in their congregations. They hunger for relationships that nurture them and challenge them to grow spiritually and for connections that move past surface pleasantries into the real joys and heartaches of life. In a society that is increasingly fragmented, they are looking for a place to take off their masks and simply belong—to come home to other people and to God.

As most pastors will readily admit, germinating a culture of honest and open conversation about life and faith, a place to be at home with one another, is not an easy task. Some are choosing to address this need by reaching back into the traditions of the church, hunting for wisdom and resources about communal life that continue to have meaning for our contemporary context. One Baptist pastor we spoke with has embraced this path with fervor, calling himself a "scavenger" of various spiritual traditions. But he also recognizes that there are untapped riches within his own historical community. In this book, we explore the history, theology, and practices of spiritual companioning in the Protestant tradition. Like gold miners who travel deep into the earth hoping to spot promising veins in the rock that are worth their time and effort, we are convinced that precious veins within the Protestant tradition, sometimes hidden or overlooked, can help to address the contemporary longing for connection at the level of soul.

This shared conviction brought the three of us together. Our relationships to one another have grown over many years. We have come to trust each other quite deeply and have even companioned one another at different points on our spiritual journeys. In the highly polarized context of American society today, we regard it as a wonderful sign of God's grace that a Baptist,

Mennonite, and Presbyterian could work together with trust and mutual criticism to write a book that speaks for all three of us. This book is different than any one of us would have written by ourselves. It is a sign and witness to the mutual enrichment of the diverse gifts of the one Spirit within the body of Christ. Is this not what our one Lord, the head of the body, truly desires? Is not this sort of unity in mission desperately needed in our world today? With this in mind, we begin with one of our own stories of spiritual companionship.

Discovering Spiritual Companionship

In my early forties, I (Marcus) faced a significant crisis in my life. After serving as the pastor of an inner-city congregation for twelve years, I seemed to "hit a wall." Even though things were going well in the congregation and in my personal life, I began to feel dry and empty emotionally and spiritually. I was still reading Scripture and praying, but my passion for ministry was gone, and preaching was becoming a colossal pain. My prayers seemed fruitless. I could not seem to connect with God anymore. I began to question whether I had done something to cause God to seem so distant.

After six months of struggle, the congregation gave me some extra time in the summer for personal renewal. I participated in several spiritual renewal settings. At the end of that time, in response to a friend's suggestion, I went on a personal retreat alone for several days in a cabin in the mountains. This was my first experience of extended solitude. I spent the time resting and relaxing, hiking and praying, pondering Scripture, writing in my journal, staring out the window, and fasting. By the second day, I recognized that the Spirit was stirring anew within me. I soon noticed that as I became more aware of God, I was also led to deeper awareness of my own thoughts and feelings.

At the end of three days I was in awe. I felt humbled and tired, yet refreshed and deeply reassured of God's presence. For me, the encounter bridged the gap I felt with God and with my own self. I discovered that it was not God who was distant, but it was *I* who needed time and focus to keep opening up to God in new ways.

This experience changed some of my thoughts about who God is and how I relate to God. I began to reflect on my patterns of prayer. I came to realize that sometimes my interactions with God at a preconscious level were still being influenced by earlier feelings of isolation, a sense of emotional abandonment and emptiness rising out of my childhood and youth. I recognized that my prayers sometimes focused more on seeking than receiving, more on my needs than on God's presence and provisions. It was becoming clear that spiritual practices including solitude, meditation, and journaling could help me on this journey.

My primary spiritual challenge was not so much to keep searching for a deeper relationship with God as to continue opening myself to God. I have since lived with the conviction that if I take time to keep opening to God, God is present. God truly desires to be in communion with me. The retreat also changed something about how I understood my role in ministry. I needed to face the realities of my work habits. As the pastor of a growing and thriving congregation in the inner city, I had become overextended for too long. I constantly faced many demands. It began to dawn on me that I was doing more than God was asking of me. I was working hard *for* God but not always *with* God. Although it has been a challenge for me to live into this way of being a minister, my awareness and desire to work *with* rather than *for* has always been before me since then.

Embracing spiritual practices helped me to reimagine my approach to ministry. I wanted to find a way to invite the congregation into renewal also. In the months following the retreat, I offered an open invitation for a small group of persons to commit to a spiritual practice for a period of nine months. During this time, each one would meditate on an assigned Scripture for twenty minutes several days a week, write in a journal, pray about the encounter, and meet weekly to share experiences and pray together. I had no idea what to expect from the invitation, but sixteen people responded, including key lay leaders in worship, Christian education, and mission.

After a week of using these simple exercises for meditation and prayer, I was awed by the spiritual desire and hunger stirred up within the group. At first I was anxious in the face of this spiritual hunger. I did not feel adequately prepared to shepherd them. But I soon relaxed as I was able to acknowledge that God's Spirit alone brings renewal. Our task as a group of spiritual companions was simply to keep opening up to God and one another and to trust that God would nurture us.

Years later I still feel awe when I think of my experience with that group. These leaders had been very active in the congregation. Our worship often seemed to be touched by a visitation of the Spirit. We regularly studied Scripture, and our Christian education program was very strong. We had already been a congregation with a vital small group program and a significant mission in the inner city. And yet when we committed ourselves to a particular time for reflection, meditation, journaling, and prayer each week, something new began to happen. Our deeper hunger for God percolated to the surface, opening us to a rich movement of God in our lives.

During this time, I also began to lead quarterly weekend retreats for members of the congregation. They included similar practices of silence, meditation on Scripture, journaling, and sharing our experience of encounter with God. These retreats were completely voluntary, and they were always attended by fifteen to twenty persons.

The structure of the retreats was influenced by Bonhoeffer's thoughts in *Life Together*, where he writes: "Let him who cannot be alone beware of community. He will only do harm to himself and to the community. But the reverse is also true: Let him who is not in community beware of being alone. If you scorn the fellowship of the brethren, you reject the call of Jesus Christ, and thus your solitude can only be harmful to you."[1] The pattern of solitude, meditation, journaling, prayer, sharing about encounters with God, confession, mutual support, and deep renewal in Christ was bringing those involved to a new *life together*. This became a significant resource in building up the congregation as the body of Christ.

These events occurred back in the 1970s. For many years, I pondered that experience as a pastor. I wondered how to understand the witness of Psalm 65:4: "Happy are those whom you choose and bring near to live in your courts. / We shall be satisfied with the goodness of your house, your holy temple." How was it that a thriving congregation with vitality in community life, worship, and mission was not adequate for the spiritual needs of its members? What was missing from and so badly needed in the programs of the church? Why was I twelve years into my sixteen-year term as pastor before I recognized this spiritual hunger in myself and others?

This story pinpoints the tension pastors often face between the demands of shepherding a vital and viable church program and of discerning how to respond to the spiritual hungers of church and society. Underlying the yearnings of all our members, recognized or not, is the continual desire to know God better and to experience the presence of God in all of life. It is the human heart's yearning for genuine relationship and deep communion—always seeking but never fully finding in this life. The ministry of spiritual companioning is an important element in the life of the congregation to help us learn how to keep opening up to God and to one another.

The Renewed Interest in Spirituality

During the 1970s and '80s, a growing interest in spirituality began to emerge in the Western world. A plethora of books and articles were written, seminars

1. Bonhoeffer, *Life Together*, 77, 78.

and workshops were offered, interest in Eastern religions began to grow, and the language of spirituality became an accepted part of therapy and self-help groups. On the surface, this curiosity about spirituality seemed like a boon to American religion and culture. As we look back, however, we recognize that it also has an ambiguous side. The search for spirituality tended to be subject to whatever meaning and experience seekers chose. It was often consumer oriented, focusing primarily on personal fulfillment.

Eugene Peterson described the growing interest in spirituality as early as 1993. He observed that "there is a groundswell of recognition spreading through our culture that all of life is at root spiritual; that everything we see is formed and sustained by what we cannot see."[2] Many had begun to realize that secularism marginalizes two essentials of human wholeness: the need for *intimacy* and *transcendence*. The revival of interest in spirituality emerged almost overnight in order to meet these two needs. But, Peterson noted, the result had a certain obscurity about it. "It should be no surprise that a people so badly trained in intimacy and transcendence might not do too well in their quest. Most anything at hand that gives a feeling of closeness . . . will do for intimacy. And most anything exotic that induces a sense of mystery will do for transcendence. . . . Contemporary spirituality desperately needs focus, precision, and roots: focus on Christ, precision in the scriptures, and roots in a healthy tradition."[3]

Peterson's words continue to resonate with us more than two decades later. In a time of enormous social, cultural, and religious change, the challenge facing the church is to provide clear foundations for Christian spirituality and to become a vital expression of the living Christ in our midst. We need depth and vitality in our church life that is rooted in the core beliefs and practices of the church that have stood the test of time.

Toward Spiritual Practices in the Church

Princeton sociologist Robert Wuthnow offers a helpful historical perspective on the contemporary renewal of interest in spirituality in *After Heaven: Spirituality in America since the 1950s*. He defines spirituality broadly as "all the beliefs and activities by which individuals attempt to relate their lives to God or to a divine being." He points out that "spirituality is not just the creation of individuals; it is shaped by the larger social circumstances and by the beliefs and values present in the wider culture."[4]

2. Peterson, "Spirit Quest," 27.
3. Ibid., 28–29.
4. Wuthnow, *After Heaven*, viii.

During this period, we have begun to see some Americans describe themselves as spiritual but not religious. This trend has accelerated with the rise of the "nones": persons who claim no religious affiliation. They no longer seek the guidance of religious institutions to give shape to their spirituality. They pursue their own spiritual reality in recovery groups, bookstores, films, talk shows, classes on world religions, self-help groups, therapy, and other venues.

Wuthnow describes this as a general trend away from a traditional spirituality associated with inhabiting sacred places to a spirituality of seeking the sacred wherever it may be found. The religious scene now consists of *dwellers* and *seekers* who experience God and the world very differently. In a *dwelling-oriented spirituality* the central image is a *spiritual house*. This form of spirituality was dominant in America through the 1950s. A spirituality of dwelling emphasizes habitation. God occupies a sacred space where humans too can dwell—a sacred space for worship, traditional programs, and communal gatherings. Here the spiritual life is rooted in lifelong membership in a church where many people are cradle-to-grave members of a particular tradition.

In a *seeking-oriented spirituality*, the central image is the *spiritual journey*. This shift from sacred house to sacred journey began to emerge during the tumultuous years of the 1960s and has continued to the present. A spirituality of seeking emphasizes moments of mystery, awe, and transcendence that reinforce the conviction that the divine exists. Yet these moments are fleeting. Rather than knowing the territory, people keep searching for the divine in a diverse spiritual marketplace. Churches and religious institutions may still be viable options, but individuals feel free to switch churches frequently. They view their chosen church not so much as a home but as a supplier of spiritual goods and services. In the face of the enormous problems confronting the world today, many seekers view the church as having little purpose. Some even see organized religion as part of the problem. So they seek spiritual meaning elsewhere.

In our congregations, we have both dwellers and seekers worshiping and working side by side. But they are strikingly different in the ways they relate to God and in their vision of the church. This sometimes creates tensions and disappointments. But they need each other, for neither dwelling spirituality nor seeking spirituality is entirely satisfactory by itself. Dwelling spirituality encourages dependence on communities that are inherently undependable in a complex, changing world, while seeking spirituality is too fluid to provide individuals with the social support and spiritual depth they need. It does not encourage the stability and dedication required for spiritual growth and mature character.

Wuthnow argues that we need a *practice-oriented spirituality* as an alternative to dwelling or seeking alone. As he puts it, "Spiritual practices require individuals to engage reflectively in a conversation with their past, examining who they have been, how they have been shaped, and where they are headed."[5] A practice-oriented spirituality roots people in socially shared activities of spiritual depth that link them to the wisdom of past centuries. Such practices are inevitably embedded in religious institutions. But they will have little attraction for individuals in our present context unless they are personally meaningful and create space for divine awe, mystery, and immediacy. Practice-oriented spirituality is best nurtured by congregations that provide people with ways of entering a relationship with the living God in the context of genuine fellowship and spiritual companioning. As we saw already, through Bonhoeffer's writings, this involves living in solitude and community, integrating both the personal and the communal, and providing people with both roots and wings.

We believe the practices of spiritual companioning discussed in this book are an essential ingredient of congregations today. Helping church members gain glimpses of the immediacy of God in their lives serves both dwellers and seekers. In this book we are especially interested in promoting vital personal and congregational spiritual practices in the context of the Protestant tradition.

A number of excellent books have been written in recent decades on the nature and practice of spiritual guidance and direction. Many of these writings rely heavily on resources from the Roman Catholic tradition because it has maintained a practice of spiritual direction through the centuries. We do not write to position ourselves against this tradition in any way. As authors we are greatly indebted to Roman Catholic writers and teachers in our own learning and development. Nor are we writing a book that focuses solely on classical forms of spiritual direction between one director and a directee. Instead we explore spiritual companioning at various places in congregational life and in a variety of practices, including group spiritual direction, spiritual friendships, and many spiritually formative activities.

It is our intention to take what we have learned about spiritual companioning from various traditions and personal experiences and to focus this learning on congregations in the Protestant tradition. Along the way, we explore the purpose and process of listening deeply to one another and reflecting together on the movement of God in our lives. This, in turn, can lead to increased awareness of God in all of life and to the ongoing renewal of congregations.

5. Ibid., 16.

Chapter Sections and Summaries

The chapters that make up this book explore various facets of spiritual companioning by incorporating sections on cultural context, Scripture, the Protestant tradition, practicing spiritual companioning, congregational stories, and exercises for companionship. The importance of Scripture in the practice and theology of spiritual companioning has long been affirmed in the Protestant tradition by the theological tenet *sola scriptura*, which teaches that Scripture contains all that is necessary for salvation and holiness. While this tenet has been interpreted in different ways in the Protestant tradition, it points to the importance of the Bible as the authority of authorities in the Christian life. Accordingly, we include a section on Scripture in each chapter.

Each chapter also includes reflections on the Protestant tradition by exploring resources from the past that continue to have relevance for today. Sections on the contemporary context and the stories of congregations are also included in each chapter. They reflect the Protestant commitment to bear witness to the gospel in a manner that is culturally relevant. Protestants have a long-standing commitment to "translate" the gospel into the language and lifestyle of a particular time and place. From the beginning, for example, Protestants gave priority to translating the Bible into the vernacular language. The home of this ongoing process of translation and embodiment of the gospel is the congregation.

Protestants do not view the church in terms of the institutional continuity of church hierarchy but in terms of the faithfulness of congregations seeking to hear God's Word and heed God's call to mission in a particular time and place. It is here—in the congregation—that spiritual formation and companioning should take place. Accordingly, we explore the broader social context of the church today and the stories of particular congregations that provide insights and possibilities for spiritual companioning in the present.

Finally, we describe practices and exercises for spiritual companioning to provide concrete guidelines and examples. We invite readers to imagine how these might be used in their own particular congregational settings, a process that requires the "translation" and creative adaptation we are describing.

Each chapter addresses one particular aspect of spiritual companioning. Chapter 1 lays the groundwork for understanding companioning as a relationship of presence that encourages deeper awareness of God's work in the soul of each person and community. We reflect on the significance of companioning in a culture of isolation and suggest approaches to connecting with others that have broad application for the church.

Chapter 2 introduces a vision of the church that is rooted in a culture of intentional spiritual companionship. We discuss the foundations of human sociality and consider the process of nurturing congregational spiritual companioning through key concerns, like developing a language for the spiritual life and supporting various companioning relationships.

Chapter 3 focuses on one-with-one spiritual direction, a special kind of formational relationship. We describe the historical tradition of spiritual direction and consider the skills and art of walking alongside another person in the spiritual life. We also discuss the personal preparation of the spiritual director, which is critical to the process.

Chapter 4 attends to spiritual companioning in small groups. In the Protestant tradition, small groups have historically provided support for the spiritual life and ministry of the laity and have played important roles in movements attempting to renew the church. While congregations have many types of small groups, we identify key elements of groups in which genuine spiritual companioning takes place.

Chapter 5 focuses on spiritual companioning in everyday life. Many contemporary churchgoers have a strong desire to know that God is present with them in their daily journeys and has a unique personal calling and purpose for them, a vocation. We offer a theological and practical framework for discerning God's presence and activity in daily life through shared spiritual practices and accountability.

Chapter 6 deals with spiritual companioning over the course of life. It portrays the spiritual life as a journey and considers the forms of spiritual companioning a congregation might offer individuals as they travel this journey. It also emphasizes the importance of gathering the stories of others in spiritual companioning.

Chapter 7 addresses the necessity of companionship for spiritual leaders. Leaders who want to provide companionship for others must commit to seeking companions for themselves. The chapter considers the unique challenges and demands of life in spiritual leadership and discusses the process of developing relationships of accountability and vulnerability that nurture spiritual health and well-being over time.

The Language of Spirituality

In light of the wide variety of traditions of spirituality that are present in Christianity today, it may be helpful to clarify at the outset some of the terms we use in this book. In the following descriptions, we provide some simple, working definitions. We fill out the meaning of each of these terms as the book unfolds.

- *Christian spirituality* is about living all of life in the presence and by the power of the Holy Spirit. It creates a foundation for seeking to be conformed to Christ, to love God and neighbor as self, and to live in communion with the Triune God in Christian community.
- *Spiritual companioning* is a way of accompanying others in intentional relationships of prayerful reflection and conversation that help them notice God's presence and calling in their personal lives, local communities, and the world. It involves the provision of support and accountability in responding to God's invitations. We use the term "companioning" in *verb form* because these kinds of relationships are much more than casual connections—they require an intentional, *active* commitment to a way of being with others and with God. People companion one another through one-with-one spiritual direction, small groups, peer spiritual friendships, family and congregational connections, and other forms of relationship.
- *Spiritual guidance* is the assistance a person or group offers others in a spiritual companioning relationship. While this sometimes includes counsel and direction in learning spiritual practices, it more typically involves helping persons notice the movement of God's Spirit in their lives. It is more evocative than directive, a process of drawing out their own sense of God's presence and guidance rather than telling them what they ought to do or think.
- *One-with-one spiritual direction* is an intentional relationship of spiritual companionship between a director and a directee in which the total focus is on the presence, activity, and invitations of God in the life of the directee.
- *Spiritual friendships* are relationships between peers who commit to providing spiritual companionship for one another.
- *Spiritual practices* are patterns of communal and individual action that open people's lives to God's forming and transforming presence through Word and Spirit.

About the Authors

Angela Reed was raised in a Mennonite congregation in a small rural community in Manitoba, Canada. She became very involved in the church as a child and was companioned in her spiritual life by members of her family and congregation. In her late teens, she began to sense a calling to some form of vocational ministry, though opportunities for women were limited in her context. While she attended college, her eyes were opened to new possibilities, and she was commissioned for pastoral ministry in her midtwenties. In the years that followed, she longed for a richer and broader spiritual life and began to understand more deeply her need for ongoing spiritual companionship. She decided to pursue training in spiritual direction, and one of her instructors was Marcus Smucker. A desire to continue studying led her to complete a PhD at Princeton Theological Seminary under the guidance of Rick Osmer. Her research focused on the significance of spiritual direction training for pastoral leaders and their congregations. In 2010, she accepted a call to join the faculty of George W. Truett Theological Seminary at Baylor University. Along the way, she embraced the Baptist tradition. She teaches spiritual formation and directs a formational program that includes providing spiritual direction to students and local ministers.

Rick Osmer was raised in a Presbyterian church and received spiritual companionship from his parents, church school teachers, and the youth group leaders in his congregation. Through his involvement in a parachurch organization as a young person, he was mentored in the practices of prayer, small group Bible study, and relational evangelism. As a student at Harvard Divinity School, he participated in a training program in which he received spiritual direction from a Jesuit who taught him how to pray the Scriptures imaginatively in the Ignatian tradition. Later, as a student at Yale Divinity School, he had the good fortune of studying with Henri Nouwen. As a professor at Princeton Theological Seminary, Osmer has taught courses in small group Bible study and has participated in small groups with colleagues and students. For many years, he also received one-with-one spiritual direction from a Presbyterian pastor. More recently, he participated in the Kairos School of Spiritual Formation, a program led primarily by Mennonites and influenced by Ignatian approaches to spiritual direction. In this program, he met Marcus Smucker.

Marcus Smucker was raised in the Anabaptist tradition (Amish and Mennonite) and was deeply rooted in the connectedness of a communal spirituality. Through several years of involvement in service projects, including working with refugees in Europe, he sensed God's calling toward a spirituality of service. He served as the pastor of an inner-city congregation for sixteen years and trained as a pastoral counselor. This led him to embrace a relational spirituality. During this time in the pastorate, he also began a journey into the contemplative tradition. Later, as a professor at Anabaptist Mennonite Biblical Seminary, he taught pastoral studies, helped develop a program in

spiritual formation, and taught courses in spiritual formation, including training in spiritual direction. In retirement, he taught spiritual direction for Kairos School of Spiritual Formation and served as a spiritual director. He also
taught spiritual formation courses for Eastern Mennonite Seminary, Lancaster
campus, and was involved in the completion of this book's manuscript prior
to his death in 2014.

Cases and Stories

Throughout this book, we share many cases and stories. These are based on
real persons and events with whom we are familiar. To preserve the anonymity
of persons and congregations, we have changed the names of all parties and
modified our descriptions slightly. We have attempted to maintain the central
dynamics of the relationships and situations in order to base our reflections
on actual cases and stories that are familiar to readers who participate in and
lead congregations.

1

Spiritual Companioning as Presence

Susan was serving as a lay member of the pastoral care team at Living Word Community Church when she received a call from Rose. They had become acquainted through a Sunday morning Bible study in previous years, and Rose was aware that Susan provided spiritual direction to a few people in the congregation. Susan was surprised to hear that Rose was seeking her out for spiritual companionship since she had not seen Rose in some time. Even when Rose did attend church regularly, she seemed to keep to herself, coming and going with only the necessary pleasantries. Susan did not feel that she knew her very well. She had an inkling that it took a great deal of courage for Rose to reach out to her, and she felt privileged to walk with Rose, wherever their shared journey might lead.

Susan began the first meeting with prayer and silence, and then she waited. Her open acceptance and hospitality of spirit gave Rose a sense of safety, which allowed her to release pent-up thoughts and feelings. Rose began by telling her story. She had been raised in a Christian home and attended a theologically conservative congregation. Her mother, who struggled with ongoing depression, embraced the morally strict view of God held by the congregation and their larger Christian community. The religious culture Rose was steeped in communicated grace verbally, but in practice embraced the notion of God as a strict judge. Rose's father was an alcoholic who sometimes terrorized the family. He wanted to change, but he could not overcome his addiction even though he had been admitted to a state mental hospital on several occasions. He died when she was a child.

The sense of shame in the family was pervasive. Rose felt responsible and sought to be a peacemaker and caretaker, wanting to make everything right for her mother and siblings. Reflecting back, she acknowledged that she had felt emotionally numb from childhood into adulthood. As a teenager, Rose began to doubt God, but did not feel safe discussing her spiritual struggles within the church. In her early twenties, she married a student attending a fundamentalist Bible college. In that environment, she tried hard to be a good evangelical Christian. She thought that if she only believed what was right, God would deliver her from what seemed like a lifetime of suffering. This did not work out.

Rose's desire to free herself and others from suffering extended beyond her own family. Early in life, she had grand visions of alleviating world pain. She wanted to make a difference by caring for needy persons, addressing issues of injustice, and seeking to protect the earth. She began a nursing career in her twenties because this was an acceptable caring vocation for a woman in her community. Rose did not find this satisfying. Unfortunately, her marriage also failed. By the time she reached her midthirties, she was divorced with three children. One child had serious health issues in her teens. Another had chronic mental health problems in his twenties and continued to be very dependent upon his mother.

Rose carried the shame of her childhood into her adult years and found it difficult to form genuine relationships. Now in her fifties, she felt isolated and very alone in life. She was depressed and disillusioned by her experiences of life and religion. The claims of the church and even her own belief in God had become oppressive, making demands but seeming to give little in return. Through the years, she had been involved with counselors and psychiatrists, but they did not help much with her sense of personal futility. By the time she called Susan, she attended worship services and other church events only sporadically. However, somewhere deep within she never fully gave up hope in faith and in God. She continued to pray the Jesus Prayer, which she learned in a Bible study group, and she reached out to Susan for spiritual companionship.

Understanding the Cultural Context

While Rose's life circumstances may seem especially challenging, her sense of isolation and struggle while seeking to experience God is not uncommon.

This is true both inside and outside the church. We live in times of significant stress at work, at home, and in the larger community. In such times, our sense of personal isolation and loss of support increases, and we tend to hold these losses privately with a feeling of quiet desperation. At the same time, we long to be understood and valued by others—this is part of what it means to be human. We all want friends who will accept, enjoy, and love us in good times and in bad. Most people would like to be genuinely known and respected by others for who they truly are, not only in their goodness and competence, but also in moments of weakness, failure, and personal need.

This longing for companionship runs deep. We watch for persons we can trust and who express interest in the whole of our lives—our social, physical, spiritual, familial, and professional selves. We may find companionship through marriage, meaningful friendships, family and church connections, work and school relationships, and special interest groups. When these relationships are healthy, they involve reciprocity, mutual respect, and the normal give and take of sharing, caring, and mutual support.

Yet even in caring relationships, the pathway to a deeper level of companionship is often unclear, and for some it is laced with struggle or anxiety. In our society, it is common for people to have many casual relationships but no close friends with whom to explore the intricacies of their lives, particularly in times of stress and struggle. We may be comfortable sharing hobbies or casual lunches, but hesitate to trust others with our private thoughts, desires, fears, and hopes. This is especially true for men. Many of us do not know how to establish the kinds of deep friendships that allow for genuine companionship, particularly companionship that delves into the spiritual life. Frequently we turn to professional "helpers" for support and care in critical life moments. The astounding growth of the counseling industry during the past several decades confirms this fact.

Diagnosing Social Isolation

The problem of social isolation has become the focus of a significant number of sociological studies in recent years. Around the turn of the twenty-first century, research conducted by Robert Putnam found that our society is becoming increasingly disconnected from family, friends, and neighbors, a fact that is impoverishing our personal and communal lives.[1] This research shows that we belong to fewer organizations, meet our neighbors less often, connect with friends less regularly, and even socialize less frequently with our

---

1. Putnam, *Bowling Alone*. Putnam's research team completed nearly five hundred thousand interviews over a quarter century.

families. According to Putnam, changes in work, family structure, suburban life, television, and digital technology, among other factors, contribute to this decline. The notion of friends and family gathering to chat on the front porch at the end of the day seems a thing of the past.

Other research suggests that over the last thirty years, fewer and fewer Americans are likely to have confidants with whom they discuss what really matters to them. In fact, from 1985 to 2004, the number of people who reported not having anyone with whom they discuss important matters has tripled.[2] Those who do confide in others rely increasingly on spouses and parents, a very small social network compared to generations of the past. Sociologists are confirming what many of us have already noticed: larger support systems in our culture are disintegrating, leading to widening chasms of social separation.

This sense of disconnection is accentuated by our economic and cultural circumstances. Changing patterns among emerging adults are a good example of this. In an article for the *New York Times*, Jennifer Silva put it this way:

> Young working-class men and women . . . are trying to figure out what it means to be an adult in a world of disappearing jobs, soaring education costs and shrinking social support networks. Today, only 20 percent of men and women between 18 and 29 are married. They live at home longer, spend more years in college, change jobs more frequently and start families later.
>
> These are people bouncing from one temporary job to the next; dropping out of college because they can't figure out financial aid forms or fulfill their major requirements; relying on credit cards for medical emergencies; and avoiding romantic commitments because they can take care of only themselves. Increasingly disconnected from institutions of work, family, and community, they grow up by learning that counting on others will only hurt them in the end. Adulthood is not simply being delayed but dramatically reimagined along lines of trust, dignity and connection and obligation to others.[3]

Regardless of age, human beings are wired to depend upon committed relationships. As these relationships grow scarce, individuals experience a deep sense of unhappiness and dis-ease that can be debilitating.

This kind of social isolation also tends to impact the spiritual life. When individuals have fewer committed relationships, their awareness of God's presence and commitment to them is often diminished as well. As they disconnect from others, they also tend to lose a sense of connection with God. Our experiences of committed, loving relationships with others help us to imagine

2. McPherson, Smith-Loven, and Brashears, "Social Isolation in America," 353.
3. Silva, "Young and Isolated."

that God might also be loving and committed toward us. Jesus himself used these kinds of comparisons when he talked about the sort of gifts a father gives to his child (Matt. 7:9–11). If we think back to Rose's story, we might hazard a guess that a lack of supportive, committed relationships throughout her life contributed to her impression of God's absence, something she hoped to begin addressing through spiritual companionship.

A Calling to Congregations

Without a doubt, what happens in the larger society directly affects the church. The reordering of fundamental social structures presents a tremendous challenge for congregations in our time. Leaders want to create genuine Christlike communion, but they often do so by focusing on programs rather than people. What we need most today are spiritual companions. If we are honest with ourselves, this is what all of us need and desire.

The church can be a significant arena in which to pursue and explore deeper relationships with others. Congregations are intended to be communities of genuine, even intimate relationships. In the context of such relationships, the gospel can take root more deeply and bring greater transformation, especially during troubling times. The ministry of spiritual companioning is particularly important for helping to provide a genuine spiritual presence and a growing awareness of God. A congregational companioning ministry can also be a means for training members in various kinds of relationships to care for one another. The skills of listening, praying, and responding may become so embedded in the lives of individuals and congregations that spiritual companioning becomes part of a community's way of being.

Listening to Scripture

Central to our understanding of spiritual companioning is Scripture's portrait of human beings designed for fellowship. At the heart of human life is a deep and abiding longing for spiritual communion, animating an underlying hunger for intimacy, love, and meaningful relationships.

Human beings created in God's own image (Gen. 1:27) with God's own "breath of life" (2:7) are made for communion with God, one another, and their own selves. This is evident already in Genesis 2 when God sees that it is not good for "man [Adam] to be alone." So God creates a "helper" to be his partner (ezer; 2:18 NIV), a counterpart who is equal to and even mirrors and corresponds to Adam, and they have the ability to communicate with one another. This is a picture of intimate companioning, a partnership between the man and the woman in face-to-face relationship. In "the garden," there is companionship and communion not only between two humans but also between the humans and God.

However, in Genesis 3 this intimate, harmonious relationship is shattered. With human failure comes shame (3:7), hiding from God (3:8), casting blame (3:12–13), and alienation from self, human relationship, and the Creator (3:17–19, 24). The description of toil amid thistles and thorns, and eating only by the "sweat of your face" (3:17–19), speaks of the hard work humans must do to survive and also symbolizes the spiritual and emotional struggles inherent to human existence. This is a graphic description of the human condition.

The discord commencing with Adam and Eve is further magnified in their sons when Cain kills his brother Abel, breaking the most fundamental bonds of the family (Gen. 4). God confronts Cain, and he attempts to hide from the truth. In just two generations, this is now the second example of the effort to hide in the face of costly mistakes. As human community continues to develop over time, we see new challenges arising. The builders of the first city attempt to create a tower that will reach all the way to heaven to make a name for themselves and to penetrate God's dwelling place (Gen. 11). Again God is not pleased, and human beings are scattered across the earth, speaking many different languages. Human community is marked by misunderstanding and confusion. God continues to express concern for the social dimensions of sin when he gives the Ten Commandments, which are all, fundamentally, about maintaining healthy relationships with God and with others (Exod. 20).

Many biblical stories depict the brokenness of communities resulting from the fundamental breach of humanity's relationship with God, but Scripture also tells the story of God's faithfulness. The God described in the Bible does not give up on human beings but reaches out in love to restore them to right relatedness with himself and with others. We see this at the very beginning of the story Scripture tells. When Adam and Eve "hid themselves from the presence of the LORD God among the trees of the garden," God called out, "Where are you?" (Gen. 3:8–9). This call was like the cry of a parent urging a lost child to come home. This cry of God reverberates throughout Scripture and history, calling all humankind to come home again—a call that continues to the end of time, when God's "family" finally returns to the place where God dwells (Rev. 21:3–4).

The biblical story portrays God's restless and relentless initiatives to connect with humans and assist them on the journey home. God calls into being a new community, Israel, which is elected to show the rest of the world how human beings are to engage with one another, interconnected through a covenant commitment with God. The prophets cry out again and again, urging the people to remember their covenant with God and to be faithful. When Israel fails in its mission, God sends his Son, Jesus Christ, to restore a sinful humanity to right-relatedness to God and one another in a wondrous act of reconciliation. It is an invitation to receive forgiveness and cleansing through Jesus, a chance to be at home with God, to love God with all our heart and to love our neighbor as ourselves. In the human condition of alienation, blame, fear, and hiding, the call to come home is a call to reconciliation and renewal.

As Jesus was preparing his disciples for his departure, he promised them another "helper" (or "paraclete," from the Greek word *paraklētos*) to be alongside them, within them, and among them (John 14:15–17), even as he had been. The word *paraklētos* is variously interpreted as meaning counselor, comforter, helper, advocate, or one who convicts. It also might be translated as convincer, encourager, and mediator, one who suffers with, consoles, challenges, and guides. Jesus chose this term for the Holy Spirit (John 14–16) in order to convey the manner in which the Spirit would continue to companion his followers and they, in turn, would companion one another.

The significance of this is clearly evident in the New Testament picture of church as a community of people who are vitally engaged with "one another" as they are gradually being transformed into the image of Christ (2 Cor. 3:18). Brothers and sisters in the Christian community are called to be in lively interaction with one another as co-laborers in God's work of transformation both personally and communally. They are to help each one to be faithful to God as they "love one another," "encourage one another," "exhort one another," "bear with one another," "forgive one another," and so on. These "one another" passages are scattered throughout the writings of the epistles, occurring nearly two dozen times.

It seems clear that New Testament Christians were to be spiritual companions to one another, providing whatever was needed (exhortation, encouragement, and mutual care) as they continued on the journey of homecoming. In this mutual companioning, they joined with the Holy Spirit to mediate the grace of God to one another and to the world around them.

This is an astounding picture: human beings driven by an abiding desire to be "at home" while on the other side of the divide a relentless God cries, "Come home!" In this drama, people often seek to satisfy their "hunger and thirst" in all the wrong places—in material abundance, a need to control people and circumstances, absolute security, and sensual desires. Human beings are like the prodigal son searching for something in a foreign land while his father watches and waits for his return. This picture may be true even for those who embrace the Christian faith.

The journey home is not simple. It is a process of growing self-awareness, release of ego-driven ways, and increasing freedom to love God and neighbor as self. The journey home is not only an individual journey but also a road taken with others as we join together in the work of the Holy Spirit for renewal and transformation.

Mining the Protestant Tradition

When we think back to Rose's journey, one of the more striking elements is her desire to seek spiritual companionship even when she had experienced much pain and disappointment in relationships. With her doubts about God and her sense of being oppressed by the church, why would Rose seek out Susan as a spiritual companion? What would this kind of relationship have to offer someone who is no longer sure she even believes in God?

Susan is a member of a Protestant congregation and an active participant on its pastoral care team. In her response to Rose's request, she provides a helpful introduction to two basic theological themes that are central to spiritual companioning in the Protestant tradition. First, Susan agrees to enter into a companioning relationship with Rose out of an awareness of the human dilemma: the deep longing and need for communion with God that offers healing, transformation, and hope in human relationships that are broken and distorted. Second, she responds to Rose's cry for help as a person who shares in the ministry of bearing witness to the gospel of Jesus Christ.

Responding to the Human Dilemma

Spiritual companioning in the Protestant tradition takes very seriously the human dilemma created by the reality of sin. It affirms that God's grace is greater than human sin, but it does not seek to minimize or trivialize the brokenness of relationships with God and with others. Rose's story is filled with the sorrow and pain that come from this reality. While her story is uniquely her own, it reflects a condition that is universal.

In the previous section, we explored the Genesis 3 story of the fall of humanity. When Adam and Eve took life in their own hands and sought to be equal to God, they experienced a deep sense of shame, a sign of their broken relationship with God (Gen. 3:7). When God came to fellowship with them in the garden, they were afraid, so they ran and hid (3:8). In their fear and alienation from God, they began to blame their problems on each other and on the One who had created them (3:9–13).

Thus began the dance of human history: longing to be in God's presence but also feeling afraid to be seen and known. Adam and Eve wanted to be with God, but they dreaded exposure. So they hid from God. This underlying sense of shame, this fear and hiding, defines the struggle of the human soul. In spite of being created in the image of God (Gen. 1:27)—created for fellowship with God and one another—human beings are caught up in a profound ambivalence: an inner desire for intimacy and closeness while also wanting to remain hidden and "safe."

This story identifies the "push-pull" reaction we all have in our relationships. On the one hand, we cannot experience fullness of life without deep connections; we feel the pull of our longing for divine love and for relationships of genuine closeness and fulfillment with others. On the other hand, we fear the exposure and risks that come with closeness; we feel the push of shame and fear that drives us away from God, leading us to hide from our Creator and one another.

Spiritual companioning in the Protestant tradition gives attention to this human predicament, and it offers insight into Rose's experience. She is estranged in many ways, yet she longs for meaning, for relationships that bring closeness and fulfillment, and for what is transcendent. Augustine's famous statement is certainly true: You have made us for yourself, O Lord, and our heart is restless until it rests in you. Our yearning to experience divine love is a God-given desire that remains with us always.

Susan heard Rose's underlying desire for a meaningful experience of transcendence in spite of her struggle and doubt. She realized that Rose's struggles with God did not grow primarily from intellectual doubts but from profound disappointment in her experiences of God as God was communicated through her relationships and the events of life. This left Rose with a hunger for the divine, but also fear and resistance to embrace the divine—the push-pull dynamic noted earlier. As a companion, Susan came to recognize that Rose was dealing with profound and difficult issues, yet she was confident that God was already present in Rose's life. Helping Rose attend to God's presence and hear this call lay at the very heart of their relationship.

Reflecting the Gospel of Jesus Christ

Susan also responded to Rose out of her understanding of Christian spiritual companioning as a ministry of the gospel of Jesus Christ. This christological focus is central to the Protestant tradition. Companioning in this tradition is not a form of therapy or a way of helping people deal with their generic spiritual needs; it is at heart a ministry of the gospel of Jesus Christ. The gospel is the "good news" that God loves us while we are still weak and alienated (Rom. 5:6–8). As parents have compassion for their children, so the Lord has compassion for us. He remembers that we are made of dust (Ps. 103:13–14). Five biblical themes central to the Protestant tradition can inform Susan's ministry of spiritual companioning with Rose.

Jesus as Savior

As a minister of the gospel, Susan recognizes that the divine connection we long for comes through Jesus Christ, who died for our sins and offers forgiveness, reconciliation, and new life. Christian spiritual companioning is rooted in the recognition that we ourselves cannot resolve the dilemma of lostness and alienation in the depths of our own being and in the human community. This is something God in Christ has done on our behalf and in our stead in a wondrous exchange: Christ entered into the sin and death of our condition that we may stand with him in a reconciled relationship with his Father.

Spiritual companioning in the Protestant tradition is based on the belief that Jesus Christ is the Savior of the world. It is in this truth, definitively, that we hear the call of God to come home. This call is not based on our own goodness or success. It comes to us as a gift based upon what God has done for us and in our place. Susan responded to Rose's request for help in a Christlike way, which embodied the most basic pattern of the gospel. She did not offer Rose her companionship because she deserved it or was a promising directee or might become a productive church member. Susan chose to enter into Rose's deeply troubled life as a witness to the way Christ entered our world of pain and sin.

The Love of God

Susan soon became aware that Rose had not experienced God's unfailing love in her life, nor had she seemingly experienced much love from others. Her relationships were relatively utilitarian in nature—Rose believed that she would be valuable to others for what she could do for them. This raised questions about whether Rose had ever really experienced or understood the nature of unconditional love—the love of people close to her and the love of God.

Love is at the heart of all Christian experience of the companioning of Christ through the Holy Spirit. Scripture tells us that "love is from God; everyone who loves is born of God and knows God. Whoever does not love does not know God, for God is love" (1 John 4:7–8). To truly know God is to experience God's love. In the created order, the beginning of the experience of love is designed to come through family. We often learn to know God's love through caring interaction with others, and we learn to love God back by loving others. Through our participation in love we can grow in appreciation for God and become more responsive to God.

Jesus said that love for God and love for our neighbors as ourselves are the two greatest commandments (Matt. 22:37–39). His statement implies that all of us, including Christians, also need to love ourselves. Love of oneself is often missing, as it appeared to be in Rose's life. Some find it difficult to believe that God cherishes them and to value themselves accordingly. It requires not only welcoming Jesus as a savior, but also embracing the ongoing work of the Spirit in our lives. This is a necessary step toward healing wounds as we embrace new ways of regarding ourselves and learn new patterns of living. Loving ourselves as God does is part of the journey back home to God. This is not a call to selfishness, egocentricity, or undue attachment to self. It is a call to care for our own life as God values and cares for it.

The love commandments became a practical guide for Susan in her work with Rose. They served as a window for observing and remaining aware of Rose's whole experience of life. They reminded Susan to keep attending prayerfully to Rose's life in its inward, outward, and upward dimensions. In this way, Susan, under the guidance of the Holy Spirit, was able to join Rose on her personal journey of spiritual growth that embraces every aspect of life. Facilitating the experience of love for self, others, and the divine was crucial in the companioning ministry with Rose.

JESUS AS MEDIATOR

Christ alone is the one mediator who stands between God and human beings, for he alone is truly God and truly human. This truth embraces all aspects of his work as prophet, priest, and king. In this context, we focus especially on Christ's priestly ministry. While Christ alone is our one true sacrifice and high priest (Heb. 2:14–18; 7:25), the people of God are called to participate in this priestly ministry (Rom. 15:16; 1 Pet. 2:9). In the Protestant tradition, priestly mediation is not just concerned with the role of priests or ministers; it is a part of the calling of every member of the Christian community. We are called to pray for, encourage, and bear the burdens of one another in Christ, mediating God's forgiving love and bringing the special needs of each person to God in intercessory prayer.

Susan understood spiritual companioning to include the "mediation" ministry of Jesus (Heb. 2:18–19). The companion joins Jesus through the Holy Spirit to reach out to another on behalf of God and to talk with God on behalf of another. With this in mind, Susan was able to serve as an important presence that helped to build Rose's connection to God.

RECONCILIATION THROUGH CHRIST

The ministry of mediation is closely related to the ministry of reconciliation. In the second letter to the Corinthians, we read that God has reconciled us to himself through Christ and given us a part to play in the ministry of reconciliation (2 Cor. 5:17–20). Through a process of prayerful reflection and interaction, spiritual companions offer support for an individual's journey of reconciliation with God, others, and their own selves. This even includes being reconciled to one's enemies.

In spiritual companioning, guides become ambassadors for Christ as God reaches out to others through them. They offer a ministry presence for Christ's sake, and their relationships with directees may become the primary relationships through which directees begin to experience reconciliation. For example, Susan recognized that Rose was angry, disappointed, and alienated in virtually every relationship in her life. She was burdened and weighed down by a lack of fruitful connection. Susan must discern how best to help Rose notice God's movement in her life, gently nudging her toward new patterns of relationship grounded in an awareness that she is forgiven, accepted, and loved by God. Rose was invited to live into the reconciliation God offered her so that healing and hope would pour out and over into her relationships with others. It would be slow and painful work, and Susan could not rush Rose along. Susan had to seek the guidance of the Holy Spirit as she worked toward the reality of reconciliation in Rose's life.

THE UNIQUE PRESENCE OF JESUS CHRIST
IN HUMAN RELATIONSHIPS

Jesus is not a dead man of the past. He is the risen Lord, who lives and reigns at the right hand of his Father. Jesus told his disciples, "Where two or three are gathered in my name, I am there among them" (Matt. 18:20). This suggests that Jesus will be present whenever human beings desire that God be with them.

Jesus takes this one step further in John 14:23, saying, "Those who love me will keep my word, and my Father will love them, and we will come to them, and make our home with them." Here is the remarkable promise that as we live and walk with Jesus Christ, our desire to be "at home" with God will be fulfilled.

In these biblical passages, Jesus teaches about the sacredness of relationships in the Christian community. When we openly acknowledge Christ and invite him into a relationship, he sows a seed of divine presence, renewal, and constructive potential. In Christian spiritual companioning, the responsibility of directing or determining that potential is not up to those providing companionship. They have the more modest and manageable task of discerning and observing the movement of the divine presence in the life of the other person. Often, both are aware of this presence.

This is a sacramental relationship in the sense that the relationship is imbued with divine presence and becomes a visible expression of something invisible. The spiritual companion does not create Christ's presence but mediates it in the companioning relationship. Christ is at work and the companion simply joins him through the power of the Holy Spirit in that work. God always makes the first move. We participate by offering ourselves to be in a companioning relationship with another "in the service of God," thus becoming a means for mediating God's forgiving, redeeming, and renewing presence.

Susan's understanding of the gospel of Jesus Christ informed her response to Rose's request that she be her spiritual companion. Susan brought these convictions into her companioning relationship with Rose, and the convictions informed their relationship throughout. Susan's agenda was not primarily to teach or persuade but to walk alongside Rose: to mediate Christ's presence and to observe and facilitate the "birthing" process of the Spirit. Susan chose to be a companion on this spiritual journey of healing and renewal with the conviction that the relationship would be imbued with the love and energy of God. She hoped her visible presence would become a sign of God's presence and compassion for Rose. This would be true regardless of whether Rose ultimately acknowledged God's interest and presence in her life. It was Susan's prayer that as she touched Rose's life on behalf of God, Rose would also be touched by Jesus Christ.

In Western Christianity today, the ministry of spiritual companioning is critical to the vitality of the church. In spite of the many activities of the church, it is entirely possible for Christians to go through life without having a setting, a place, and a people with whom to have conversations about their deeper personal struggles or experiences of God. Some people have extraordinary experiences of God that they do not share for fear of being regarded as strange or outside the norm. Some feel scared to admit their doubts and struggles because they fear that they will be viewed as lacking in faith. Yet it is often in conversation about the deepest cries of our hearts—be it struggle, fear, embarrassment, failure, or deeply moving spiritual experiences—that we encounter God most easily. To have a relationship with a trusted and trustworthy spiritual companion or companions, where the deeper matters of the heart and soul can be expressed, is a sacred gift. Having a faithful spiritual companion to accompany us on our journey can facilitate continuing spiritual renewal and depth in our walk with God.

While a theology of Protestant spiritual companioning is certainly Christ-centered, it is also trinitarian. Spiritual companioning ought to offer a tiny sampling of the kind of relationship shared by the Father, Son, and Holy Spirit. Trinitarian theology suggests that the Father, Son, and Holy Spirit live in a relationship of radical love in which each person of the Trinity is fully open to and mutually implicated in the others. In the threeness of the Godhead, there is oneness, a communion that is full and complete in eternity.

This is a picture of God at the core of the divine being: in unbroken relationship, total love, and profound communion. We are given a glimpse of this through the Holy Spirit as we are joined to Christ and, through him, to the Father. In spiritual companioning we are called home to this God who is at work in all of our experiences, inviting us to notice, trust, respond, and be transformed over and over. The ministry of spiritual companioning serves this movement of the Triune God, who calls us out of our lostness and alienation back home to the community we were created for and the communion that will be fully complete when God is finally "all in all" (1 Cor. 15:28).

Practicing Spiritual Companioning

The vision of community through Christ can be lived out in companioning relationships in many different ways. Rose's particular story and specific need for a healing relationship were unique, and so were the gifts that Susan brought to the encounter. The companioning relationship is dynamic, diverse, often complex, and tailored to the particular journey of individuals and the unique personhood of the companion. It cannot be adequately described in a few pages, but there are several common steps that help to create sacred space for life-giving spiritual companionship.

Being Fully Present

The process of spiritual companioning begins very simply by being ourselves and giving our full attention to another. The companion welcomes the other person into an open relationship of acceptance and caring, committing to attentive listening, respect, and confidentiality. This kind of soulful hospitality enabled Rose to let her guard down enough to risk sharing her story.

How a companion invites the other into his or her personal space, as one human being with another, has deep spiritual significance. We employ skills that are fundamental to human social interaction, skills that nearly all of us can develop. We intentionally commit to meeting, greeting, noticing, attending, and accepting as one human being with another on behalf of God. It begins not by doing or saying anything especially profound, but by focusing on simply *being* with the other.

The companion engages the other, over a period of time, in a manner that says, "I am with you"; "I care"; and "I am interested in your life." We communicate this nonverbally with facial expressions, eye contact, posture, general attentiveness, and responsiveness in conversation. This kind of presence engenders trust, which is an absolute necessity for open conversation.

As Susan and Rose are getting to know each other, Susan initiates a conversation about how they will treat one another and what to anticipate in the relationship. Because Rose has experienced significant relational wounds, she needs to understand what to expect from Susan, including the time, place, length of meetings, and the particular role each one will play in helping to make their interactions effective. In this case, a casual "let's get together again soon" will not be sufficient. This conversation may also involve some discussion about how they will relate when they meet each other socially at church events or around town. A mutual understanding about the relationship is necessary to provide adequate structure for this ministry and assure Rose of continuity.

Being fully present in companioning brings a kind of immediacy to others, a welcome, safe moment to let their guard down and reveal a bit of who they truly are and what they feel and think about God, themselves, others, and the world. Many of us, like Rose, have become consummate actors, able to share casual pleasantries while hiding away our isolation, confusion, and curiosities about the spiritual life. Susan's most important gift to Rose is her commitment to a simple, intentional presence.

Being a Prayerful Listener

A second element in companioning is listening in a prayerful way. Part of being human is having a spiritual nature and an ability to learn to hear from God. The companion attends not only to the other person's story but also to God's presence and interaction in the relationship. This helps the companion to keep in mind the big picture of God's greater purpose as well as it can be discerned in what is expressed through ideas and feelings. Prayerful listening often creates a deep spiritual bond.

Through this kind of listening, the companion touches the depth of the other without being intrusive. Instead of becoming a "helper" to solve problems or analyze dilemmas, the companion, through the practice of prayerful listening, helps to make the interaction less active and more reflective. Prayerful listening engenders humility as both persons "bow" before God with a heightened awareness of being in the presence of God together. The process invites us to slow down, pay attention to our inner selves, engage in reflective interaction, and become more open to noticing God in the present moment. As Susan listened alongside Rose, she was reinforcing the belief that God wanted to communicate with them, and she was teaching Rose to practice this way of listening for God on her own.

Being a Respectful and Empathic Presence

A third way of engaging in a companioning relationship is by listening with respect and empathy. Offering respect is a way of valuing one another as God values us. The companion befriends the other by listening with empathy, being attentive to the person while his or her "story" emerges and continues to unfold. Empathic listening also involves identifying with another's experiences, feelings, and concerns without becoming personally attached to or attacked by them. In the companioning relationship, this includes inviting in-depth self-disclosure in whatever way the other person chooses. It communicates personal interest, creates a safe environment, and is an offer to be present no matter what joy or pain is expressed. We hope to be genuinely present emotionally. As we express empathy, we make it easier for others to tell their stories.

Through empathic listening, Susan accompanied Rose as she explored the difficult parts of her life journey and, ultimately, the depth of her own being. Susan joined Rose not primarily to solve problems but to be emotionally present as Rose continued to unearth the layers of her life. With Susan's help, Rose could identify and name the movements of her inner life—fear, despair, depression, and hopefully pleasure as well—getting in touch with some of her deepest desires.

Empathic listening also gives us the courage to face whatever is present in our lives and helps us to name constructive ways to respond. This is true for experiences of suffering, moments of great joy, and the acceptance of what is routine or feels boring. In her empathy, Susan might also find that she begins to feel what Rose feels right alongside her—both the pain and the joy. It is important that she release those feelings to God, who can hold them when she cannot. Caring for another in this way reflects the compassion of God for each of us.

This kind of listening may happen in various contexts and formats, including formal sessions and informal encounters, through years of walking with another or in brief moments of shared conversation and prayer. Of course, relationships will normally grow more fruitful as trust is built over time. The process of significant personal sharing and listening always requires a basic commitment between companions, implicit or explicit, that the other person's story is of interest, that what is shared will be held in confidence, and that no matter what is said, it will not change the value and appreciation the companions have for each other.

Being Reflective Together

Being reflective together is another significant element in spiritual companioning. Like priming a pump, the respectful listening of the companion often facilitates greater self-reflection by the other person. It provides opportunity for others to listen to their own words and ponder the significance and meaning of their experiences and concerns. It is an invitation to deeper awareness of the events of daily life. Some reflective questions that may be useful include the following:

- What do you hear yourself saying?
- What comes to your awareness as you are speaking?
- What are you experiencing right now?

The benefits of reflection increase when it becomes a mutual process. Such *reflective interaction* may include dialogue or discussion, but it is often a simple pondering over life, including encounters with family, at work, or in any other context. The reflection process addresses how God seems present or absent in these experiences of life.[4] Pondering the questions of life together, with each one initiating and contributing, creates a relationship of mutual solidarity. The companion may ask questions, not necessarily for discussion or to seek information, but to join with the other in solidarity. The process strengthens the person's confidence in his or her own observations and insights. Together they can delight in any "aha moments" that arise. This is not a relationship of dependence but of lively spiritual interdependence.

We can understand the practice of reflection in life more fully as we ponder the biblical notion of Sabbath. In the creation story, God worked six days and rested from his labors on the seventh day, which was set aside for refreshment (Gen. 2:2; Exod. 31:17). The word in the original language that is translated "refreshed" in Exodus 31:17 is used as both noun and verb, to mean breath,

---

4. The term "reflection" is used in pastoral-care literature in a variety of ways. Most writers agree that it is an active, conscious practice. Some suggest that it is a cognitive process for clarification of thought and intention. Others say that it is a process of pondering, somewhat similar to the biblical understanding of meditation, which is a conscious process but moves more toward being open and receptive than toward mastery and control.

desire, vitality, or soul. When God took a deep breath on the seventh day and considered what he had created, God was refreshed.

This was not a time for God's physical renewal, but rather a time when activity gave way to reflection, mastery to receptivity, and doing to being. Thus, in the order of creation, God instituted a rhythm of work and rest, doing and being, mastery and receptivity that is essential for human well-being. God invites us to embrace this same rhythm so we can be revitalized through times of reflection, time to simply *be* in the presence of God, time to be with one another and the world around us, and time to continue opening up to that which transcends us.

The Sabbath provides an excellent word picture for understanding the purpose of the reflective process in spiritual companioning. Whether the one seeking companionship feels fragmented, distracted, or burdened, or is simply hungering and thirsting for God, the manner of the companion's presence welcomes the other to experience this Sabbath rest. "Rest" in this case is not an escape or a reprieve from difficult things. It invites the divine presence to break into daily experience again and again, bringing new life. The companion facilitates this continued birthing of a new way of being in life.

One significant resource Susan brought to Rose's journey was the ability to step back and glance over the larger picture of Rose's life. She might raise various kinds of questions designed for deeper reflection on Rose's unique story: How did she experience God in her earlier years? What prompted her to begin considering agnosticism? Had there been a moment recently when she was reminded of God in some way? What were some of her deepest desires or hopes in life?

Ideally Susan's questions would help Rose get in touch with divine transcendence. Personal and spiritual growth often occurs at the frontier of human experience. All of our experiences, those that are typically identified with spirituality and those that are not, may become like clay in the hands of God to help mold and shape us. Pondering one's life in a companioning relationship can help evoke deeper awareness of God's active involvement in daily experience. It fosters the conviction that God is present in all of life (Rom. 8:28). Not only is God in all things with us, but all of life is ultimately fulfilled in union with God (John 15:1–11; 17:21–23; Acts 17:28). This is the vision the companion brings to the relationship.

Speaking the Truth in Love

Companioning is also about speaking challenging truths for the sake of love (Eph. 4:15). As trust and openness in the relationship evolve, companions may offer observations, speak "candidly" about what they see in the life of another, or even gently confront issues that need to be addressed. This is always done in the context of a bond of trust between companions. It is never a process of persuasion. The words spoken must first of all be offered to God and then, with reliance on the Holy Spirit, shared with the other person.[5]

This can serve as both affirmation and challenge. When companions speak a difficult word out of love, they do so "with" rather than "to" another. Such a soulful, prophetic presence may sharpen our ability to imagine what God sees when he looks at our lives, so that we can make clear decisions and strengthen our personal commitments. No doubt Susan may notice issues of concern in Rose's life that she can gently identify at some point. An issue may be anything from an unhealthy habitual pattern to an inaccurate belief about oneself.

Whatever the case, Susan will need to give careful thought and prayer to voicing a word of concern and not be quick to do so until there is a history of trust and commitment. In fact, she may not sense the need to name the issue at all but may simply choose to hold it prayerfully with the hope that Rose will recognize the need to change for herself. Either way, Rose will have to know that she is loved by Susan before she hears a word of challenge. In cases of abuse or other such extreme concerns, companions must be quick to act and identify what they see to the ones they care for and to others in authority within the larger community. There are times in which safety trumps confidentiality.

Naming and Describing Experience

As our conscious awareness of ourselves, others, God, and all creation grows, a companion will encourage us to put our encounters into words. Naming and describing our experiences can enhance our interactions with God and others, and enrich our understanding of God's work in the soul. It can also increase our sense of collaboration with God in our own growth and in the choices we make in everyday life.

Finding words to describe experience helps us notice the intricacies of life. Naming our inner awareness of self and God further enables us to recognize what we hope for in relationship with others—with family members, friends, at church, and at work. As we develop this skill, we also become more cognizant

5. Some church traditions include a form of "binding and loosing," holding members responsible for significant moral failures that they refuse to confess and change, even to the point of removing them from membership (Matt. 18:15–18). Spiritual companionship as we describe it functions somewhat differently. Companions do not impose or demand. In some cases, a companion may choose not to continue meeting if the relationship is not proving to be life-giving and fruitful.

of the experiences of others, particularly those we spend time with. Gaining clarity in place of ambiguity strengthens all of our relationships and creates opportunities for us to empathize with others.

At the core, companioning employs skills that are learned and passed on, helping us build committed, caring relationships in ever-widening circles that get beyond the surface and address isolation. Susan's conversations with Rose will help Rose develop her own ability to listen for the presence and activity of God in the lives of her children and others she relates to. We have seen this many times in spiritual companioning relationships. The purpose may not be to teach, but the skills for becoming a spiritual companion to others are learned by example and practice.

Encouraging Spiritual Practices

At the appropriate time, a companion may coach the other person in the pursuit of spiritual practices that nurture the soul and help that person continue opening up to God. The companioning relationship will attend to the other's maturing experience with Scripture and prayer. For example, it may be helpful for Rose to discuss her choice of the Jesus Prayer as a regular practice. Why is she drawn to it? What happens when she prays in this way? She may also be interested in talking about a Scripture passage that is especially meaningful or draws her to pray. It is often helpful to start by reflecting on practices that a companion already uses.

When we introduce new practices, it is important to discern the process carefully so that the new thing is actually life giving and does not become a burden. Idealistic plans for prayers at five in the morning or for lengthy fasts, when one lacks prior experience in these areas, are bound to fail and bring more guilt than grace. Like the newborn child who learns to sit before standing and to walk before running, we all learn by increments, and it is no different in the spiritual life. In chapter 5, "Spiritual Companioning in Everyday Life," we will explore in detail specific practices for companions.

Exploring the Stories of Congregations

Susan's relationship with Rose did not develop in a vacuum. The women are connected to a community of faith, a congregation, even if Rose's attendance has become sporadic. Rose became aware of the opportunity to meet with Susan because of a Sunday morning class, and Susan received support for the companionship she offered through the pastoral care team and the congregation as a whole.

The congregation offers spiritual companionship in many other ways as well, sometimes in ways we would not expect. These relationships function a bit like the strands in a spider's web. The spider cannot depend on one strand alone to create its home; many strands are necessary, woven back and forth, designing a remarkable web characterized by strength and support. All of us exist within a web of relationship, but for many us the webs are small and have fewer connections than in generations past. The congregation can enlarge and strengthen our webs of relationship through intentional forms of companionship. Throughout this book, we explore the possibilities for companionship in a number of congregational settings. For now, we will consider a few of the ways Living Word Community Church could care for Rose and others seeking spiritual nurture.

Pastoral Care

Perhaps one of the most obvious approaches to spiritual companionship with Rose is pastoral care. As Rose grows comfortable with Susan, she might welcome a visit from another representative of the congregation, such as the pastor or a member of the care team. Living Word has two pastors and a few deacons who are available to make visits. This team meets regularly to discuss particular needs in the congregation, and Susan participates in those meetings. If Rose gives permission, Susan might mention to others on the team that Rose, and possibly her dependent child, would benefit from a visit. This would be another meaningful connection in Rose's web of relationship to address her sense of isolation and disconnection.

The caregiver can learn a bit of Rose's story, ask clarifying questions, explore options for congregational engagement and other support, and offer a prayer if Rose is willing. Rose may even welcome an invitation to meet occasionally, just to see how things are going. This approach tends to focus more on problem solving than does Rose's relationship with Susan, but that is probably helpful, especially if Rose has particular physical needs the congregation can provide for. The caregiver may also come to realize that Rose has a passion for helping others and can then assist her in identifying possible areas of involvement in the congregation's life and mission. Rose's healing journey may actually be strengthened by opportunities to pass on the gifts of care and companionship.

Pastoral Counseling

Rose may also be companioned through pastoral counseling, a particular form of pastoral care. One of Living Word's pastors is a trained pastoral counselor. He may be able to meet with Rose to explore feelings, thoughts, motivations, unconscious drives, and unresolved issues from her family of origin, such as the experience of losing her father and her sense of responsibility to care for her family. Though these events happened long ago, they may still be hindering her personal and spiritual freedom in life. This in-depth relationship could become a significant resource for transformation. Developing this relationship for a time and then possibly supporting her through referral to another counselor will show Rose that the congregation wants to commit to companioning her.

Preaching, Teaching, and Worship

We might not think of the worship service or Christian education class as a form of companionship, but for Rose they could become important ways to receive new insights about her relationship with God, others, and the world she lives in. Because her inner conflict has been severe and her circumstances harsh, she has pulled away from these contexts. As the other intentional relationships develop, she will probably be more likely to return to regular church services and activities. Preaching and teaching that attends to honest experiences of people and their struggles in relationship with God will be critical for helping Rose know she belongs. If sermons, prayers, and other elements of worship acknowledge loss and pain, speak about family systems in broad ways (e.g., allowing for single divorcees), and make space for questions about God, Rose will recognize that her story fits in the community.

Support Groups

A small support group that meets regularly for sharing and prayer may be one of the most important forms of companionship for Rose. Over the last few decades, congregations have recognized needs for deep healing and the value of gathering people together to support one another in the hurts of life. Rose will benefit from various kinds of groups, perhaps a grief group for addressing the losses of childhood or a group designed for families facing mental health issues. The extent to which the group will be an effective spiritual resource for persons in a deep struggle or a "dry" place will depend upon the nature and level of the group's interactions, their use of Scripture and prayer, and their depth of personal relationship with God. Some groups have the longevity, commitment, and skill to go beyond mutual support to engage in the deeper work of soul making—many do not.

In each of these ministry tasks, relationships are nuanced and encouraged in particular ways to support specific elements of the congregation's purpose.

At the same time, no ministry task stands alone. All tasks are interconnected within the larger activity of the church, and they ought to complement and strengthen one another.

Exercising Our Companionship: Practicing Presence

The following exercises provide opportunities for practicing the interactions we have just considered. They represent only some of the relational exchanges that can help facilitate spiritual growth. There are many other ways to engage a person in a companioning relationship. We always keep in mind that we serve as vessels for God: we accompany others on the spiritual journey, and we try to focus not on our own wishes but on what God is already doing and wants to do in the lives of others.

A. Being Fully Present
   1. Agree with a friend to have her tell you a story about herself.
   2. Be fully present by doing the following:
      • Arrange chairs a comfortable distance from one another.
      • Sit in a relaxed manner, maintaining good eye contact.
      • Use nonverbal and verbal communication to respond to the person and her story (e.g., eye contact, facial expressions, nodding to indicate listening).
   3. At the end, reflect together on the experience.
      • On a scale of 1 to 10, how present to your friend did you feel?
      • What was it like for you to be present with the other?
      • What was it like for your friend to experience your presence?
B. Expressing Empathy
   1. Agree with a friend to have him share something about his spiritual life.
   2. Listen carefully and, as appropriate, paraphrase what you are hearing.
   3. Let yourself be aware of what the other person is expressing (feelings, concerns, etc.).
   4. Toward the end of the time together, tell him your sense of what he was expressing; invite your friend's correction as needed.
   5. Invite your friend to reflect with you about what he experienced in the session, particularly the process of having you listen.

C. Listening While Praying

    1. Agree with a friend that she will share something about her spiritual life.

    2. Sit with your hands on your lap, palms up, in a posture of prayer while the other person is sharing. Keep verbal responses to a minimum. As much as possible be aware of God (or Jesus specifically) in the room with you.

    3. At the end, reflect together on the experience and discuss the following:

- What did your friend experience as you were listening prayerfully?
- What was it like for you to practice "prayerful listening" with your friend?

D. Using Reflective Questions

    1. Agree with a friend that he will share something about his spiritual life.

    2. Listen carefully and, as appropriate, paraphrase what you are hearing.

    3. As the story unfolds, ask a few reflective questions, including the following and one or two of your own:

- What was that like for you?
- What was your experience (of that event or moment)?
- What were you feeling or thinking as this was happening?
- What are you experiencing now?
- How does this (or has this) affected your life?
- What do you desire from God in this situation?

E. Describing the Experience of God

    1. Agree with a friend to have her share about an encounter with God.

    2. Listen carefully and, as appropriate, paraphrase what you are hearing.

    3. Ask a few of the following questions:

- What did God seem like in that encounter?
- How do you suppose God feels about that?
- What do you suppose God is doing (or wanting to do) in your situation?
- What might be God's desire for you (or someone else) in this situation?

For Further Reading

Augsburger, David. *Caring Enough to Confront: How to Understand and Express Your Deepest Feelings*. 3rd ed. Ventura, CA: Regal Press, 2009. An exploration of how to build trust and be honest with another about concerns or issues, including anger or blame, and how to communicate in a healing way.

———. *Caring Enough to Hear and Be Heard*. Scottdale, PA: Herald Press, 1982. An introductory text that teaches readers how to listen and be heard, and to reach out across a void to really learn to know the other person.

Brenneman, Terri J. *Practicing Presence*. Harrisonburg, VA: MennoMedia, 2012. Twelve study sessions that highlight how to be present with one another and with God, examining biblical texts that illustrate the importance of companioning one another.

Dutton, Marsha L., ed. *Aelred of Rievaulx: Spiritual Friendship*. Trappist, KY: Cistercian Publications, 2010. A classic text that defines human friendship as sacramental, beginning in creation and showing how God sought to place his own love of society in all his creatures.

Edwards, Tilden. *Spiritual Director, Spiritual Companion: Guide to Tending the Soul*. Mahwah, NJ: Paulist Press, 2001. An examination of ways to nurture the soul and recognize a true spiritual experience, with suggestions for how to be genuinely present with another.

Hart, Thomas N. *The Art of Christian Listening*. Mahwah, NJ: Paulist Press, 1980. A discussion of contemporary spiritual theology and modern psychology. It is written as a guide for anyone who wants to assist others in their spiritual growth.

Jackson, Cari. *The Gift to Listen, the Courage to Hear*. Minneapolis: Augsburg Fortress, 2003. A powerful and persuasive book on the efficacy of listening that creates an environment of safety and promotes a willingness to enter into deepening relationship.

2

Spiritual Companioning
in the Congregation

Tracy is a South Carolina native in her midtwenties who moved to a Midwestern state for graduate school. For the first time, Tracy set out to choose a congregation without the input of family or close friends. She has been involved in various congregations through the years, including Presbyterian, Evangelical Free, and a local "community" church. After Tracy first moved to town, she visited numerous churches over several successive Sundays. When she discovered the congregation Christ the Savior, she stayed. Tracy found herself drawn to this congregation because it is exploring contemplative traditions and practices in worship and small group life. She was especially attracted to the simple, quiet atmosphere of corporate worship, so different from the contemporary worship services she was accustomed to.

Tracy finds that she is experiencing spiritual growth by attending to God's presence in her life in new ways. She remembers that during Good Friday this year, she sat in the sanctuary for the Tenebrae service. As the Scriptures were read, then held in silence, and the candles extinguished one by one, she had a moment of clarity about her own struggle to open herself to God amid the demands of work and school. She felt physically depleted and distant from God. An anguish rose up within, and the themes of Good Friday drew her to consider in a new way what separation from God might be like. As the room grew darker, she prayed silently, "God, don't leave me!" Almost immediately she sensed a kind of communication, an inner knowing that God never leaves her alone. It was a relief.

Tracy is quick to say that these kinds of experiences are not common for her, but owns that she has noticed them more often since coming to Christ the Savior Church. She finds herself reflecting on these moments and on her spiritual growth as a whole with a few new friends from church and in a small group that practices various forms of prayer together. The church does not plan many social events for young adults, and Tracy misses that, but she experiences encouragement in honest conversations that delve into the genuine joys and challenges of life with God. She notes that many church members seem comfortable with these conversations in a way she has not encountered before, and it is refreshing. As Tracy feels more at home in this church, she is paying increasing attention to her own sense of call to serve God and has recently started caring for developmentally delayed children in the congregation.

Understanding the Cultural Context

At root, what Tracy is looking for in a congregation is connection. She longs to connect with God and become increasingly aware of how God is with her. She desires meaningful connections with others that go beyond pleasantries to matters of the soul. We might also say she is seeking connection with her own sense of call, including opportunities to participate in the purposes of God. Tracy is less motivated by denominational affiliation or even social programming than by genuine encounter, and she isn't the only one.

Congregations That Facilitate Connection

Researchers with the Gallup organization have been exploring "congregational engagement" for over a decade to understand what causes people to want to stay in a congregation and become active participants. After extensive study, they developed a list of twelve statements that express what people need in order to be engaged in the life and ministries of a local church.

1. As a member of my congregation, I know what is expected of me.
2. In my congregation, my spiritual needs are met.
3. In my congregation, I regularly have the opportunity to do what I do best.
4. In the last month, I have received recognition or praise from someone in my congregation.

5. The spiritual leaders in my congregation seem to care about me as a person.

6. There is someone in my congregation who encourages my spiritual development.

7. As a member of my congregation, my opinions seem to count.

8. The mission or purpose of my congregation makes me feel my participation is important.

9. The other members of my congregation are committed to spiritual growth.

10. Aside from family members, I have a best friend in my congregation.

11. In the last six months, someone in my congregation has talked to me about the progress of my spiritual growth.

12. In my congregation, I have opportunities to learn and grow.[1]

These items create a picture of communities where connection is at the heart of what matters, and the spiritual life is intimately tied to community and service. We notice several statements that have the ring of spiritual companioning to them: personal spiritual development is encouraged in individual relationships, people ask each other about their spiritual growth, leaders express care for each individual person, close personal friendships flourish within the life of the larger community, and people acknowledge and affirm one another as they use their gifts to serve.

All of these items appear so simple and fundamental to life in community that any church should be able to implement them. But somehow congregations lose touch with core commitments like these or do not know how to measure whether they are actually practiced. The reality is that we get bogged down because we explore our questions about the life of the church in the wrong order. Often the "what" questions get our first attention. What will be the shape and time of our worship? What curriculum should we use in the youth group? As any committee member knows, we also spend considerable time raising the "how" question. How will we run the children's ministry or the mission initiative in our neighborhood? The time and energy of nearly any church can be caught up with these issues. We give our primary attention to what we are accomplishing, what we are *doing* for God.

The questions we address more rarely, often when things aren't working, are "who" and "why." Who are we, as God's people, made to be? Why do

---

1. See, e.g., Albert L. Winseman, "Congregational Engagement Ascends," Gallup, February 15, 2005, http://www.gallup.com/poll/14950/congregational-engagement-ascends.aspx.

we even gather together? Whom do I talk with about my spiritual life? Why should I participate in this particular congregation's community? Perhaps these questions can simply be too theoretical, time consuming, or even divisive to answer. They have a place in seminary, but do not seem pertinent amid the everyday demands of keeping up with hospital visits and Sunday school preparation. Yet this is precisely the point. We need to raise these questions because they help us to move past institutional maintenance to the deeper purpose for the existence of the church. They help us get at the core of congregational engagement.

There could not be a better time to ask "who" and "why." A century ago, the majority of Americans were raised in a traditional Christian or Jewish context, and they remained within that tradition all of their lives. Most Protestants worshiped as adults in the denominations they were raised in, often in the same churches. Individuals had a firm sense of religious identity and a strong commitment to the local church, which was a place to worship and nurture a social life. The church was a natural home for long-term friendship and spiritual companionship, a home that members were loyal to. This reflects the *dwelling-oriented* spirituality we described in the introduction.

Much has changed. Many of us experience a transient life, as Tracy does. We move from place to place and from church to church. As we have already noted, *seeker-oriented* spirituality tends to encourage our use of well-honed consumer skills to "shop" for a congregation we feel best meets our spiritual needs. Making matters more complex, there are a multitude of options outside of congregations that nurture personal spirituality, including retreat centers, parachurch groups, and spiritual guides hanging out a shingle. Protestants are flocking to Roman Catholic monasteries these days, to spiritual-formation training programs, and to myriad other voluntary gatherings addressing specific concerns, such as grief support groups. Some gather together to form new congregations with particular goals or niche interests rather than join existing ones. This was true of the church Tracy attends. The practice of forming new churches is an especially Protestant one that continues to be popular in our time.

Within the context of innumerable options for pursuing spirituality, congregations may have doubts about the roles they are called to play. We can lose sight of the "who" and "why" questions while feeling the pressure to "compete" for members in a consumer-driven spiritual marketplace, to draw new members in, and to keep those we already have (as if they are ours to own). We focus on programs and activities people seem to desire, but don't ask the core questions that speak to genuine connection—to engagement. These questions are actually the foundation of our sense of calling to each other. They are rooted in the fact that we are fundamentally relational beings. We begin our journey into the "who" and "why" of spiritual companioning by exploring our human makeup.

Forming "Good Enough" Relationships

Scientists of every stripe have long been convinced that companionship is critical because we are fundamentally communal beings. This becomes obvious from life's earliest moments. There are few things more awe-inspiring than the birth of a child. With it comes the reminder (and just a bit of terror!) that this child cannot survive without us. Many novice parents feel uncertain the first time they are alone at home with their newborns. They wonder if they will know how best to respond to their child's cries and if they can learn to tell one kind from another. They come to realize that this tiny person's life depends on their limited knowledge of baby care and, most important, their willingness to love and sacrifice for the child's sake, whatever time of day or night.

Fortunately, most parents quickly learn to provide for the basic needs of their children. They also discover that children require much more than food and shelter; they need physical touch and human modeling to develop into healthy, purposeful adults. Nearly a century ago, pediatrician and psychoanalyst D. W. Winnicott reflected on the gift of the "good enough mother," the primary caregiver who responds adequately to the child's essential need to be held and cared for.[2] A "good enough" response allows the child to grow a relationship of dependence on the caregiver and develop a healthy sense of self. If you have ever seen a baby who will relax only in the arms of a father or mother, you know what we are describing. This trustful dependence expands into the ability to relate in meaningful ways to a widening circle of human beings among family, friends, and ultimately larger society. Over time the support of caregivers enables children to learn the norms and practices of culture that allow them to participate fully in human community.

Winnicott goes on to describe what happens in the inner world of the child when the caregiving response is "good enough."[3] Babies who are reassured and embraced regardless of how they express themselves come to realize that communicating what they desire is safe and welcome. They grow up learning to live more naturally out of their true selves, able to express honest feelings and thoughts. Those without "good enough" caregiving tend toward a false self, a kind of mask they put on to meet the perceived expectations of others. They learn to internalize and imitate the behavior of others in order to please

2. Winnicott, *Playing and Reality*, 13–14.
3. Winnicott, *Maturational Processes*, 139–45.

those around them. The life journey of every individual person is certainly unique and complex, but there is no doubt that we are biologically wired to need community for survival. Even more, the quality of that community makes a critical difference for how well we can actually live in a manner that reflects our true, authentic selves.

As a culture, we tend to focus on the role of human community for physical and emotional development, but the profound influence of human modeling extends to the spiritual life as well. We would have very few ideas about relating to God if not for the examples of others. All kinds of interactions, from meal-time prayers to Sunday school classes to the informal mention of God, teach us something about who God is and how we believe God interacts with us. Even our images of God tend to reflect our experiences with primary caregivers.

The impact of community upon our spiritual lives also goes beyond parents, mentors, friends, and congregations that interact with us directly. The very fact that we can read the story of God's people in the Scriptures points to centuries of Christian communities committed to preserving these documents and teaching them to the next generation. The Spirit of God undoubtedly guided the process, but God allowed human beings to play a critical role. Communal practices like the Lord's Supper are rooted in another time and place, but they continue to play a central part in the life of most congregations because they have been passed down over time. All spiritual development bears the indelible stamp of human relationships, a truth also evident in the biblical narratives themselves.

Listening to Scripture

In the previous chapter, we explored some of the ways our understanding of spiritual companioning is grounded in Scripture. We painted this picture in broad strokes, describing the Bible's depiction of the human dilemma of sin and the resulting distortion of our relationships with God, neighbor, and self. By God's grace, we are called to come back home to him, an invitation that is possible through Jesus Christ, in whom God is reconciling the world to himself. Christ's presence in our lives is rooted in a trinitarian framework of the communion of Spirit, Son, and Father. Just as God is by nature community, so human beings are also invited to community and to particular kinds of intentional relationships such as spiritual companionship. Through effective companionship, we live into the good news of God's healing, forgiveness, and transformation. In this chapter, we give special attention to the way Scripture portrays the congregation as the primary community in which spiritual companioning takes place.

We begin by turning once more to the example of Jesus Christ. Not only does Jesus's death provide a pathway to reunion with God, self, and others, but his life and ministry also give us a window into the nature of a new kind of spiritual fellowship. Jesus models an intimate relationship with God, his Father, taking critical time away to pray even when his schedule is busiest (Mark 1:35–37; Luke 5:16). For the first time, human beings get an "on the ground" look at what it means to be a companion with God and to share that companionship with others.

The mission of Christ continues in a new way with the sending of the Holy Spirit at Pentecost. While the Spirit is involved in Jesus's life and work from beginning to end, the Spirit is now poured out more fully on Jesus's followers. The Spirit is present and active in their lives, working toward redemption, calling human beings to return their attention to God, and becoming a Counselor and Comforter to those who invite the Spirit to guide their way (John 14:26). Through the Spirit's presence and power, it is possible to begin putting aside broken ways of relating and to grow relationships that show evidence of the Spirit's fruit (Gal. 5:22–23). It is the Holy Spirit who strengthens and guides the first church gatherings as they are getting started.

We see many examples of how effectively the Spirit builds up the Christian community in the book of Acts and the letters of Paul. In the early days of the church, Christians in Jerusalem spent considerable time together (Acts 2:42–47). They met at the temple, and their fellowship spilled outward. They did everyday things: eating and praying, learning from one another, and sharing life with God. They did not become hermits in their new beliefs. The example of Christ and the guidance of the Holy Spirit led to the birth of the church, a community of loving, committed relationships pointing to God. Yet even in this remarkable fellowship, sin is still part of the story. We discover that two members of the community, Ananias and Sapphira, chose to lie to their leaders about their gift to the church. They paid for their dishonesty with their lives (5:1–11). This was a shocking development that must have shaken the fledgling church to its core. Life in the Christian community is hardly idyllic. It is not without pain and mess.

In spite of struggles, early followers of Christ continued meeting together. The letters of Paul offer many poignant images of spiritual fellowship. He encourages members of the congregation to use their different gifts for the common good and to "bear one another's burdens" (Gal. 6:2). As we have already noted, Paul uses "one another" language frequently to talk about the mutual commitment and encouragement God is calling the community to foster. The Greek verb *oikodomeō*, which means "to build up," is employed to explain this process. In Paul's time, construction workers and engineers would use this language to describe their work. Paul adapts it to clarify his leadership role in building up the congregation as a spiritual fellowship. In 1 Corinthians 3:10, for example, Paul calls himself a "skilled master builder" who lays the foundation of the Corinthian congregation, on which others continue to build. Paul also believes the task of building up the spiritual fellowship of the congregation is not his alone. It belongs to everyone in the congregation. As he tells the Christians in Thessalonica, "Therefore encourage one another and build up each other, as indeed you are doing" (1 Thess. 5:11).

During the early centuries of the church, the gospel spread in part because of the special kind of community found in Christian congregations. The mutual care and support members offered one another and their neighbors stood in stark contrast to the way people ordinarily treated each other in the Greco-Roman world. In fact, Christian participation in community became a very practical matter at many points when believers faced intense persecution. Some lost their families, their freedom, and even their lives for choosing to embrace the faith. The new community became like a family, gathering in those who needed relationship and encouragement to live the Christian life faithfully, just as the New Testament describes.

Mining the Protestant Tradition

The Christian church has regularly returned to the biblical portrayal of the first church for wisdom and renewal. The Protestant Reformation in its many streams was one such attempt to recover the kind of Christian community described in the New Testament. Martin Luther spoke of the priesthood of all believers to describe the way every Christian serves as a minister to others: bearing burdens, praying for one another, and providing mutual encouragement.

The early Anabaptists were especially concerned about developing Christian community. They took great risks to bring to life the New Testament's vision of spiritual fellowship among Jesus's followers. To keep their unlawful meetings a secret, they gathered in hidden places and hillside caves. At these meetings, they recited Scripture, sang, prayed, and testified to God's presence in their lives. They believed that giving and receiving spiritual companionship was worth the risk. In spite of real dangers, they created voluntary communities characterized by commitment and accountability to Christ and one another.

Other movements have emerged in the Protestant tradition that have also attempted to keep alive the vision of the congregation as a living fellowship of spiritual companioning. The Pietist movement is one example, as is the Methodist movement, initiated by John Wesley. Sometimes, the recovery of spiritual fellowship in the congregation was not part of a larger movement but came to expression in a single congregation or an organization of Christians from many congregations. Sometimes, it was articulated in the vision of a single individual.

Committed to Companionship

One leader whose vision of spiritual companioning in the congregation stands out in a particular way was born into an upper-class German family in 1906. His father, Karl, was a neurologist and psychiatrist, and his mother, Paula, was a teacher with a passion for her children's education. Young Dietrich longed for the elusive attention of his father and older brothers, and he often experienced a sense of intense loneliness. He began to claim a deep personal faith in Christ in his young adult years and grew to develop close personal friendships. A passion for discipleship and Christian fellowship would set the course for life choices in the years to follow.

A bright scholar, committed teacher, and faithful church person, Dietrich Bonhoeffer was drawn into a confluence of events that tested his commitment to Christlike community in a remarkable manner. Even as a young man barely in his twenties, he revealed a fascination with Christ-centered relationships in his doctoral thesis, "The Communion of Saints." He seemed poised to head into a meaningful career as a Lutheran pastor and teacher when the Nazi party began to gain strength. While he had opportunities for teaching and ministry elsewhere in safer places, he chose to risk his own life for the sake of others.

Bonhoeffer returned to Germany to direct a clandestine seminary for the Confessing Church, a movement defying the Nazi government's attempts to control German Protestants. We feel the conviction of his commitment in a letter to Reinhold Neibuhr: "I must live through this difficult period of our national history with the Christian people of Germany. I will have no right to share in the reconstruction of Christian life in Germany after the war if I do not share in the trials of this time with my people."[4]

During this period of subversive leadership and, later, imprisonment, Bonhoeffer continued to give himself to the cause of Christian community. Along the way, he explored spiritual companioning in thought and practice. This is evident in the treasure trove of surprisingly hope-filled letters Bonhoeffer wrote from prison to Eberhard Bethge, his closest friend from the underground seminary. Bethge responded to these gifts of friendship by taking great risks to hide the letters and then devoting himself to their preservation and publication in later years. This relationship, formed in a clandestine Christian community, bolstered them through darker days.

Like many spiritual companions, Bonhoeffer shares with Bethge both the mundane activities of everyday life and profound spiritual insights. He reflects also on the nature of spiritual friendship, something truly bittersweet given the solitude of his prison cell. Bethge's companionship must certainly have been

4. Coles, *Dietrich Bonhoeffer*, 24.

on his mind when he wrote the poem "The Friend." Bonhoeffer suggests that true friends function as "playmates . . . on the spirit's long journeys." Even in the midst of plentiful "vermin that feed on envy, greed, and suspicion," it is possible for a human being "to cast aside all deceit, open his heart to the spirit he trusts, and unite with him freely as one." This form of friendship is like a fortress that provides the "refuge and comfort and strengthening" needed to face the world and act resolutely in the kind of work that brings life meaning.[5]

Bonhoeffer's words are a fitting testimony to the type of companionship he shared with his closest friend. While they had different ways of seeing life, Bonhoeffer with the intellect and Bethge through the senses, they naturally understood and supported one another in the use of their gifts because of their "long spiritual fellowship."[6] Bonhoeffer recognized from experience that we may know a bit of God's presence through the trusted spiritual companion.

Christ the Mediator of Relationship

This practice of spiritual companionship is undergirded by rich theological convictions. Bonhoeffer suggests that regular fellowship in the Christian community is a gracious gift from God that cannot be neglected or taken for granted. In fact, he notes that Christian community is a gift that "any day may be taken from us," words that foreshadowed his own journey.[7] For Bonhoeffer, genuine fellowship is essentially a spiritual, not a human reality. When we love out of our human nature, we cannot fully separate ourselves from the motivation to meet our own desires for affirmation and acceptance. In our attempt to mean something to others, we all too consciously cultivate relationships that can lead to what Bonhoeffer calls the "cult of the human."[8]

Whether aware of it or not, we are driven by our own need to be needed, and ultimately people become more important than anything else. We all have a God-given desire for relationship, but our brokenness makes it impossible to share the kind of fellowship God imagined for us at the beginning of creation. As Bonhoeffer suggests,

> We are separated from one another by an unbridgeable gulf of otherness and strangeness which resists all our attempts to overcome it by means of natural association or emotional or spiritual union. There is no way from one person to another. However loving and sympathetic we try to be, however sound our psychology, however frank and open our behaviour, we cannot penetrate the

5. Bonhoeffer, *Letters and Papers*, 387–90.
6. Ibid., 384–85.
7. Bonhoeffer, *Life Together*, 20.
8. Bonhoeffer, *Letters and Papers*, 386.

incognito of the other man, for there are no direct relationships, not even between soul and soul.[9]

Failed relationships in our own lives and all around us reveal the truth of Bonhoeffer's words. We visit counselors and use psychological tools such as Myers-Briggs in an effort to understand and be more honest with one another, but we still fail to live according to the social mandate at the heart of the Ten Commandments.

By the grace of God, we do not have to give up on our efforts to cross the gulf that exists between ourselves and others. Bonhoeffer reveals another way to envision a soul-to-soul connection in the Christian community. It begins by keeping in mind that our fellowship in the congregation is based completely upon what Christ has done for each of us. It is what God has done, rather than our own grasping efforts, that binds us together. Jesus Christ is a Mediator not only between God and humanity (1 Tim. 2:5) but also between human beings—in the messy middle of our engagement with one another. When Christ stands between us, our relationships are transformed entirely. We are able to see others with a compassion that does not come from within us. This is true even in the most intimate relationships of life. Genuine spiritual companionship becomes possible by grace through the in-breaking of Christ. This has significant implications for our approach to spiritual companionship. Our soul conversations, in particular, depend upon Christ to mediate between us. Perhaps we might even think of Christ as a kind of interpreter, the One we invite to stand between us so that we might catch a glimpse of what he sees and hears when we listen to each other.

Bonhoeffer brings the notion of Christ as Mediator into the everyday life of a community by offering several concrete suggestions for building spiritual fellowship. First, he states that intercessory prayer forms the foundation for relationship. If God is truly mediating between us, we do well to recognize this in the way we spend our time together. We may petition God for others while on our own, but it is especially effective in community. For Bonhoeffer, corporate prayer is the purest form of fellowship. When we pray together for one another, Christ is recognized as present and accessible, at the center of our gathering.

Second, intercessory prayer must be accompanied by a willingness to listen well, a skill Bonhoeffer believed was sadly lacking among Christians in his time. Not much has changed. If anything, our attentiveness to one another has deteriorated amid the distracting noise and activity all around and within us. God not only gives us his Word but also listens to us, and we are called to

9. Bonhoeffer, *Cost of Discipleship*, 97.

pass this gift on to others. Bonhoeffer argues that our inability to listen to our brothers and sisters in Christ suggests that we may soon cease listening to God as well. The death of the spiritual life lies in "spiritual chatter and clerical condescension arrayed in pious words," something none of us enjoys listening to.[10]

We feel the mediating love of God in conversation partners who do not presume to know what we will say before words are spoken, but who wait with patience, honoring us with prayer-filled attention. In essence, this becomes a three-way conversation as we attend both to God and the other. If we listen in this way, our attitudes toward each other reflect the kind of attention we hope God also gives to us.

Third, these practices must be accompanied by the ministry of bearing. It is clear that Bonhoeffer had Paul's letters in mind when he wrote about this. He reminds us to appreciate one another in those characteristics we find odd or weak along with those we find pleasant. Even, or perhaps especially, when weakness results in sin, we must bear with one another by lovingly creating space for confession and reconciliation. Bonhoeffer taught that confession before a fellow believer is essential. A privately held sin is so much more difficult to eradicate than one we have shared with someone who cares for us.

The success of groups like Alcoholics Anonymous attests to this. These private sins actually harm our fellowship with the whole community by creating separation. We participate in God's mediating acts between us when we confess in the presence of another. Confession before one brother or sister in Christ restores fellowship with the whole community. Bonhoeffer offers this compelling reminder: "If a Christian is in the fellowship of confession with a brother he will never be alone again, anywhere."[11]

Leaders of Christian communities have a special responsibility to model a ministry of bearing. At one point, Bonhoeffer urges ministers not to complain about their congregations, not to God or to anyone else. Church leaders have not been given communities of faith in order to evaluate them constantly, in essence, taking their spiritual temperature. Some ministers need to be reminded that the community of faith does not belong to any individual person. It is not "my church" because I am a leader. The congregation belongs to God. Rather than complaining, leaders ought to examine themselves first and then intercede for the communities they serve.[12]

Bonhoeffer's ideas about Christ's mediating presence and the gifts of intercession, confession, and bearing are reflected beautifully in one minister's

10. Bonhoeffer, *Life Together*, 97–98.
11. Ibid., 112–13.
12. Ibid., 29–30.

description of practicing companionship through spiritual direction. Sarah has been serving a congregation as an associate pastor for three years, and she offers spiritual direction to a handful of church members. During a day full of pastoral tasks, she sometimes feels tired and preoccupied by the time she sits down across from a directee and enters into silent prayer. At that moment, the silence is as much for her as for the directee. Sarah asks God for the ability to listen well and see the other through the eyes of Christ, with the compassion of Christ. In the silence, she invites Christ to join the conversation, in essence, pulling up a chair to make a circle of three.

As Sarah begins to listen to the directee, the weariness somehow melts away, and she gains a focus that she struggles to describe. Sarah hears and feels alongside the other, leaning forward in her chair to catch the next bit of insight, praying silently for God to move and minister. At times she offers a word of encouragement, hears a confession, or raises a challenge. She often invites the directee to pause for moments of silent listening before God, and she always ends their time together by naming the other in spoken prayer before God. Directees often seem relieved and encouraged after hearing their names spoken aloud before God.

Even after years of experience, the empathic energy arising within her still takes Sarah by surprise. She never doubts that this kind of compassion comes from the Spirit of God. Sarah cannot own or manipulate it—she does not always sense God's presence to the same degree. All she can do is trust in the mediating Christ to build a bridge between herself and the other, at least for those precious moments. While this kind of prayerful attentiveness seems to come most naturally for her in the spiritual direction setting, she tries to open up to Christ's mediating presence in all kinds of ministry interactions.

Practicing Spiritual Companioning

The witness of Scripture and the wisdom of theologians like Dietrich Bonhoeffer help lay the groundwork for us to imagine spiritual companionship community. What we are saying essentially is that the "who" and "why" questions we need to ask about congregational life are rooted in these core ideas: (1) human beings are designed by God to be fundamentally social; (2) human relationships are disrupted by sin; (3) God offers an invitation to restoration in relationship to himself and to one another through the mediating presence of Christ; and (4) the congregation is specially set apart by God to meet the human need for restored connectedness through spiritual companionship.

We must not underestimate the role of the church in the process of reclaiming relationships with God and others. While we may get caught up in running programs, parsing out the minutiae of doctrine, or focusing on the image we portray to the community, a foundational calling of the church is to create a space where people can know and love God and each other. Ultimately, the spiritual growth of church members depends less upon the quality of our music in worship or the fabulous activities in our children's ministry and more on the genuine relationships between children and adults and the attention music leaders give to who we are and what will create a space for encountering God. Congregations are easily distracted by peripheral concerns that do not matter much from a God's-eye perspective.

In truth, congregations are intended to be guided by the Holy Spirit to bear witness to the gospel in what we say and do, in our teaching, in our administration, and in how we treat one another and our neighbors. Spiritual companionship in the congregation is a critical part of this witness. It sets before the world the possibilities of a human community that has begun to reorient itself to God's reconciliation of the world in Jesus Christ. It represents provisionally, not perfectly, what a community might look like when it lives out the forgiveness, healing, mutual care, peace, and service that flow from a restored relationship with God. In this way, spiritual companioning is a means to spiritual development, and it is also an embodiment of what God has in mind for the Great Restoration, when God's purposes for all creation are finally complete. As our congregations grow confidently into these core ideas, we can move forward to create space for genuine engagement and explore the "what" and "how" questions we described earlier.

The Climate of a Congregation

So how does the average congregation practice living out this vision? What does spiritual companionship actually mean at the level of nuts and bolts, of people and programs? Not long ago, a pastor of an established congregation raised these questions with some frustration. He had already caught the vision for spiritual companioning and had developed significant spiritual friendships in his own life, but he was unsure about how to invite others to get on board. Unfortunately, there is no one answer or set process that makes sense for every congregation or guarantees meaningful spiritual companioning. What we must do is pray for God's guidance and then start to create spaces where individuals can choose to engage with one another and grow. We begin our discussion of the possibilities by exploring the importance of atmospheric conditions.

There is no doubt that climate makes a dramatic difference in our perspective on life. This past winter has been no different. Unusually dramatic swings in temperature in many parts of North America have brought out strong feelings about the weather. When the coldest days blow in with considerable wind or snow, we bundle up and wish for warmth, complaining about how uncomfortable it feels. We wrap our coats tightly around us and hurry inside, frowning at the unpleasant sensation of biting temperatures. A few days later the sun comes out and the weather warms by thirty degrees. We smile again and remove outer layers, hurrying a bit less in our travels. We talk about how pleasant it is outside and encourage each other to enjoy the weather. When the temperature swings dramatically, it is especially easy to see how much we are influenced by the pains and pleasures of our climate.

Congregations develop a kind of climate that becomes evident in casual conversations, meetings, and small group gatherings. Do we take time to chat and check in about family members or important events? Do we open up our lives to one another and bask in the warmth of a pleasant climate, "breaking bread" together as the believers did in the book of Acts? Do we risk exploring our prayer lives and areas of spiritual growth or challenge with others, as Bonhoeffer described? Or are we quick to come and go, tightening our coats in self-protection and holding back from sharing our true selves with one another?

One thing we, the authors, have noticed is that congregations can sometimes appear hospitable but not actually be open places where genuine spiritual companionship is welcome. These are communities or pockets of communities where virtually everyone is wearing a smile and claims to be "fine" most of the time. Images on church websites show happy families playing together and members experiencing deeply religious moments, sometimes on mountaintops with hands raised and light streaming all around.

Of course, few congregations would want to be known for unhappy families or the absence of God. Yet our images and expectations can lead participants to put on false selves, as Winnicott describes, appearing to have it all together and masking the pain and struggles that are not easily fixed. Talk of broken hearts and lives is mostly avoided. The joy-filled parts of Scripture are chosen much more frequently than the painful ones. While congregations like these appear warm, they have cold spots that prohibit genuine relationship.

Some of us tend to expect wintry conditions in congregations. We hesitate to warm up to others because we have had painful church experiences or we fear that we will not be accepted for one reason or another. Winnicott's description of the "good enough mother" is an apt metaphor for describing the church. Not everyone has experienced a "good enough church," which provides genuine spiritual companionship through people who extend the love and grace of Christ in spite of faults and failures and who offer the companionship that incorporates confession, intercession, and bearing with one another. We are not talking about people who provide the perfect experience of community. Every church, just like every parent, does some things better than others, and probably has a few regrets and blind spots. But the "good enough" church strives to create a warm climate with open spaces for honest conversation about things that matter, so that even painful stories find a safe and comforting place to be told.

Caleb is a church member who describes this experience with clarity. Some years ago he found himself struggling deeply with doubts about his faith. He wrestled with questions about God's goodness in the face of tragedies and wondered if God is really present and active in the world today. These were not the kinds of doubts and questions frequently named in Sunday school classes or in conversations in church hallways. Sometimes he wondered if he should continue attending church.

Caleb's pastor surprised him by beginning to talk about naming pain and raising tough questions in a series of sermons. When she opened up about her own faith struggles, he took a risk and decided to speak to her directly. Instead of offering the kind of judgment he feared, she created a warm and hospitable space that helped him to name his questions openly. By accepting him in spite of his doubts and affirming his honesty, she allowed him to begin setting aside the false, "church-appropriate" self to live out of the true self. Years later, he describes the experience as an important form of spiritual companionship. It was not any particular wisdom she offered or advice she shared, but simply a willingness to walk alongside him as he struggled with God. The experience has helped him develop deep roots in the congregation and has drawn him to become part of small groups and individual relationships dedicated to intentional spiritual companionship. He now looks for opportunities to become a spiritual companion to others.

Creating a Culture of Spiritual Conversation

A warm and nurturing climate alone is not enough. Another part of fostering spiritual companioning in a congregation is creating a culture of spiritual conversation. Some congregations tend to focus on ideas *about God* more than on describing the relationship *to God*. There may be several reasons for this, but two stand out. First, the seminary training of church leaders does not always adequately prepare them for talking about experiences of connecting with God. Seminaries tend to teach more abstract theological language for God and expect pastors-in-training to experience the communal spiritual nurture they need through a local congregation. Seminary students get the message that personal spiritual formation is not essential for leadership preparation, or they deduce that developing a relationship with God is a private matter that does not need to be discussed in community. Meanwhile, the congregations they serve generally assume that seminaries are a place for learning about and nurturing the spiritual life. The end result is that graduates bring the practical skills and theological analysis they train for into the congregation but may downplay language for a personal experience of God, and congregations may not receive the nurturing they thought their leaders had been equipped to give. This is a great loss to the church.

Accurate theological perspectives are critical, but so is a growing communion with God that deepens as we share in it with one another. We have already discussed examples of this in the Acts texts that describe the believers speaking of God over meals and informal fellowship. We see intentional practices that nurture conversation about the spiritual life in Bonhoeffer's commitment to interceding for one another in person, listening attentively, and practicing confession. The church today is called to do much more than provide correct theological language about God; it is meant to create trusting spaces for learning to speak with and about God personally.

A second reason we tread carefully around language for relating to God is the terrible damage done when people presume to declare exactly what God wants in complex circumstances. Did God really want Christians to embark on the deadly Crusades in his name? Could God allow a child to die because he needs "another angel in heaven"? Human beings have often failed miserably at putting words to God's will. Instead of reflecting biblical theology and nurturing the spiritual life, we have said and done things that distorted God's purposes. Because of this, many of us have become wisely cautious about declaring that we know what God is saying or doing in individual circumstances, ours or anyone else's. This seems dangerously close to stripping God of mystery and transcendence. We can know God's purposes only in part, as if we are looking through a fog when the sun has not yet burned through the mist (see 1 Cor. 13:12 in *The Message*).

These concerns make us guarded about presuming to know how God is communicating with us. In fact, we may shy away from exploring language for our spiritual journey altogether and feel uncomfortable when anyone else does. What we lose in the process is our ability to explore how God is still with us, still actively involved in our lives, and still revealing himself to us in our time and place. As in every generation gone before, people today are hungry for a word from the Lord. Learning to talk about this enables us to grow in intimacy with God and each other. It is possible to develop a language for God with humility rather than presumption.

Rediscovering Historic Christian Spirituality

One way to begin creating space for spiritual conversation in congregations is to explore historic traditions of Christian spirituality. Great riches in historic Christian spirituality are being recovered today, but many people in our congregations are still unfamiliar with them. Developing the ability to talk about our spiritual lives is greatly enriched by learning from the stories of those who have sought God before us. We gain a great deal from a broad range of writings like Dietrich Bonhoeffer's *Life Together* and Brother Lawrence's *The Practice of the Presence of God*. We look not only for ideas but also practices and the stories of lives lived in relationship with God. We can draw from contemporary spiritual writers in familiar theological traditions alongside those from times and traditions very different from ours. Often they provide language we can relate to somehow that helps us give voice to our own experiences. Congregations that take this approach need to begin slowly. Some participants will be more receptive than others. Starting a study group or drawing upon historic Christian figures in sermons can help nudge the congregation forward.

Every community develops its own unique language and terminology for the spiritual life. In our experience, it is critical to listen for language that our communities are already comfortable with, and then gently expand it alongside new practices. In one of our seminaries, we talk about "praying with Scripture" as a way to present *lectio divina* to new students unfamiliar with the term. A student who embraced the practice decided to bring it to a group of older women in her conservative Protestant congregation. If she had invited them to practice *lectio divina*, they might have hesitated, but all seemed comfortable exploring new ways to do two things they already knew well: reading Scripture and praying about it. Ultimately they discovered that this unfamiliar practice was closely related to what they had been doing privately for decades. Sharing what they sensed in the silence created inroads for deepening companionship.

Whatever our approach, we also take the time to discern how the new thing we introduce belongs within the theology and communal life of our congregations. We must think through the relationship between practices and beliefs and be able to give an answer for this to anyone who asks. There will always be people in our circles of fellowship who need to understand what we are introducing theologically and reflect on the implications for the community before they feel comfortable participating. We cannot impose spiritual practices or theories about the spiritual life on our communities simply because they have become popular. We risk treating the church as a consumer environment where we offer up the latest product because it worked somewhere else. Rediscovering historic traditions of Christian spirituality is a process requiring prayerful discernment and reflection on how these spiritual resources belong in our contexts.

The importance of this issue became evident in the experience of a middle-aged couple. One spouse embraced the growing spiritual direction ministry in their congregation, finding it deeply encouraging personally and communally. The other spouse was skeptical. She worried that congregational members would turn increasingly inward and lose sight of their commitment to community service. They agreed to disagree, but acknowledged that each did not truly understand or value the other's perspective. What leaders needed to offer this couple and the larger community was an opportunity to reflect on how the new ministry would fit alongside the commitments the congregation already cherished. They needed to explore a theology of spiritual direction and ask important questions about how the practice can actually support community service. Perhaps safeguards could be put in place to protect the calling to both forms of ministry, including commitments to talk, pray, teach about, and practice both regularly.

One congregation encouraged spiritual companioning groups to lead worship at a nearby assisted living facility, drawing upon their life together to prepare worship and build relationship with others. Theological discussion and engaged practice belong together, and they help to strengthen our ability to provide genuine spiritual companionship to one another.

Forming Character

Spiritual companionship cannot develop by language and practice alone. It requires the hard work of growing in character, which directly affects how we treat one another. On this point, no one says it better than the apostle Paul, who reminds believers that they can speak the language of angels and have the ability to fathom great mysteries but it is all empty, irritating noise without a commitment to love (1 Cor. 13:1–2). Those who are unwilling to develop qualities of patience, gentleness, self-control, and other signs of the Spirit (Gal. 5:22–23) will hardly be desirable spiritual companions. Who of us seeks counsel from someone who has a vast knowledge of Christian spirituality but cannot be trusted to hold a confidence? All of our "spiritual" words are useless without godly character.

Jeffrey, the leader of a small young-adult group, experienced this firsthand. The group was learning to practice silence and prayer in weekly meetings alongside brief Scripture readings. A young man started coming with a friend and seemed to express interest in the group. After a time, it became clear that his focus in the meeting was debating theology. While others moved into personal exploration of God's presence and calling in their lives, sharing in personal confession and a desire to grow, the young man could not get beyond argumentative opinions. Jeffrey grew frustrated and irritated, and he was convinced that he had personally discovered the noisy gong and clanging symbol of 1 Corinthians 13.

Growing in character in a small group like this means treating others with the kind of love that Bonhoeffer describes. Love includes listening in a way that invites others to speak the truth about themselves, including areas of vulnerability and brokenness. It seems the young man was unable to participate in this kind of love. Ironically, love also dictates accepting others in their weakness, something Jeffrey kept in mind in his decision to continue welcoming the newcomer. Jeffrey hoped that the group's companionship would help the young man to grow, to learn compassion and begin sanding away some of his sharp, arrogant edges. Jeffrey's experience reminds us that spiritual companionship is possible only because the mediating love of Christ enables us to treat one another in new and different ways. We choose to embrace the character that God is developing within and welcome the fruit of the Spirit's presence. Living the fruit makes us trustworthy spiritual companions.

Forms of Spiritual Companionship

Perhaps it goes without saying, but spiritual companionship can flourish in many places in the church. One of the most formal types occurs between a trained *spiritual director and directee*. Within the congregational setting, a spiritual director might be a pastor, another staff member, or a layperson who is commissioned or somehow recognized for the work. The director sets aside time to meet with directees one-with-one, generally monthly. This form of relationship can be complicated in congregations because directors must wear multiple hats in people's lives. It is a bit like the experience of counselors or psychologists who see individuals in their practice and at church. Open conversation about handling these roles is critical. While the congregation is called to be a home for spiritual companioning, it is also perfectly appropriate to seek a director from outside the congregation. This may be necessary at times, especially in the case of laypeople who have leadership roles alongside the pastor.

A second, somewhat less formal approach to companionship is the *spiritual companioning group*. The group allows for less individual focus time and intimacy, but provides an opportunity for developing several spiritual friendships. We recommend that the leader have some kind of training or experience with this kind of group. It is also extraordinarily helpful for the group to read about the practice of spiritual direction as they get started. It can be a challenge for participants to learn some of the basics of the process, such as welcoming silence while sitting with others and not giving advice or offering opinions.

Spiritual direction is not like Bible study. It takes focused effort to learn the art of reflective spiritual conversation about the things of God when we are most accustomed to analyzing biblical texts and practically applying them. While a church staff or committee may not be tasked with the mandate to provide spiritual direction to one another, they could learn some of the basic skills and experiment with this kind of process during a retreat or as part of regular gatherings. Spiritual companionship in a group creates space for vulnerability, soul conversation, and a growing consciousness of God's presence in our lives in a way that few other church settings do. It also strengthens the ability of the group to work together at other tasks.

A third type of companionship is *spiritual friendship* between peers. Just as Dietrich Bonhoeffer and Eberhard Bethge came to share significant fellowship, we too can open up to a deepening level of companionship with a select few people in our lives. If we cannot yet fathom who might be interested, it may become clear as we pray and watch for opportunities. Congregations can help their members deepen these relationships by providing sacred spaces for existing friends to become more intentional about their time together, such as retreat days for practicing the skills of spiritual direction. They can also facilitate opportunities for interested persons to find spiritual friends. One congregation experimented with this for both groups and individuals, a process that led to several significant companioning relationships. Sometimes we find these relationships on our own through existing spheres of church, work, community, or family.

A practical approach to intentional connection is to set a regular time in which companions take turns sharing how they sense God's presence and are growing in their faith. The listener temporarily sets aside his or her own agenda to reflect back what is heard and ask probing questions. The most important thing to keep in mind is that we must be intentional about our purpose. Spiritual conversation as we have described it is very different from casual talk; it requires a decision to attend to the other while watching for signs of God's presence. Through the nurture of spiritual friendship, we get a small taste of the love and affirmation of God. Genuine spiritual fellowship in a congregation grows beyond the initial relationships to touch many more lives, something every leader hopes for.

Exploring the Stories of Congregations

Many of the ideas we explore in this chapter are reflected in particular ways in the journey of Christ the Savior, the congregation we introduced in the beginning of the chapter. Again, there is no one way individual congregations must proceed; each one will find a unique path for developing a ministry of spiritual companionship. This congregation held its first gathering about two decades ago when a handful of friends assembled to discuss the meaning and purpose of church life. They were growing increasingly exhausted from participating in heavily programmed congregations, yet none were willing to give up engaging in spiritual fellowship. Several founders admit that they never intended to start a new congregation, but that is ultimately the path they chose.

What the group most yearned for was a straightforward way of being the church. They began to identify themselves as "sacred and simple." "Simple" did not mean effortless. The members completed all of the tasks of church life and worship themselves with the exception of preaching. Early worship experiences included several typical Protestant elements—a worship order with sermon, hymns, and prayer—but everything was chosen by the members themselves, who offered up their gifts, celebrating the importance of each one's contributions.

The church's first pastor was called a few years after its founding. He suggests that the congregation did not have a very clear vision of who they wanted to become beyond "sacred and simple." They were a diverse group in terms of denomination and politics, and they were open-minded, longing to move past institutional maintenance toward connection with the divine and with each other. In his words, "When they began to meet, they had a contemplative experience around being together. . . . They would sit and talk about their pain . . . and talk about faith in ways that didn't seem to be encumbered by someone quoting from Karl Barth. They were more personal."

In addition to the emphasis on relationship, they gradually began to work out the "sacred and simple" concept in deeper theological and practical ways. The pastor's own crisis of faith caused him to seek guidance to deepen his spiritual life. For the first time, he discovered the life stories of the desert fathers and mothers and the works of spiritual masters such as Thomas Merton, Cynthia Bourgeault, and others from many segments of the Christian church who were writing about the encounter with God and ways of praying. He recognized his need for time alone to attend to his own spiritual health and to build relationships with people trained in spiritual direction. He began making visits to retreat centers and Benedictine monasteries and gave significant time at home to contemplative prayer and study.

The pastor knew that his own personal transformation was critical for his health and well-being, but it could never be for him alone. He wanted to companion his congregation and see the same good things he experienced come to pass among them. He began to wonder about how to create a congregational space that nurtures spiritual formation for individuals and the larger soul of the community. He started preaching about growing in the spiritual life, drawing on writings from ancient spiritual masters that had revolutionized his own journey. Simple choruses, moments of silence, and *lectio divina*[13] in worship drew participants to prayerful reflection and encounters with God. Members came alongside one another in groups formed for developing spiritual practices strengthened by mutual accountability.

Over time the church has grown and changed, facing the challenges of larger numbers with the inevitable push toward programming and a loss of the kind of intimacy that can be shared only by a few. Yet new members and original founders still describe the congregation as a place to encounter God in and through the companionship of a community sharing the vision to be "sacred and simple."

Exercising Our Companionship: Understanding One-Anothering

While developing practices of companionship, it may be helpful to learn the "one-anothering" passages of the New Testament. Whether you are alone, with a spiritual friend, or in a larger group, read slowly through the list, pausing briefly after each reference. Repeat. Do not hurry; take time to listen for any invitations from God along the way. Is there a particular area of one-anothering in which you personally are flourishing? Any specific area of struggle? How about in the life of your community? Journal or discuss with others what you notice.

> "*Love one another* with mutual affection; outdo one another in showing honor" (Rom. 12:10).[14]
>
> "*Live in harmony with one another*; do not be haughty, but associate with the lowly; do not claim to be wiser than you are" (Rom. 12:16).
>
> "Owe no one anything, except to *love one another*; for the one who loves another has fulfilled the law" (Rom. 13:8).

13. We describe *lectio divina* in chapter 5. In the context of corporate worship in this congregation, *lectio divina* involves the repetitive reading of a brief Scripture passage with pauses between readings for silent meditation and prayer.

14. We have added italic for emphasis throughout the quotations in this list.

"*Welcome one another*, therefore, just as Christ has welcomed you, for the glory of God" (Rom. 15:7).

"Put things in order, listen to my appeal, *agree with one another*, live in peace; and the God of love and peace will be with you" (2 Cor. 13:11).

"For you were called to freedom, brothers and sisters; only do not use your freedom as an opportunity for self-indulgence, but through love *become slaves to one another*" (Gal. 5:13).

"*Bear one another's burdens*, and in this way you will fulfill the law of Christ" (Gal. 6:2).

"*Be kind to one another*, tenderhearted, forgiving one another, as God in Christ has forgiven you" (Eph. 4:32).

"*Be subject to one another* out of reverence for Christ" (Eph. 5:21).

"*Bear with one another* and, if anyone has a complaint against another, forgive each other; just as the Lord has forgiven you, so you also must forgive" (Col. 3:13).

"Therefore *encourage one another* and build up each other" (1 Thess. 5:11).

"See that none of you repays evil for evil, but always seek to do *good to one another* and to all" (1 Thess. 5:15).

"But *exhort one another* every day, as long as it is called 'today,' so that none of you may be hardened by the deceitfulness of sin" (Heb. 3:13).

"And let us consider how to *provoke one another to love* and good deeds" (Heb. 10:24).

". . . not neglecting to meet together, as is the habit of some, but *encouraging one another*, and all the more as you see the Day approaching" (Heb. 10:25).

"Do not speak evil against one another, brothers and sisters" (James 4:11).

"Beloved, *do not grumble against one another*, so that you may not be judged" (James 5:9).

"Therefore *confess your sins to one another*, and pray for one another, so that you may be healed" (James 5:16).

"Above all, *maintain constant love for one another*, for love covers a multitude of sins" (1 Pet. 4:8).

"We know love by this, that he laid down his life for us—and we ought to *lay down our lives for one another*" (1 John 3:16).

"Beloved, *let us love one another*, because love is from God; everyone who loves is born of God and knows God" (1 John 4:7).

For Further Reading

Ackerman, John. *Listening to God: Spiritual Formation in Congregations*. Lanham, MD: Rowman & Littlefield, 2001. A guide for leaders who want to help both individuals and congregations learn how to attend to God by first learning to listen to God in community.

Bonheoffer, Dietrich. *Life Together: The Classic Exploration of Faith in Community*. San Francisco: HarperOne, 2009. A classic text that provides practical and theological guidance for living in Christian community.

Dwight, Judy H. *A Quiet Pentecost: Inviting the Spirit into Congregational Life*. Nashville: Upper Room, 2013. A resource that considers stories from over forty congregations that are being transformed by drawing upon spiritual practices.

Reed, Angela H. *Quest for Spiritual Community: Reclaiming Spiritual Guidance for Contemporary Congregations*. New York: T&T Clark, 2011. A text that explores features of contemporary spirituality, stories of congregations, and reflections on historical practices and theological foundations to direct congregations in the recovery of spiritual guidance practices.

Standish, Graham M. *Becoming a Blessed Church: Forming a Church of Spiritual Purpose, Presence, and Power*. Lanham, MD: Rowman & Littlefield, 2004. A resource that considers the process of discerning God's will in the life and ministries of the congregation and inviting the congregation to participate in God's purposes.

Vennard, Jane E. *A Praying Congregation: The Art of Teaching Spiritual Practice*. Lanham, MD: Rowman & Littlefield, 2005. A guide that helps congregation leaders teach various prayer forms in their communities of faith.

Wilhoit, James. *Spiritual Formation as if the Church Mattered: Growing in Christ through Community*. Grand Rapids: Baker Academic, 2008. A comprehensive introduction to spiritual formation, especially in relation to the congregation's role in supporting transformation in each of its members.

3

Spiritual Companioning
in Spiritual Direction

By the time Matt was in his early fifties, he was experiencing considerable stress. In his more honest moments, he had to acknowledge that
he was actually overwhelmed with everything going on in his life. As
a husband, parent, chairperson of the congregation's elder board, and CEO
of his own company, Matt felt the weight of many demands. He was also
feeling the pinch of the "sandwich generation," providing emotional support
and care for both aging parents and young adult children who were passing
through major life transitions. Matt's experience of God and his life in the
church were beginning to lose the meaning they once had. While he could
not fully put it into words, he had begun to feel discouraged and vulnerable.

Matt asked Fred, a trained spiritual director, to talk with him about his life.
They began meeting once a month, and Fred listened carefully to Matt's story,
periodically raising questions about present and past experiences. Fred soon
discovered that Matt had been fairly successful over the years in many aspects
of life, normally accomplishing whatever he set out to do. His experience as a
husband and father was generally satisfying. He had a reputation as a respected
leader in the church and community, something he found deeply gratifying.

Over time, Matt's commitment to family, church, and work had firmly
guided him and given him a sense of purpose. He was diligent about spiritual

practices, praying and reading Scripture regularly, participating in corporate worship, and serving the church. Matt saw himself as a follower of Jesus, and he believed he had often experienced the flow of the Spirit in his life. But now something had changed. At times, Matt felt as though he was losing control of his life, and he recognized how important a sense of control over his affairs had always been for him. The familiar habits and structures no longer worked as well as they once had. Scripture reading and prayer had actually become difficult. Sometimes he felt like he had to drag himself to worship and church meetings.

Matt was anxious to get back to life as it had been before. He wanted to find a better way to live, to do more than just survive, but he felt stuck in a cycle of demands, responses, and reactions that were draining him physically and spiritually. Matt's energy, creativity, and spiritual vitality seemed to be dwindling. He recognized that all of this had something to do with his relationship with God, and he expressed a strong desire to see this relationship become more vital, but had no clue how to get there. Matt was genuinely puzzled about why he could not, as usual, pray his way through this new challenge. He wanted to be close to God, but was feeling a keen sense of failure as a spiritual person and follower of Christ.

So we ask, what kind of help did Matt need? He could have chosen to ask his small group for support, to talk and pray with him. He could have shared his concerns with the group of elders, asking them for counsel and guidance. He could have met with his pastor for several sessions to talk and pray. He could have sought help from a counselor to find ways to reduce stress and better care for himself. Any of these might have provided some significant help.

Matt considered these options, but chose to seek out an experienced spiritual director who was trained to attend to spiritual health and well-being. Perhaps Matt had an inner sense that he needed something more than the kind of support that primarily addresses problems. Perhaps the Spirit was nudging him in another direction toward a kind of reorientation of life. Matt had to admit that he did not yet feel fully comfortable sharing these matters with people who looked up to him as a leader, someone who should have a strong and fervent faith. When he made the decision, Matt was not fully sure of all the reasons himself, but he chose to begin a long-term journey of monthly spiritual direction sessions with Fred. As time passed, Matt recognized that Fred was helping him open his life again to the nearness of God in the midst of stress and distress, discovering anew what it was that God actually wanted of him, and discerning how best to respond.

As Fred describes the relationship from his perspective, he remembers that he paid special attention to exploring not only "spiritual" things but the whole of Matt's life in all of its inner and outer dimensions. As a spiritual director, he holds the conviction that all human experience is of interest to God and that God is somehow present within all experience. The sessions were a practice of spiritual direction, as distinct from other forms of caring, because of Fred's chosen pattern of responses. With a quiet, gentle demeanor, Fred attended to whatever Matt had to bring. He listened with empathy and support, observing the details of Matt's mind and heart by noticing which words he chose and his attitude and spirit as he spoke. When the time was right, Fred gently invited Matt to bring his experiences and concerns directly to God—specifically and in detail.

Fred suggests that his role was to be *with* Matt rather than intervene in his life. He offered a quiet space in which Matt could ponder his concerns and challenges. This included attending to weaknesses, fears, and perplexities about himself and about God. Along the way, Matt reports, he became more aware of God's interests and desires. In fact, after a while he began to see that many of the expectations he believed God had of him were really demands he had placed on himself. When almost everything else was stripped away, Fred asked Matt what, in the end, he believed God really required of him. Matt's response came out unexpectedly and stirred him to the core: *very little*. God expected very little. In one sense, God wanted it all, his whole life; but in another sense, God would accept him regardless of his successes or failures. God expected *very little*. With these few words, Matt felt a remarkable peace and growing strength.

These moments set aside for encountering God brought deeper intimacy, a keen sense of being loved, greater meaning in life, and also some significant challenges. As Matt became more aware of Christ's presence, he could see how his whole life came into play in his interactions with God. At the end of a session with Fred, Matt often reflected on the practical changes he believed God might be inviting him to make. He came to recognize that it was time to let go of some things and allow others to help with responsibilities or take his place and, most of all, that he needed to continue to persevere in prayer even when God seemed more distant than present. There were moments when Matt felt like pushing back against Fred's questions, when the challenges seemed too great or the direction of the conversation was less than helpful. Always the two found their way back to listening for God. For Matt, renewal came at a cost, but he embraced it as good.

As we consider Matt's journey, we see the significance of the one-with-one ministry of Christian spiritual direction. It builds upon spiritual companioning as we have already described it. Spiritual direction has a place in the life and nurture of the church. In fact, it is meant to be a complement to the other ministries of the church, not an alternative. We would never recommend to Matt that he cease going to worship or participating in church boards and small groups because spiritual direction is enough—quite the opposite. Matt's relationship with Fred opened up conversations that enlivened Matt and renewed his vision for congregational participation while also giving him opportunity to prayerfully discern his contributions. The practice centers on a directee who is pursuing an ever-deepening experience with *both* God and God's people. We view spiritual direction as a kind of mentoring or a form of discipleship that may be offered by a pastor or layperson within the church or, as in Matt's case, a person belonging to another congregation.

As we have come to know and experience spiritual direction in modern times, the term itself does not seem to be the most apt description for this ministry. This is particularly true in our mainline Protestant, evangelical, and Anabaptist contexts. The term "spiritual direction" suggests a kind of heavy-handed approach to guiding the spiritual life of another that is not especially welcome in our time. Spiritual direction is not "spiritual" in the sense that it deals only with rare esoteric moments or particular activities like prayer and worship. Nor is it "direction" in terms of the director telling the directee how to please God or what life decisions to make. It is spiritual in that it looks for the Spirit's presence and activity in all of life, and it is direction in the way that the director comes alongside the other who seeks God's direction for life.[1] We choose to use the term "spiritual direction" because it connects us with a practice that has been a rich part of the church's heritage. In contemporary times, numerous books, training programs, and practitioners also use this language. More broadly, we can talk about spiritual guidance, spiritual friendship, spiritual mentoring, and other labeling words to describe the same or similar forms of companioning ministry.

Understanding the Cultural Context

Thomas Paine's famous words, "These are the times that try men's souls," have at least a faint echo in our day.[2] The American psyche is afflicted by violence, terrorism, wars, poverty, broken families, racism, economic insecurity, failure of governments, erratic weather patterns, shootings, and more. Post-9/11 America feels less secure, has greater anxiety and fear, and feels grief and anger at the losses it has suffered. Not unlike Matt, we are also beset by many

1. Reed, *Quest for Spiritual Community*, 8–9.
2. These words were written in the heading of each of a series of pamphlets Thomas Paine wrote on "the American crisis" in 1776 and 1777.

stressors inherent in our personal lifestyles: fear of job loss, homelessness, financial struggles, tense relationships at home and work, long work hours, discrimination, death, divorce, chronic illness, and more. We are an anxious nation and need help to keep anchoring our lives in the God who walks with us.

One way we deal with these concerns is to fill our minds and lives with many activities. The Protestant work ethic remains deeply embedded in our culture and congregations and has long driven us to think that if we only work harder and do more, life will improve. Even with all of the technological advances that should make life easier, we feel rushed. In truth, we are also more distracted than ever because the world is literally at our fingertips as we fly from one website to another. Hurry has become a sickness among us. As C. J. Jung reportedly said, "Hurry is not of the Devil; it *is* the Devil."

Research reveals how big this problem is in our contemporary context. Nathan Stucky, for example, explores the impact of sleep deprivation on adolescents.[3] Contrary to popular perception, he reports, research now indicates that adolescents require between 8.5 and 9.25 hours of sleep every night. In 2014, the National Sleep Foundation found that the average fifteen- to seventeen-year-old gets 7.1 hours of sleep. Sleep deprivation in adolescence is associated with decreased academic performance, obesity across the lifespan, reduced immune function, increased stress, and other problems.

The reasons for sleep deprivation are complex. In part, this trend reflects a cultural ideal, expressed aptly in a slogan on a coffee mug sold at Starbucks: "Sleep is for the weak." For many adolescents, busyness is a badge of honor, a sign that they are working hard and striving for the American dream.[4] It also is related to the need for constant connection fostered by the increased use of smartphones. Stucky summarizes some of the most important research on the relationship between sleep deprivation and the widespread use of these technologies among young people:

> In a study of over 1,600 young people, Jan Van den Bulck found that 62% reported using cell phones after "lights out," and he discovered a strong association between cell use after lights out and daytime sleepiness. In her work with college students, Sue K. Adams at the University of Rhode Island found that over 45% of college students admitted to answering texts during their sleep, over 40% answered calls during sleep, and several of her research subjects acknowledged that they slept with their phones under their pillows. The National Sleep Foundation reports that 20% of teens are awakened by cell phones after falling asleep "at least a few nights a week," and researchers at Harvard

3. Stucky, "Disorienting Grace." The studies cited here come from chap. 2.
4. Ibid.

have documented cases of "sleep texting"—similar to sleep walking—in which people send and receive texts during their sleep and then have no memory of the activity the next morning.[5]

We find a similar picture of hurriedness and drivenness among adults. Decades ago, Meyer Friedman and Ray Rosenman coined the term "hurry sickness" on the basis of their research on the effects of stress on the heart. They found a particularly strong association between "hurry sickness" and Type A behavior, which they describe as "a continuous struggle, an unremitting attempt to accomplish or achieve more and more things or participate in more and more events in less and less time, frequently in the face of opposition—real or imagined—from other persons."[6] Such behavior is no longer confined to a particular personality type. It is pervasive in a culture in which people feel the need for constant connection to work and other people through digital media, 24/7.

Our hurried, sleep-deprived, hyperconnected lives often cause us to run roughshod over family, friends, and our own inner being, leaving us little time to be reflective and prayerful. Like the seeds falling among thorns that choked the plants into fruitlessness (Mark 4:7), our spiritual vitality is choked out by busyness and hurry, sometimes even our hurry on behalf of Christian community. Sunday mornings and Wednesday nights at church can become hurried times that prevent us from really noticing our families, friends, and the stranger who just walked in. It also can prevent us from hearing what God is trying to communicate in and through times of worship and study. Likely, Matt felt this way on occasion.

At the core of our being, we have been created for fellowship with one another and communion with God. But when anguish and hurry continue unabated, our spirits feel smitten, even ravished, often with a growing sense that God is absent and uninterested in our lives. By nature, anxiety and hurry captivate our minds and our attention. When this happens, we begin to lose a sense of the immediacy and immanence of God. Scripture reading is dry and our prayers seem empty. Today, as much as ever, we need to step alongside one another and help each other press the pause button on our activities, so that we may open up to the God who wants to renew us. This is the vision of spiritual direction.

This ministry is not just for those who seek healing in their relationship with God. It also is important for persons who simply want to grow in Christ and need a place to explore the mysteries of the Spirit's presence. Sometimes our divine encounters border on the mystical. In divine-human interactions,

---

5. Ibid., 78–79.
6. Friedman and Rosenman, *Type A Behavior*, 31.

God cannot be tamed. When the presence of God lights up the soul, that person may have unusual experiences that seem mysterious, out of the ordinary, and hard to explain. At such times, spiritual direction can be used by God to affirm and guide the soul. We benefit from a safe space that allows us to set aside fears of being misunderstood or viewed as spiritual misfits.

Listening to Scripture

When we look at the larger story of God's people that emerges in Scripture, we notice that one-with-one relationships were essential for opening to God's will and purposes. In the records of the Israelite people, wisdom came through the Torah, mediated by priests, prophets, community leaders, and family members. But it was also passed on through mentoring relationships. This is seen in the relationship of Eli with Samuel, Samuel with David, Naomi with Ruth, and Elijah with Elisha. There are many instances in which one-with-one relationships are a source of clarity and guidance.

The teacher-student or master-disciple relationship rooted in Hebrew tradition remained essential in the New Testament. We see this most clearly in Jesus's relationship with his disciples, especially the inner circle of three. In the interactions between Jesus and Peter, for example, we find Jesus mentoring Peter as he travels a long journey before finally realizing that Jesus is God's Son and Messiah. This is a journey filled with impetuous enthusiasm, as well as misunderstanding and denial. Finally Peter comes to full recognition and a deep faith in Jesus. It is an important reminder that mentoring and one-with-one spiritual direction can move through many phases over an extended time.

Paul's story offers guidance for a variety of helping and mentoring relationships that may be part of a person's journey to Jesus and continuing path as a disciple. When Saul (later Paul) met Jesus on the Damascus road, his life was in chaos. He was struck down by a flashing light as he heard the voice of Jesus saying, "Saul, Saul, why do you persecute me?" (Acts 9:5). He became totally disoriented, and for three days he was blind and would not eat (Acts 9:9). Saul needed help to understand what was happening to him, to recognize that it was indeed God he was encountering in these mystifying and mysterious circumstances. He needed to learn to keep opening himself to the true ways of God in his life. Saul was desperate for spiritual companionship—the presence of someone representing God to help him find his way.

God called the disciple Ananias to play this role, coming to him in a vision with the call to go to Saul. Though Saul was known to be a fierce persecutor of Christians, Ananias was called to place his hands on Saul, restore his sight, and pray that he be filled with the Holy Spirit. At this pivotal moment,

Ananias became a spiritual companion to Saul as he headed in a new direction and opened to the new invitations of God in his life.

Ananias was a disciple, perhaps a very ordinary one, who was attuned to God. He was obviously a person of prayer who listened to God and took seriously the highly unusual and risky message that he was to meet Saul. It is not surprising to find that Ananias protested, but the Lord urged him, "Go!" and so he did. He was willing to follow the lead of God. He was chosen by God to represent God's interests. He helped Saul understand what was happening and joined him in prayer for the restoration of his sight (Acts 9:10–19). Saul, the persecutor of the church, was on his way to becoming Paul, the great apostle to the gentiles.

Later, Barnabas, nicknamed "son of encouragement," also took Paul under his wing and mentored him. When Paul first began his ministry, the disciples in Jerusalem remained afraid of him. It was Barnabas, a trusted leader of the church, who introduced Paul to the Jerusalem church and opened doors for his future ministry to the gentiles (Acts 9:26–27). He later brought Paul with him to Antioch and invited him to share in his ministry in this important center of missionary activity (11:25–26). Together, they were commissioned to spread the gospel throughout the empire (13:2–3), in the cities of Pisidia, Iconium, Lystra, and Derbe. Later, Paul chose Timothy and others to join him in his missionary work (16:1–5). The mentee now served as a mentor. Over the years, Timothy would become one of Paul's most important coworkers, trusted by Paul to provide leadership in the communities they founded (1 Cor. 4:17; Phil. 2:19; 1 Thess. 3:2).

Paul's story is a vivid example of the importance of spiritual companioning in the early Christian community. One-with-one relationships are critically important for the growth of the church and its people. Ananias companioned Saul/Paul at a pivotal moment in his life, helping him understand the life-changing events on the road to Damascus. Barnabas became his mentor, allowing Paul to be accepted by the Jerusalem disciples and inviting him to share the work in Antioch and other missionary locations. Paul passed on this gift of mentorship, guiding several others into relationship with God and the work of ministry. His story is a witness to the importance and power of one-with-one spiritual companioning in the development of the spiritual life and the calling to service.

Not all guiding relationships fulfill the same purpose. The connection between Ananias and Paul was brief but all-important at the point of conversion. Paul's interaction with Barnabas and then Timothy stretched over many years. Typically, spiritual direction relationships tend to stretch out over time. They unfold as mutual trust and awareness of God's presence deepens. These relationships involve helping another to notice God's initiatives, listen to God's communication, enter a dialogue with God, and respond to God's love and guidance, all the while praying, "Your will be done on earth as in heaven."

Mining the Protestant Tradition

A growing number of Protestant leaders and laypeople are interested in bringing one-with-one spiritual direction into the contemporary church. As we pursue this path, it is important to gain some sense of this ministry's Protestant heritage against the backdrop of the longer Christian tradition. We begin to do this with a brief overview of the history of spiritual direction leading up to and continuing in the Protestant tradition.

As we have seen, one-with-one spiritual companioning was an important part of the New Testament church. This continued in the centuries that followed. As the church gained acceptance after its adoption by Emperor Constantine, however, it faced many new challenges. It moved from being a minority community representing an alternative way of life in the dominant culture to becoming the religion of the empire, helping to hold the empire's diverse population together. Over time, some Christians began to believe that the church was losing its connection to God and was no longer taking the spiritual life seriously.

A significant movement arose during the fourth and fifth centuries in Egypt, Palestine, and Syria in response to these concerns. A desert tradition of spiritual direction emerged as individuals fled the immorality of the cities and the established churches to pursue God in the wilderness. Others followed, seeking words of guidance from an *abba* or *amma* (father or mother), the most holy people they knew of. Relationships of obedience and trust developed, which focused on the interior life of the directee. Over time, communities of spiritual companionship developed around these spiritual guides.

By the sixth century, set patterns of spiritual direction that had developed in the desert became increasingly institutionalized. The Rule of Saint Benedict describes the guidelines followed by many communities. Monks submitted to an abbot who was officially charged with providing direction to individuals and the community as a whole. This rule of life also offered instruction on how to practice obedience, silence, humility, and brotherly and sisterly love. More mature members were encouraged to provide accountability and help in discerning God's guidance to others.

Over the centuries that followed, monastic contexts continued to be the most common places for intentional one-with-one spiritual direction. But change was afoot in the twelfth to fifteenth centuries, when new movements, including the Dominicans (1216) and the Franciscans (1221), gave particular attention to the needs of laypersons. Leaders provided spiritual guidance to all who sought them out, teaching and offering individualized spiritual counsel. This was relatively uncommon in the church at that time.

In the sixteenth century, Ignatius of Loyola developed the *Spiritual Exercises*, a resource designed to help individuals rid their souls of inordinate attachments and discover the will of God. His writings became a classic tool for spiritual directors, who guided individual retreat-goers through a process of meditation, prayer, and contemplation on the life of Christ. The Ignatian approach to spiritual direction was shaped further by later writings, such as Francis de Sales's *Introduction to the Devout Life*, written in the seventeenth century.

Around the same time, the Council of Trent (1545–63) brought about significant change to the typical spiritual direction relationship. Some Roman Catholics, especially those associated with monastic communities, continued to pursue broad forms of one-with-one direction. But many more received spiritual guidance that focused more narrowly on penitence and confession. Obedience to the director was required, and the process became firmly associated with an office of the church, in contrast to the less structured approach of seeking out a spiritual guide with a gift for discernment.[7]

This hierarchical model of the Roman Catholic Church was particularly disagreeable to the early leaders of the Protestant church, to such a degree that they dropped the language of spiritual direction altogether. At the same time, they were still vitally interested in attending to the spiritual hunger of people. While these leaders emphasized the importance of finding God through preaching of the Word and administration of the sacraments of baptism and the Lord's Supper, they also provided personal spiritual care and encouraged pastors and laypeople to do the same. Stories and teachings about the historical Protestant church often overlook this.

Many of the first Reformers gave diligent attention to one-with-one communication. Martin Luther, for example, exercised an extensive ministry of personal direction by word of mouth and letter. It was not uncommon for him to urge a student to reveal "the condition of [his] soul."[8] Ulrich Zwingli was another leader who recommended consulting with other wise and mature Christians for assistance on the spiritual journey. John Calvin was careful to emphasize that Christians should serve God alone and not submit blindly to church leaders, including spiritual directors. But he offered one-with-one

---

7. Further discussion of spiritual direction models from the early church to the Reformation can be found in Janet Ruffing, *To Tell the Sacred Tale*, 3–18.

8. Leech, *Soul Friend*, 85.

spiritual companioning to individuals in person and through letters and spoke highly of its value.

The Anglican tradition is one stream of the Protestant community that held on more tightly to historical practices of one-with-one spiritual direction. Individuals seeking guidance would converse with a priest about their spiritual lives. The process often incorporated both prayer and confession. Numerous Puritan writers also called upon local pastors to guide and enlighten the individual conscience, perhaps most notably Richard Baxter in the seventeenth century. Baxter urged pastors not to "slubber over" the ministry of personal spiritual counsel, but rather to attend to it energetically.[9] Indeed, Baxter was known to invite his wife, Margaret, to share her insights on the spiritual guidance of individuals. She seemed to have a particular gift for resolving cases of conscience, better than most "divines" Baxter knew.[10]

The Radical Reformers and the traditions that followed them also attended to spiritual direction in some form, though they used different language. Essential to the Anabaptist way of life was fraternal admonition, often referred to as "giving and receiving counsel." This was a practice of personal direction within a communal covenant and context. Quakers also developed a tradition of individual and corporate direction and discernment. Early communities held to a core belief that the light within, the Spirit of God, would guide them in their spiritual journey into truth. Special emphasis was placed on mutual guidance and admonition. The Quaker meeting was the centerpiece of this discernment process, but one-with-one relationships were important as well. George Fox, the founder of the Quaker movement, was known to have a gift for discerning God's presence in a person's spirit.

While certain Protestant leaders emphasized some form of one-with-one spiritual guidance, intentional relationships like these have been spotty. Public worship and Bible studies, among other practices and programs, have received more attention. This is slowly changing. Perhaps because of our experiences of isolation and the general resurgence of interest in spirituality, people are again looking for intentional spiritual companions. In a sense, we are a bit like the early Christians who went out to the desert. We seek spiritual guides in retreat centers, monastic communities, and counseling offices. Ironically, we do not often find what we are looking for in a local congregation. It is time for congregational leaders to be informed about the practice of spiritual direction and to give leadership to this important ministry in their congregations and larger communities.

9. Ibid., 86.
10. Ranft, *Woman's Way*, 158.

Practicing Spiritual Companioning

In the twentieth century, spiritual direction across the spectrum of denominations has generally become less institutionalized and more reliant on the spiritual gifts of the individuals involved. Today spiritual directors are expected to understand spiritual growth and development, know about prayer from personal experience, be able to assist the directee with discernment, and have some awareness of psychological issues. Even though one person serves as "director" to another, the director's role is really to come alongside and point to God. God is the true Spiritual Director, and it is God's action that is primary and necessary.

One-with-one spiritual direction is truly both art and skill. Each of us writing this book remembers some of our first stumbling attempts to minister in this way. Though we had been trained for pastoral ministry in Protestant seminaries, or perhaps *because* we had been trained in those contexts, we found it difficult in those first encounters to simply listen, holding back from drawing upon our storehouses of practical and theological wisdom. Like many who have gone before us, we were more accustomed to analysis than reflection.

I (Angela) remember well my first spiritual direction session, when the courageous woman who agreed to be my directee burst into tears within the first few minutes and could barely speak for what seemed like an eternity. In reality, it was probably only about fifteen minutes, but I could not stop thinking that my instructor (Marcus) had not prepared me for this! A few days later, Marcus listened to an audiotape of the session, and he made several helpful suggestions about my skills, especially the notion that I did not need to fill the silence. What surprised me was that he also noticed something else: he saw the creative side of the encounter—the unique gifts I brought to a ministry of presence.

Tools for Spiritual Direction

There are several practical tools or interactions we want to explore that are consistently useful for building the skills of spiritual directors. At the same time, there are artful elements to the spiritual direction relationship. Every director has been gifted differently, and all function out of unique personalities, church experiences, religious beliefs, and journeys in ministry. Both skill and art come together to form our way of being directors. Each of the following interactions also builds upon the general practices for spiritual companioning that we explored in the first chapter. As we describe them, we imagine how Fred and Matt might experience them. We believe that spiritual direction facilitates a deeper life with God when we offer the following gifts: (1) welcoming, (2) covenanting, (3) listening and probing, (4) noticing God, (5) lingering and savoring, (6) discerning, and (7) consulting.

WELCOMING

Welcoming is about offering the gift of hospitality on several levels. When Matt came to see Fred, he was welcomed into a special space that invited him to be at home with himself, with Fred, and with God. The *physical space* for spiritual direction should be comfortable and inviting, a space that is attractive and private, uncluttered and without distractions. We are wise to turn off our cell phones and limit other external noises. Pictures or symbols may be helpful for inviting a contemplative atmosphere. Practical needs like a box of tissues and a glass of water or a cup of coffee help people to relax and begin letting go. Just as we want guests in our homes to feel welcome and comfortable, in the same way, on God's behalf, we provide an environment that communicates to directees that they are valuable to God and to us.

Personal space is also important. No matter what frame of mind Matt was in when he came to a session, Fred's quiet, receptive demeanor helped him prepare for contemplative interactions. Often a directee comes to a session feeling distracted, harried, or distressed. Many times we have seen directees sit down across from us, ready to begin, but struggle to actually settle down internally. The peaceful demeanor of the director provides a balm in the midst of chaos, which enables the directee to gently release tensions and embrace a measure of inner quiet.

Attention to both personal and physical space helps to establish what is most important: *spiritual space*. The décor of the room and Fred's prayerful presence set the tone for their time together so that Matt could more easily open to the Spirit's gentle and renewing ways. In order for Fred to create this kind of space, it was helpful for him to prepare ahead of time. He might plan to arrive early, quiet himself, and pray in the meeting room, asking that God prepare both participants and enable them to notice what God desired for them in this time and place. This kind of prayer helped to settle Fred and enabled him to remember that the Spirit of Christ was always present. Sometimes an empty chair nearby also helps to keep this in mind. Fred could choose to pray aloud to begin the session or suggest that they both pray in silence. Some directors begin with conversation; it all depends on the director's artful ways and the comfort of the directee.

Finally, it was critical that the director provide a *safe space* so that Matt could freely explore his life in light of God's love and care. Whether he was sharing a pleasant joy, a deep suffering, a perplexing problem, or a mystical encounter, it was of utmost importance that Matt be in a safe space that included strict confidentiality and behaviors appropriate and conducive to his well-being and care. For the good of both the directee and director, appropriate boundaries in the relationship are absolutely necessary.

Directors must not lose sight of the fact that caregiving relationships tend to give power to the caregiver. How directors ask questions or respond to comments can have significant implications for how directees process the events of their lives and understand God's guidance. In some cases, directors recognize that directees need other kinds of supportive relationships, such as psychological counseling or psychiatric examination. The best care may be a referral to another trained professional. In every case, it is the director's responsibility to safeguard the relationship from any kind of sexual, romantic, or emotionally intimate form of relating that crosses professional boundaries. The frequency of clergy sexual misconduct points to the reality that caregivers must give serious thought to their roles and act according to appropriate ethical standards. If healthy boundaries cannot be kept for any reason, the direction relationship must end, and other kinds of healing support should be pursued. With principles like these in mind, directors can faithfully come alongside directees as representatives of a trustworthy God.

COVENANTING

The spiritual direction space is more easily safeguarded when a mutual agreement is made about the purpose and procedures of the sessions. The notion of a covenant is helpful in such instances. "Covenant" is a word representing promises and commitments in the Christian tradition that extend to all kinds of relationships between God and humanity and between human beings. When we covenant with one another, we hold up the relationship as sacred, and we commit to treating it as such before God. The covenant to give and receive spiritual direction is important, but it is not permanent and it certainly may be updated or renewed from time to time. It does not require a signed agreement in most cases, but simply involves a conversation between participants when both are ready to make a commitment to multiple sessions.

The covenant-making process begins by addressing the reasons the directee is seeking spiritual direction and considering whether the director is well suited to provide guidance. For example, Fred could begin by asking Matt, "What brings you to spiritual direction at this time?" Another way of asking this, after a session or two, might be, "What are your deepest desires in life?" With thoughtful questions and careful listening, Fred could patiently assist Matt in clarifying and expressing his expectations in the initial sessions.

The director also explains in simple, specific language how she or he views spiritual direction and what the relationship offers. The covenant includes an agreement regarding the length and frequency of sessions (usually one hour each month, though there may be more than one session in the first month), where the sessions will occur, issues related to boundaries in the relationship, understandings about confidentiality, expectations of remuneration (if any), a process for evaluating the relationship, and procedures for closure of the direction relationship. A covenant is necessary so that the two have a mutual understanding of what to expect during the sessions. As in all specialized ministry relationships, it is important that participants agree on the procedures.

It is important for both the director and directee to keep in mind that self-disclosing conversations create significant vulnerability in the directee. This gives the director power in the relationship. When directees are vulnerable, the responses of directors have a significant impact on the directees' view of themselves. As the direction relationship progresses, the directee may encounter the Spirit in ways that can lead to "purifying" or "perfecting" his or her life (Matt. 5:48). Each one has his or her own inner "timetable" for self-disclosure of various aspects of life. As this occurs, the interactions need to remain open and free for the individual to find words to describe and prayerfully discuss personal experiences. A simple axiom in the spiritual life is that the deeper we go with God, the deeper we also need to go within ourselves to face the truths of our life that God is touching for transformation. Spiritual direction is a journey of collaboration with God's agenda to transform us into the likeness of Christ (2 Cor. 3:18).

Listening and Probing

We have already discussed the foundational role of prayerful listening. As the spiritual direction relationship deepens, it helps to listen carefully and begin probing a bit deeper for specific elements of the directee's spiritual life. Fred listened to the specific issues Matt brought to each session, and he also watched for bits and pieces of Matt's larger story as it unfolded. Early in the relationship, Fred could review with Matt his religious background and experience, beginning to gather his story. Sometimes the director will invite the directee to offer a brief personal history in the first session or two. On occasion Fred invited Matt to expand or explore particular aspects of his story in greater depths. As he listened, Fred paid attention to Matt's words, but he also noticed body language as Matt told the story.

Spiritual directors often listen for what is not said as much as for what is said. Some directees are not very aware of their own emotional responses to life events. Recognizing and naming these feelings before God can deepen the directee's sense of trust and connection with the divine. As appropriate, Fred commented on what he was hearing and observing. He was attentive to major milestones in Matt's story, times of joy or accomplishment and moments of God's loving and grace-filled presence. He also listened for the difficult elements of the story, such as confusion, regret, temptation, or avoidance. This storytelling might focus on current or past experiences.

In this process Fred probed gently, encouraging storytelling by asking exploratory questions, such as the following:

- What have been some key moments and events in your spiritual life over the years? In your church experience? In other religious contexts?
- Could you say more about this event or experience?
- What was the impact of this event or experience as time went by?

It was important that Fred's words and body language communicate interest and compassion. This would enable Matt to gain a deeper understanding and appreciation for his life experiences. This is never done just to satisfy the director's curiosity or to allow the director to allude to her or his own story.

As directors develop skills for listening prayerfully, they are learning to focus both on God and on the directee at the same time. This does not mean they are fully aware of exactly what God is communicating (or, for that matter, what the directee is communicating), but they are listening for God's response as best it can be discerned. Directors may hold the image of Jesus's presence in their mind's eye. Prayerful listening helps directors keep in mind "the big picture" of God's purposes. This approach provides significant freedom for directors, allowing them to be less engaged verbally. We all know that it takes more energy and focus to pay attention to more than one person or thing at a time. We will naturally comprehend what we notice more slowly. Directors may want to communicate to directees that slowing down the conversation and allowing for moments of silence is appropriate in the direction relationship, even though it would seem awkward in most other kinds of conversations. When directors listen in this way, they are providing a priestly or mediating role, listening for God alongside directees (Rom. 15:16; 1 Pet. 2:5, 9).

As listening and probing continue, painful events may surface. If the circumstances causing pain move beyond the parameters of spiritual direction, directors will normally encourage directees to seek counseling. Spiritual direction is not an appropriate context in which to address deeper psychological issues or sustained emotional pain. While spiritual direction may touch on painful events, the process focuses on the presence and activity of God in those events, not on appropriate responses or problem solving. Even when the director is skilled in psychological counseling, if the sessions shift into a counseling mode, returning to a spiritual direction relationship becomes very difficult. This is not to suggest that God's movements in people are more significant in direction than in counseling—only that they are different. Each has a unique role in the ministry of the congregation or community.

NOTICING GOD

Over the years, we have observed that when directees express a desire to see, hear, or experience more of God, some of what they desire is already present, but they do not have the eyes to see or ears to hear it. Our culture's obsession with scientific explanations for every event discourages us from seeing the divine movements in our midst and learning to interpret them in light of God's presence. In contrast to the shepherd David, who wrote many psalms reflecting his experience of God, many Christians today have difficulty seeing and hearing.

One purpose of spiritual direction is to observe with the directee how God may be present and active in his or her life (Eph. 4:6; Col. 1:17). The director holds the conviction that God is present in all of life. One way to facilitate awareness is through the use of evocative questions—questions that help the directee pay attention to the possibility, or certainty, of God's presence in a given moment or circumstances. For example, from time to time, Fred might ask evocative questions, including the following:

- What is your sense of God's presence or activity in this story, event, or experience?
- If you can imagine God being with us now, how do you think God might be responding to this situation? To you?
- What is God like in this experience? What images of God emerge for you at this moment?
- What might God be inviting you to do? To be? To become?
- Would you be willing to bring your experience (feelings, concerns, or pain) to God right now?

This final question is especially important when the directee seems ready for it. Directees may be invited to name the experience, imagine holding it in their hands before God, invite God to be with them, and then listen for several minutes to see if and how God may be responding. Through this prayer exercise, the sense of God's immediacy may become very strong; at other times nothing perceptible happens. Directees may also be invited to continue practicing the prayer process regularly at home for a period of time.

LINGERING AND SAVORING

Whenever the directee becomes aware of God, either in the current moment or in some past experience, it often helps to invite the directee to linger with the experience, savoring it and finding words to describe it. It is perfectly appropriate to stop in such moments and hold in silence what has been identified. After pausing for a time, Fred could check with Matt to see if he was ready to respond reflectively to one or two questions:

- What are you noticing about God right now? About yourself?
- What is this like for you? What are you experiencing?
- What, if anything, would you like to say to God in this moment?

These evocative interactions allow the directee to rest in God's presence and learn how to pay attention to the ways God may be moving at other times of life.

Discerning

Individuals often pursue spiritual direction when they are preparing to make a decision and are seeking a word from the Lord or some inkling of God's will for their lives. It is an honor to walk alongside others in these circumstances, but we must keep in mind that spiritual directors do not have some kind of unique, privileged access to the mind of God. They companion directees, encouraging them to remain open to Christ through worship, Scripture reading, and prayer.

These practices strengthen the relationship with God and encourage patient trust during the time of discernment. Directors come along on a journey of patient, hopeful waiting on the Lord for further "word." Along the way, directors may also help directees clarify their images of God and expectations for how discernment may be revealed. Directors invite directees to become aware of the varied ways spiritual discernment may occur.

Directees may meet with trusted friends to hear their responses and also invite the community to pray with them about the decision to be made. It is important to recognize that discernment is rooted in life with a God who seeks to be known and calls us to follow. An example of a matter for discernment could be Matt's need to gain breathing space in his life by releasing some of his responsibilities to others. Fred could invite him into prayerful reflection on the process, helping him to identify his understanding of what God expected of him. They might also explore together what kinds of service Matt is most drawn toward. Ultimately Matt would make decisions, but Fred's presence would offer needed encouragement and wise reflection.

Consulting

As we have already noted, spiritual direction is not primarily about problem solving or becoming directly involved in finding solutions to situations.

However, at times a director may choose to address emotional pain, frustration, fear, or a need for clarity in a particular situation by engaging the directee in more intense dialogue or discussion about what is happening and what interventions may be needed. The spiritual director does not propose answers, but works with the person to clarify the situation and find best practices. Providing spiritual direction to pastors or lay leaders is a case in point. In our experience, spiritual leaders sometimes need confidential spaces to discuss areas of overlap in their personal and professional lives so that they can bring their needs to God with greater clarity. In those moments, a director becomes more of a consultant, intentionally taking on a different role in the relationship.

The primary danger in this change is the director's loss of her or his own center. Both participants must guard against slipping too easily into looking at direction as a work of fixing what is wrong or solving challenging problems. For example, there were points at which Fred could offer Matt some wise advice on church leadership, but they needed to guard against trying to fix the challenges of the church that Matt encountered. That is not the primary purpose of spiritual direction.

At its core, spiritual direction is really as simple as a directee requesting to meet regularly with a director to reflect on Christlike spiritual growth in the directee's journey. In preparation for the session, the directee reviews life experiences and comes prepared to initiate the conversation. The directee, not the director, brings the agenda or discovers it along the way. In our experience, such a review of one's own life with an eye to personal and spiritual growth has profound potential for continuing personal renewal.

If enough people in any given community pursue this kind of relationship and have transformative experiences, there is significant potential for congregational renewal. In any Christian community, the maturity of members varies greatly, but it is God's agenda that all be formed in Christ and transformed by God. At the core of the life and ministry of the church is Christian formation. The ministry of spiritual direction can be one important aspect of this larger vision.

Spiritual Direction as Art

We would be remiss not to address the importance of artfulness more fully. Creativity is absolutely critical to any spiritual direction relationship. As I (Marcus) write this, I am sitting in my daughter's kitchen in Seattle looking through a patio door into the backyard. What I see is a small deck with a round table and two chairs, bounded with lattice work on two sides and bamboo curtains across the end to provide privacy for a small hot tub. I know there is a larger area beyond the deck, but from where I sit I cannot see it. Even though I know my daughter has a variety of vegetation (e.g., grass, trees, shrubbery, flowers), I cannot describe it because I can see only the deck, table, chairs, hot tub, and bamboo curtains.

If I were to walk into the yard to observe what is there and be able to describe it, I would still not know what it all means to my daughter. Only if we were to linger there as she describes what it is like to experience her backyard, the struggles involved in caring for it, the pleasure she feels in seeing the beauty, the refreshment it brings to her to sit and relax in it—only then could I begin to comprehend somewhat more fully the meaning of this in her life.

Perhaps as I learned more about her experience of her yard, I could help clarify some of her desires and intentions, ask reflective questions to heighten her awareness of herself and her yard, or even make helpful observations to enhance the experience. This is a parable of the role of the spiritual director in the life of the directee. Directors draw upon the gifts of the Spirit and their sense of God's guidance to listen, linger, join in mutual reflection, and appreciate life. Directees respond with their own gifts for listening and responding. Together with God, the great Artist, they converse and create.

In the practice of spiritual conversation, the director can observe only what the directee presents, not the deeper terrain of the person's soul, until, and to the extent that, the person chooses to reveal it. The landscape of the soul can be explored only at the bidding and desire of the directee with the help of the Holy Spirit. It is not a simple, straightforward journey. It does not follow the specific outline of a curriculum, as in Christian education, but takes a much more circuitous route. In the discipline of spiritual direction, the director joins the person in his or her conversations with honest self-appraisal of the inner and outer life.

Preparing to Be a Spiritual Director

Effectiveness as a spiritual director requires that the director practice noticing God's presence in his or her own life as well. Far and away, the most important preparation for Christian spiritual directors is vitality in their own spiritual journeys, including a commitment to regular personal spiritual practices, involvement in a congregation, and an ongoing relationship of spiritual direction for themselves. It is important to be able to reflect on their own experiences of prayer with various questions: How vital is prayer to me? What happens within me when I pray? How would I describe my experience of God in prayer (e.g., present, intimate, distant, impersonal, interested, or perplexing)? In what sense do I encounter God while praying? It is not necessary to "do well" in response to these questions, but it is important to be honest with ourselves, God, and a spiritual companion.

It is also valuable to know some of the primary literature on spiritual direction, to continue to learn about the divine-human relationship, and to be thoughtful about who God is. It is especially important to be aware of and thoughtful about our own images of God, including our convictions about who God is and how God functions in the world. All of these issues are typically addressed in spiritual direction training programs.

Exploring the Stories of Congregations

Just as Matt benefited from his growing relationship with Fred, many other congregational leaders and laypeople have sought spiritual direction for various reasons. The examples we share below are based on our spiritual direction practice with various individuals over the years.

The Depressed Seminarian

Kayla, a seminary student in her early forties, asked to meet with a spiritual director who was associated with the school. In the first session, two things became evident to James, her director. First, Kayla was experiencing an intense episode of depression, and second, she longed for spiritual vitality. James agreed to meet on the condition that Kayla also see a counselor for therapeutic treatment.

During the early sessions of the direction relationship, Kayla repeatedly expressed intense pain caused by difficult relationships with her family of origin and her demanding husband. She also struggled with the unjust criticism she seemed to be receiving as a woman doing a pastoral internship in a congregation unused to women in leadership. Kayla felt abandoned by her family and the church, and this sense of loss spilled over into her relationship with God. She expressed a deep anger toward God. Yet James sensed that something hopeful lay beyond these strong emotions. Kayla carried an intense desire for healing in relationship to herself, to others, and to God. What she was really looking for was spiritual renewal.

We may wonder, how could James best care for Kayla while she was immersed in a cauldron of pain and anger? Certainly the relationship needed to begin in a *welcoming* space: a safe, quiet place that could become a haven for body and spirit. A *covenant* would be equally important: an agreement that expressed expectations, procedures, and commitments. *Probing and listening* would become James's major work: a patient, caring, prayerful presence.

This kind of presence would be able to handle the anger and help Kayla to acknowledge and face the roots of her pain. Companioning Kayla in her suffering would require that James gently invite her to *notice God* over and over, even though it seemed to her that God was absent.

Because of the intensity of Kayla's experience, James suggested that they begin by meeting twice a month. For a while, the sessions followed a similar pattern. James was primarily engaged with empathic listening. He made few attempts to solve Kayla's marriage problems or suggest approaches to dealing with criticism. He simply listened prayerfully and helped her to name facets of her experience. Toward the end of each session, James routinely made one of several responses to help her *notice God*, with evocative questions: How do you think God feels about you or your pain? What comes to you in the silence we just held? Occasionally James would sense the Spirit moving in a particular way and share what he felt he might be hearing from God. He also read Scripture when it seemed appropriate and offered to pray for her. Sometimes Kayla welcomed the prayer, and other times not.

James's relationship with Kayla lasted for two years, until her graduation. During this time, the depression began to lift and some of her problems had been partially resolved. Through this experience, a new awareness of God's presence and love emerged, and she was able to experience joy in her graduation and in the possibilities for serving God. Later on she told James that his time with her had been the most profound spiritual experience of her life.

The Joyful Mother

Sofia, a woman in her thirties, had been receiving spiritual direction from Abby for some time. When she first approached Abby, a member at her church, she knew very little about spiritual direction but was interested in finding out more. She was curious about the prayer practices Abby led in church, and the ways she talked about the experience of relating to God. There was something about Abby's own intimacy with God that Sofia found compelling. The sessions were rich and meaningful. Sofia discovered that the monthly "check-in" for her spiritual life helped her to be more committed to prayer in between sessions, and occasionally during a session she would have a special sense of God with her somehow. It was enlightening. At times, Sofia did not feel completely comfortable with Abby's approach. Once Abby introduced a body prayer, and Sophia had difficulty entering into it. After trying it for a while though, she recognized that it helped her get out of her head and attend to God in more holistic ways.

About a year after they began meeting, Sofia found out that she was pregnant. This was a time of great celebration because she and her husband had been hoping to have children for some time. Sofia also needed to make decisions with this pending life change in front of her. Would she stay home to raise her child or continue working? Was there another opportunity in her chosen field that might allow her to work less with more flexible hours? She had a full-time job as an engineer—a career that she loved, in a good company—but she also hoped to be available to her child as her mother had been to her. Sofia prayed daily about these issues, believing that God wanted what was best for her and her child, but she could not seem to discern God's will for this situation.

During a few spiritual direction sessions, Abby invited Sofia to imagine holding (with hands cupped) one feeling or question about the future, asking God to be with her in it. They would wait before God in silence for a time, sometimes for minutes, listening for any response from God. Abby described this as *holding prayer*, a way of *noticing God*. Sometimes Sofia did not experience God in this prayer in any special way, and at other times she felt a certainty that God would be with her whatever she and her husband decided. On one occasion, she sensed that she should begin praying for God's love over her child, that God would fill her cupped hands and her whole life with joy, and that this joy would flow over to her child. Abby suggested that they *linger and savor* the image for a time in silence and then read the biblical story of Jesus's love and welcome for children (Luke 18:15–16). At the end of the session, Sofia felt a deep sense of peace that all would be well. In the days that followed, Sofia found that her mind turned less toward the logistics of the decisions to be made and more toward prayer for God's blessing in the life of her child.

Alone in the Desert

Henry, a pastor in midlife, found himself in a spiritual "dry spell" that overshadowed his daily life and ministry. He felt perplexed and uncertain about what was happening. He had been an active Christian for many years, and a minister in the congregation for over a decade. His own spiritual engagement with the people had been vital and dynamic, but now he did not feel the same passion for prayer, preaching, and providing pastoral care.

Henry met with Ellen, who had once been a Christian education director and now offered spiritual direction to a handful of local ministers in her retirement. Ellen *welcomed* Henry to their sessions in significant ways. The quiet office in her home church was a comforting space that reassured Henry of God's continuing interest and care in spite of the spiritual desert. As he talked about his life and the pressures he felt as the congregation grew and the demands increased, Ellen remained attentive to his story. *Listening and probing* with care, Ellen helped Henry look at his own life in depth and name his experiences. She invited Henry to notice and name habits and patterns, including his ways of praying.

Together they began to *discern* whether the spiritual dry spell might be an invitation from God rather than a curse. Maybe God was calling him to some reorientation in his patterns of life and ministry, including the possibility of viewing ministry more intentionally as work *with* God rather than *for* God. With a series of evocative questions, Ellen encouraged Henry to recognize and embrace God's renewing presence in old and new ways in life.

Each of these spiritual direction narratives describes a struggle of one kind or another. Changes and crises in life often bring us to a new awareness of personal and spiritual need. In such times when experiences evoke ultimate questions about God or difficult issues such as evil and injustice, the director may need to facilitate movement toward new stages in personal development and spiritual growth. There is often a need for a deeper orientation or reorientation to God. Challenging experiences can contribute significantly to our growth when we become aware of the Spirit's presence, the "breath of God" working for good in the midst of struggle or suffering (Rom. 8:28).

Exercising Our Companionship: Intentional Conversations

Developing and strengthening spiritual direction skills can begin in intentional conversation with another person. In our early days of spiritual direction training, we benefited from simple practice with conversation starters. The following exercises provide opportunities for exploring the kinds of spiritual conversations that are appropriate in direction settings.

For each conversation, find a congregational member, colleague, or friend who is willing to participate in this experiment. Plan to meet for four sessions about one week apart.

Conversation 1

1. Lead the person in a spiritual exercise for several minutes (e.g., silence, centering prayer, Scripture meditation or *lectio divina*). Introduce this as an experience of prayerful meditation.

2. Ask the person:
   - What did you experience in this time of meditation?
   - How did you sense God in this experience (e.g., as present or absent)?
   - How do you experience God in your life generally?
3. Offer a prayer related to what was discussed.

Conversation 2

1. Invite the person to tell her or his story of God in her or his life. Listen well and reflect with the person about the story.
2. Invite the person to identify significant "milestones" in her or his spiritual experiences.
3. Pray with the person about her or his life.

Conversation 3

1. Ask the person:
   - What have you found to be difficult in your spiritual journey?
   - In what ways have you felt most fulfilled in your spiritual life?
   - What are some of your deepest desires?
   - What do you desire in your relationship with God?
2. Offer a prayer related to what was discussed.

Conversation 4

1. Discuss issues that emerged from previous conversations or particular matters that the person would like to discuss with you.
2. Listen and respond in a prayerful and reflective manner.
3. At the end of the session, both of you bow before God together for several moments of silence. End with a prayer of blessing for the person's life.

For Further Reading

Barry, William, and William J. Connolly. *The Practice of Spiritual Direction*. 2nd ed. New York: HarperCollins, 2009. A well-known classic used in the training of spiritual directors that provides in-depth discussion of key interactions between directors and directees.

Guenther, Margaret. *Holy Listening: The Art of Spiritual Direction.* Cambridge, MA: Cowley Publications, 1992. An artful treatment of the practice of spiritual direction that reflects upon the nature of the direction process and the skills directors need to be effective.

Kropf, Marlene, and Daniel Schrock, eds. *An Open Place: The Ministry of Group Spiritual Direction.* New York: Morehouse Publishing, 2012. An exploration of group spiritual direction in a variety of settings within the congregation and beyond.

Lebacqz, Karen, and Joseph Driskill. *Ethics and Spiritual Care: A Guide for Pastors and Spiritual Directors.* Nashville: Abingdon, 2000. A helpful discussion of appropriate boundaries and other ethical considerations for caregiving relationships.

Leech, Kenneth. *Soul Friend: An Invitation to Spiritual Direction.* New York: Harper-Collins, 1980. A thoughtful work by one of the early leaders in the contemporary Protestant awakening in spiritual formation and spiritual direction.

Merton, Thomas. *Spiritual Direction and Meditation.* Collegeville, MN: Liturgical Press, 1960. An insightful and inspiring text in which Merton explores his own journey of spiritual growth.

Moon, Gary W., and David G. Benner. *Spiritual Direction and the Care of Souls: A Guide to Christian Approaches and Practices.* Downers Grove, IL: InterVarsity, 2004. A resource that describes the emergence of spiritual companioning and direction in various traditions of the church.

Ruffing, Janet. *To Tell the Sacred Tale: Spiritual Direction and Narrative.* New York: Paulist Press, 2011. A resource that discusses the historical development of spiritual direction and attends to storytelling in the direction relationship.

4

Spiritual Companioning
in Small Groups

Reverend Jamie McClain felt the butterflies begin to dance in his stomach while he walked toward the pulpit. As he opened his Bible to Proverbs 15, he heard the familiar rustling of hands reaching under pews to pull out Bibles and turn to the passage he was about to read. He paused for a moment, and a hush fell over the worshiping community. A deep, resonant voice broke the silence: "Listen now for the Word of God." After Reverend McClain read the passage, he said, "This is the Word of the Lord," and the people responded, "Thanks be to God." Reverend McClain then began to preach. The people looked toward the front expectantly. Some kept the pew Bibles on their laps, open to the passage they had just heard.

Halfway back in the congregation, Stephanie Adams smiled to herself as Reverend McClain began to preach. Just two weeks ago, her small group Bible study had discussed Ephesians 4:26: "'In your anger do not sin': Do not let the sun go down while you are still angry" (NIV). She remembered how the members of her group found this a challenging passage. Every one of them had experiences to share. For Stephanie, the challenge nowadays was her fifteen-year-old daughter, who seemed to be going out of her way to irritate her mother—especially at night! "How can we talk things through when she keeps her door closed and tells me that she has to finish her homework?"

Stephanie asked the group. It was helpful to learn that she wasn't the only one experiencing this problem. So Stephanie refocused her attention on Reverend McClain's sermon. She was quite interested in what he might say about today's text, Proverbs 15:1: "A gentle answer turns away wrath, but a harsh word stirs up anger."

From the beginning, the Protestant tradition has placed great emphasis on preaching the Word in public worship. It is the symbolic center of Protestant congregations. Here, Jesus Christ, the one Word of God, continues to address the gathered community through the ordinary human words of preaching, as Scripture is interpreted and applied to the lives of the hearers. Good preaching seeks to place itself in God's service. It seeks to speak the gospel into the lives of the gathered community: the forgiveness of sins, the promise of new life in Christ, and the hope that God's name will be hallowed on earth as it is in heaven.

Alongside this symbolic center of Protestant congregations—the community gathered *before* the Word in preaching—a second practice also has been important in the Protestant tradition: the community gathered *around* the Word in small groups. The first practice emphasizes *verticality*: from God to the people through the preaching of the Word. The second practice emphasizes *horizontality*: God's Word emerging out of the mutual sharing, encouragement, and insights of a group of people who meet regularly to search Scripture together.

Good preaching and small group spiritual companioning are both necessary to build strong churches. Week by week, God's people are renewed, convicted, and awakened as they are addressed by God through the preaching of the gospel. Week by week, the body of Christ is built up into a living fellowship as people companion one another in small groups. Both the vertical and the horizontal are necessary if congregations are to carry out their mission of bearing witness to the gospel. Good preaching allows them to remember they are called into being and sustained by the good news of God's grace in Jesus Christ. Small group spiritual companioning allows them to embody this grace in the relationships of their group and, subsequently, in their relationships with others.

Understanding the Cultural Context

Stephanie Adams looks forward to her small group Bible study every week. This group of ten women has been meeting for several years. During the first six months, the congregation's director of Christian education led the group. Once the members learned how to run the group themselves, she dropped out to start another group. Stephanie refers to group meetings as her "sacred time." "It's special to me," she says. "My life is pretty hectic, between my jobs as an elementary school teacher and as mother of two teenage girls. Bill [her husband] does a lot around the home, but I feel like I'm always on the go. My small group is my sacred time. It's time for me to get together with people who listen to me and really know me. They help me keep my spiritual life alive."

Stephanie is not alone in affirming the importance of a small group in her life. Sociologist Robert Wuthnow found this to be widespread in a major study of small groups in contemporary America.[1] Forty percent of all Americans over the age of eighteen belong to a small group that meets regularly, and an even larger percentage has been involved in a small group in the past.[2] Three-quarters of the participants in a small group describe their group as "very important" to them.[3] Wuthnow studied all types of small groups—from book groups to Sunday school classes to bird-watching groups to neighborhood Bible studies—and his findings offer insight into why so many Americans participate in small groups today. What are people looking for in small groups?

Above all else, people join small groups because they are on a "quest for community," as Wuthnow puts it.[4] Their personal lives feel fragmented and hectic like Stephanie's. They struggle to find and keep jobs, to work while taking care of children and aging parents, to volunteer at church or their children's school, and to still find time for a little fun. Amid these different roles and responsibilities, many Americans long for a group of people who know them for who they are, not the roles they play at work or the tasks they carry out to keep their family going. This leads many people to join small groups in search of a community where they feel connected and known.

Such groups have become especially important in recent decades as many traditional forms of community have broken down. Instead of neighborhoods with long-term relationships built up as children play together, go to the same schools, and play on the same teams, many Americans live in communities where residents and housing patterns are constantly changing. In the past, moreover, work provided many Americans with a stable community where they could build lasting relationships and anchor their identities. Today, the workplace is characterized by a high degree of instability, as jobs are outsourced and as companies downsize or reorganize to adapt to the changing demands of the global marketplace. A sense of community in neighborhoods and the workplace has disappeared in the lives of many Americans. This is a

1. Wuthnow, *Sharing the Journey*.
2. Ibid., 45.
3. Ibid., 50.
4. Ibid., chap. 2.

key reason that small groups are important in American society and religion today. Many people turn to small groups in a quest for community. Spiritual companioning in small groups responds to this need.

Yet we must add an important caveat to this understanding of the importance of small groups in the contemporary American context. Since Wuthnow carried out his research in 1994, the digital revolution has emerged with full force. This marks the shift from analog electronic and mechanical devices to the kinds of digital technology available today. The digital revolution is truly global in scope, shaping business, politics, news media, families, and friendships around the world. It has tremendous influence on the ways people form relationships and communities. This is especially true for digital natives, who have used digital technology from the beginning of their lives. Some compare the digital revolution to the advent of the printing press, which popularized print culture and made reading a part of people's everyday lives.[5] So too, digital culture and the World Wide Web are reshaping the way people think, communicate, and work.[6] This is especially evident among young people.

In a 2010 study, the Kaiser Family Foundation reported that American youth interact with digital media an average of 7.5 hours a day, seven days a week.[7] The same year, the Nielsen group reported that the average American teenager sends 3,146 text messages a month, which translates into more than 10 messages every hour of the day when they are not sleeping or in school.[8] When young people are asked why they invest so much time in digital media, they talk about the ways it allows them to stay in touch with friends and families, to join affinity groups, and to gain access to information. But a compensatory tone sometimes is found in their comments as well.[9] They speak of parents who are always working, broken homes, feelings of loneliness and depression, pressure at school, and difficult peer relationships. They share stories of sitting in front of television with their parents and siblings, everyone on a smartphone or iPad and no meaningful conversation taking place between family members. They share stories of constantly texting their friends but hiding what they are really feeling, especially their "down times."

These kinds of stories remind us of the continuing importance of face-to-face relationships. They are absolutely central to our development as human persons. We need relationships in which we encounter the otherness of real people. This allows us to construct a sense of self and acquire human capacities

5. Carr, *Shallows*.
6. Rainie and Wellman, *Networked*.
7. Rideout, Foehr, and Roberts, "Generation M²," 2.
8. Entner, "Under-Aged Texting Usage."
9. Turkle, *Alone Together*.

like empathy, mutual regard, moral sense, and the ability to work through conflicts over time. Small groups are a form of community in which face-to-face relationships are central.

Yet it is likely that the quest for community will look different among digital natives than among their parents and grandparents. Perhaps it will grow out of an awareness of the limitations of virtual friendships and affinity groups, of instant communication and constant connection. As Shirley Turkle aptly puts it, many young people in our digital age are "alone together."[10] They feel pressure to constantly stay in touch with friends. Yet amid this constant connection, many feel lonely and isolated, out of touch with themselves and lacking relationships of real depth.

Small group spiritual companioning has much to offer this younger generation. As the digital revolution continues to unfold in the coming decades, it will be important for church leaders to pay attention to the ways people are being impacted by this major cultural shift. It also will be important to shape their response in conversation with Scripture and the resources of the Protestant tradition.

Listening to Scripture

In earlier chapters, we outlined the story Scripture tells. Human beings are created for relationship with God, others, and themselves but have broken their relationship with God, damaging all other relationships. In response, God elects a covenant people and, in the fullness of time, sends his Son Jesus Christ to do what humanity cannot do for itself: reconcile human beings to God. God also sends the Holy Spirit to awaken and guide Jesus's followers, forming them into a community that trusts God's salvation in Jesus Christ and bears witness to this good news to the entire world. How are we to think of small groups in the context of this story?

The key is the role of community, or *koinōnia*, in the church's witness to the gospel. Put simply, congregations are to embody the gospel in their own fellowship so they can bear a credible witness to the surrounding world, communicating the reconciliation God offers in Jesus Christ. They are to be communities in which relationship with God is reestablished through Christ and the healing and transformation of other relationships begins through the power of the Holy Spirit. Small group spiritual companioning is one of the ways the fellowship of the congregation is built up in the service of its mission as a witness.

10. Ibid.

This fellowship has an inward and an outward dimension. Within the community, fellowship is a source of healing, forgiveness, mutual support, and transformation for its members. They receive the blessings of their life in Christ as individuals and as a community. But they are blessed to be a blessing to others (Gen. 12:2). Outwardly, thus, the fellowship of believers is itself a witness, a living parable of the gospel the church proclaims. Moreover, individuals are equipped by this fellowship to bear witness to the gospel in their daily lives.

The inward and outward dimensions of Christian fellowship are two sides of the same coin. They are inherent to God's election of a covenant people. Israel is set apart from the nations, enters into a covenant with God, and receives the law in order to serve as a light to the nations (Isa. 42:6; 60:3). Jesus calls his disciples to come and follow him so they might become the sort of community that will serve as a light on a hill (Matt. 5:14). The intimate fellowship and mutual support of small groups are grounded in this two-sided understanding of fellowship in a community whose mission is to bear witness to the gospel.

Two passages in Acts offer vivid portraits of the close-knit fellowship of the early church and its role in bearing witness to the gospel: Acts 2:42–47 and 4:32–37. Both passages describe the sharing of possessions within the community so that "there were no needy persons among them" (4:34 NIV). The community is portrayed as devoted to teaching, fellowship, and worship and as meeting in smaller gatherings: "They broke bread in their homes and ate together with glad and sincere hearts, praising God and enjoying the favor of all the people" (2:46–47 NIV). And the result was that "the Lord added to their number daily those who were being saved" (2:47 NIV). Clearly, the kind of intimacy, mutual support, and sharing we associate with small groups is evident here. And the place of this sort of fellowship in winning the favor of "all the people" and adding to their number is equally evident.

Small groups in the church are a special form of spiritual companioning. In different times and places, such groups respond to different needs, whether the hunger for community felt by so many in contemporary America or the need for authentic face-to-face relationships in a digital era. From a biblical perspective, what is important is that small groups contribute to the upbuilding of a community whose very fellowship is a form of witness to the gospel and a source of equipping Christians to share the gospel in their everyday lives.

Mining the Protestant Tradition

Small group spiritual companioning has been an important part of the Protestant tradition in all of its branches. At various points, it has been an important ministry among the Reformed, Lutherans, Anabaptists, Mennonites, Anglicans,

Moravians, and Methodists. But it also has been a point of controversy within and between different Protestant communities. In his German Mass, for example, Luther called for the establishment of small groups of "earnest Christians," only to retract this position later when some groups began to separate from the established church.[11] Among those groups breaking away from the Lutheran Church were Anabaptists, who were beginning to form their own Christian communities. In the early stages of this process, they viewed small groups as gatherings of committed Christians who made a conscious decision to join a Christian community, marked by the baptism of believers.

Our task in this brief section is not to trace these kinds of conflicts. They rest on theological differences that continue within the Protestant tradition. Rather, we will follow a path described by C. S. Lewis in *Mere Christianity*.[12] In the introduction, Lewis portrays the purpose of his book with an image. He invites readers to imagine that Christianity is like a mansion with many rooms. Each of these rooms represents a different Christian tradition or denomination. In his book, Lewis writes, he will attempt to stay in the hallway that leads to each of these rooms. He will show what different Christian traditions have in common before they go their separate ways.

There are many theological differences in the Protestant tradition. These shape the ways different Protestant communities understand and practice small group spiritual companioning. Like Lewis, however, we hope to stay in the hallway. We believe that two basic assumptions about small group spiritual companioning are widely shared across the Protestant tradition.

First, small groups support the spirituality, fellowship, and ministry of the *laity*. This reflects the biblical pattern outlined in the previous section. Historically, Protestants have taken very seriously the upbuilding of the fellowship of the community, supporting the diverse gifts, ministries, vocations, and piety of every member. They have not thought of spirituality as the special vocation of nuns, monks, or others set apart in cloistered communities. Rather, the fellowship of the congregation is where spiritual formation takes place so Christians can embody the reconciliation of God in their relationship to one another and in their witness to the gospel in daily life.

Second, small groups in the Protestant tradition have been especially important in efforts to *renew* the church when it has lapsed into routinized forms of Christianity that are out of touch with the needs of the laity or fail to carry out the church's mission. Sometimes renewal has been sparked by efforts to reach people in the surrounding culture who are ignored or alienated

11. White, "Concerning Earnest Christians."
12. Lewis, *Mere Christianity*, xi–xii.

from the church in its present form. Other times, renewal has arisen from the perception that the church had become too comfortable in its present social context, supporting forms of Christian respectability and cultural conformity that diminish its ability to bear witness to the gospel.

In the Protestant tradition, small group spiritual companioning is closely associated with supporting the spirituality, fellowship, and ministry of the laity and with efforts to renew the church. Both of these emphases are readily apparent in John Wesley's extensive use of small groups in the Methodist movement, and we will examine Wesley below. Before doing so, it is worth mentioning other Protestant leaders for whom, and movements in which, small groups were significant.[13] This provides us with a picture of the breadth of spiritual companioning in small groups within the Protestant tradition.

Among the early Reformers, Martin Bucer established small groups (*christliche Gemeinschaften*) in Strasbourg, writing a number of treatises that offered theological justification and practical guidelines for these gatherings. The English Puritans developed small group meetings called "conventicles," which included prayer, singing, study of Scripture, and discussion of sermons. Cotton Mather brought this practice with him to colonial America, organizing numerous conventicles of twelve members in his congregation. Under the leadership of Philip Spener and August Francke, German Lutheran Pietists made small groups called *collegia* an important part of their effort to renew the Lutheran church in the seventeenth and eighteenth centuries. The ideas and practices of Spener and Francke were widely influential across Europe and, later, America. During this same period, Anthony Horneck and others established "societies" in the Church of England for the promotion of spiritual growth and holiness. Under the influence of Count Nikolaus von Zinzendorf, the Moravians developed a network of different types of small groups: bands, choirs, and diaspora societies.

In a very real sense, the influence of all of these leaders and movements came together in John Wesley's development of an extensive network of small groups in the early Methodist movement.[14] The movement emerged out of Wesley's concern that the church was failing to reach vast numbers of workers who had left their homes in the countryside and were now working in factories around London. He was recruited by George Whitefield to take over Whitefield's practice of open-air preaching in the early morning in an attempt to reach these workers while they traveled to work. As people began to respond, Wesley gradually organized them into small groups of various sorts. He drew

13. See Bunton, *Cell Groups and House Churches*, for an overview.
14. Goodhead, *Crown and a Cross*; Henderson, *John Wesley's Class Meeting*; Watson, *Early Methodist Class Meeting*.

on his experience in the Holy Club at Oxford, his participation in Anglican societies, his visitation of Zinzendorf, and his interaction with Moravians on his way to Georgia as a missionary and upon his return to London, where Wesley was the co-leader of the Fetter Lane Society with the Moravian Peter Boehler. After eighteen months, Wesley and others left the Fetter Lane Society to start the Foundry Society, which met near the site of Wesley's early morning preaching. This became the organizing center of people who responded to Wesley's message. In 1740, the Foundry Society had three hundred members. By 1798, a few years after Wesley's death, Methodist societies throughout Great Britain had over one hundred thousand members. What began as a renewal movement would eventually become a new church denomination.

Small groups were a key part of Wesley's success in attracting people who were alienated from the Church of England. They also were a key part of his commitment to supporting the spirituality, fellowship, and ministry of every person who became involved in the Methodist movement.

Over time, Wesley developed a network of five different types of small groups. *Societies* were composed of all Methodists in a certain area, who gathered for basic instruction in theological beliefs of the Methodist movement. *Class meetings* were the heart of the movement. They consisted of men and women of diverse social backgrounds. They included testimony and confession of sin in a context of encouragement and accountability. Visitors were allowed, and many people joined the movement through their participation in class meetings. *Bands* were homogenous, consisting of people of the same gender, marital status, and age. *Select societies* were composed of people chosen by Wesley for special instruction and mentoring. They were leaders of other groups, and Wesley hoped they might model Christian discipleship for others in the movement.

Wesley's network of small groups reflects the distinctive theology and practices of the Methodist tradition. Yet it also represents nicely the purpose of small group spiritual companioning in the Protestant tradition. Small groups support the spirituality, fellowship, and ministries of the *laity*. And they are especially important in efforts to *renew* the church. To recall C. S. Lewis's image, these emphases represent the hallway of spiritual companioning in the Protestant tradition.

Practicing Spiritual Companioning

Small groups are found in virtually every Protestant congregation in the United States. These include church committees, Sunday school classes, Bible studies, divorce recovery groups, grief support groups, spiritual direction groups, ministry teams, new member classes, discipleship groups, and many others.

What makes a small group a place where spiritual companioning occurs? We believe that the following five core elements characterize such groups:

1. Creating boundaries through explicit statement of commitment
2. Sharing, self-disclosure, and fellowship, leading to healing, forgiveness, and spiritual growth or transformation
3. Praying for one another and listening to one another in a prayerful manner
4. Equipping for ministry beyond the group
5. Engaging Scripture in a manner that creates an open space for hearing and receiving God's Word as it addresses people in their particular circumstances

Small groups embody these core elements in many different ways, and sometimes one element is hardly present at all. Yet it is helpful to keep these five core elements in mind. They serve as guidelines, naming qualities that ought to be present in groups offering spiritual companioning. They can help us spot things that might be missing and that, if strengthened, would allow these groups to better accomplish their purpose. They also can help us become aware of some of the tendencies in small groups that may create divisions in a congregation.

Creating Boundaries

Unlike a church school class in which the membership may change from week to week, small groups offering spiritual companioning depend upon clear boundaries. The expectation is that members will be present when the group meets and that they will participate along the lines of a covenant formed by the group. The covenant, or statement of commitment, clarifies the importance of confidentiality and the expectations of the group. In a divorce recovery group, for example, the covenant might state that the group members will try to be open about their feelings of loss and grief. They will receive the sharing of others and be careful to avoid giving advice and trying to "fix" them. A small group Bible study covenant might state that members will be honest with one another about how they hear God speaking into their lives as they study the Bible together. Such covenants create boundaries that promote a deeper level of commitment and sharing. They also attempt to state how the group members will relate to one another in ways that embody genuine spiritual companioning.

Roberta Hestenes wisely recommends that every small group should review its covenant periodically.[15] This gives people the opportunity to

---

15. Hestenes, *Using the Bible in Groups*, 23–24.

clarify their expectations for the group and offer feedback to one another about how well things are going. This review also serves as a time when people can opt out of the group without feeling they have let others down. Moreover, it can give the group the chance to discern whether it wants to invite others to join or wants to form new groups that expand the circles of spiritual companioning. These kinds of practices help group members remember that their mission is not to serve themselves, no matter how rich their experience has been. They are not to become a closed circle. Their purpose is to build up the fellowship of the entire congregation and to invite others outside the congregation to have an experience of Christian community.

Sharing

The boundaries of a small group create the possibility of a deeper level of sharing than happens in groups with constantly shifting members. Bounded groups develop over time as members come to know and trust one another. The members grow comfortable with the way their particular group works and their role in it. As the group develops, a greater level of sharing and self-disclosure becomes possible. It is common for one or two people to take the lead in modeling this kind of sharing.

It is very important to the group's development, however, that this sharing become mutual. This is one of the significant differences between spiritual companioning in small groups and in one-with-one spiritual direction. In the latter, the spiritual guide focuses all of his or her attention on the directee. There is no expectation that sharing will be mutual, although this sometimes happens. In small groups, the expectation is that *everyone* will share at the same level. Of course, personality differences enter in here. Extroverts find it easier to share and often achieve insights while they are talking. Introverts are more cautious and often like to think through what they are going to say before they share. It is important over time for group sharing to be balanced and mutual, just as it is among trusted friends.

The purpose of this sort of sharing is to allow people to bring their deepest needs and longings before God by articulating them to one another. This is why we point to forgiveness, healing, spiritual growth, and transformation as taking place through sharing. As the group members learn to trust and share with one another, they also support a deeper level of sharing and trust in each person's relationship with God. This is one of the most powerful dimensions of small group spiritual companioning. Intimacy and sharing with one another support intimacy and sharing with God.

Praying and Listening

One of the purposes of all spiritual companioning in the church is to help people live prayerfully. Prayer is calling upon God. It is the paradigmatic human response to God's grace. In Jesus Christ, God has reached out to the world in love, forgiveness, and healing. Our deepest response is to call on him in all things, knowing that God is gracious and desires a relationship in which his loving care is the center of our lives. How does spiritual companioning in small groups help people to live prayerfully? We believe it does so in three ways.

First, prayer is a regular and valued activity in the group. Sometimes this involves being together in silence, knowing that even though no words are being spoken aloud, others are calling on God and listening in a centered, receptive quietness for God's special word to them. Sometimes this involves praying for one another out loud, naming issues, problems, or hopes that have emerged in the sharing of the group. Creating space for prayer is a key part of spiritual companioning in small groups.

Second, small groups intentionally help their members learn to listen to one another prayerfully, even when they are not explicitly engaged in praying. We have discussed this earlier in the book. By way of reminder, it means adopting a posture of active receptivity toward God as group members listen to one another. Listening takes place on two levels. Group members listen closely to what a person is saying, and, simultaneously, they listen for what God might be saying through the words of the person talking. It is likely that small groups will need to talk about and practice this in the early stages of their life as a group.

Finally, small groups in which spiritual companioning takes place communicate the expectation that their members will pray when they are not together. This should probably be an explicit part of the group covenant. Group spiritual companioning works best when there is a symbiotic relationship between praying by the individual and praying by the group. In the group, individuals may learn concrete things that God is calling them to do and be in their everyday lives. In the midst of their everyday lives, they call upon God as they follow up on these insights and return to the group with what is happening in their lives. The spiritual life of Christians is both individual and corporate, personal and interpersonal, which is embodied in this symbiotic relationship.

Equipping for Ministry

Small groups supporting spiritual companioning sometimes become the victim of their own success. Feelings of closeness and spiritual vitality are such an important part of the group that its members begin to see the group as an end in itself. They become a closed circle unwilling to let others join. Or they fail to see the group as a way they are equipped for ministry. This is a special temptation in a social context like ours in which people turn to small groups in a quest for community. It is never fully adequate to allow the purpose of the church to be defined primarily in terms of coping with problems created by society. The church has its own purpose: to serve as a witness to the good news of God's forgiving and gracious love in Jesus Christ. This has several important implications for small groups.

Most important, the many good things that emerge in the spiritual companioning of small groups must be viewed as a way of equipping persons for ministry to others. The church is not just a gathering of persons who receive the special blessings of God. Rather, they are blessed to be a blessing to others. The good news they receive and experience is a gift they are to share. They are built up in the fellowship in order to show and share the gracious love of God in the world. When small groups become closed circles, ends in themselves, they stop serving the purpose of witnessing to the gospel.

As we have seen, one of the most powerful examples of the relationship between small group companioning and Christian witness is found in the class meetings of John Wesley's renewal movement. Research on these groups has uncovered that many people had conversion experiences or spiritual awakenings during their initial probationary period as class members.[16] Belonging preceded believing. Spiritual companioning was not just to build up those who already were Christians. It was a powerful, concrete embodiment of the gospel that brought people to faith.

Small groups equip people for ministry in other ways as well. Sometimes these groups provide the kind of supportive context in which people can grapple with real pain. This is especially the case in grief support groups or divorce recovery groups. But it also is true in other types of groups that are not explicitly oriented toward healing, like small group Bible studies and spiritual direction groups. Sometimes these settings allow people to surface profound hurts or longings in their lives: a drinking problem, addiction to pornography, an unhappy marriage, or problems with a teenager. Through prayer and support, the group may help these members take the steps they need to deal with their problems. They begin to heal. This may take a long time.

When healing occurs in small groups, it is wonderful. It is a sign of God's grace that points ahead to the consummation, when God will heal the entire creation. But it is not enough. Eventually, such persons—indeed, all people in

---

16. Goodhead, *Crown and a Cross*, 170–74. See Watson's nuancing of this understanding, *Early Methodist Class Meeting*, 149–50.

small groups—must use their own experiences of pain, longing, and healing as a bridge to other persons who are in need. They are healed to bring healing to others. They are set free to bring freedom to others. They are forgiven to bring God's forgiveness to others. Spiritual companioning in small groups equips people for ministry.

Creating Space to Receive God's Word

Small groups offering spiritual companioning engage the Bible in a wide variety of ways. Some borrow the ancient monastic practice of *lectio divina*, in which the group listens prayerfully to the same passage of Scripture as it is read several times. Some combine the study of a book of the Bible with ample time each meeting for individuals to make connections between a particular passage and their lives. Some look at a biblical theme like divine and human forgiveness or God's promise of new life as they struggle to come to terms with a marriage that has fallen apart. Some invite the members of the group to meditate on texts like Psalm 23 as a way to open themselves to God's caring presence in the midst of profound loss. Scripture is used in many different ways that are shaped by the particular focus of the group.

It is very important to engage Scripture in small group spiritual companioning. The most basic assumption of this form of companioning is that Christ through the Holy Spirit continues to speak into the lives of people when they listen for his Word in the words of Scripture as they are searched, mediated, discussed, and prayed in times of silence and sharing. The real and true companion, Jesus Christ, uses the words, thoughts, feelings, and interactions of ordinary people to communicate himself. Small groups are communities gathered *around* the Word.

The key to engaging-Scripture-as-companioning is creating an open space that offers God the freedom to speak into the lives of those gathered. The one Word of God becomes particular at such times, speaking into the concrete circumstances of each person who is present. God's Word is inexhaustibly rich in its capacity to bring what each one needs. An open space, thus, allows room for God to be active and for the group to be receptive. It leaves room for each person to receive God's Word to him or her on this day, at this time. God alone knows the deepest needs and longings of each person.

Several practical guidelines follow. An open space is not one in which a teacher, leader, or outspoken person provides the one definitive interpretation of Scripture for the group. Rather, every person is given the chance to listen for what God might be saying. Moreover, an open space moves beyond study to prayerful receptivity. Study has a role in some small groups. It represents an important way of taking the Bible seriously, paying attention to what a passage is actually saying and its canonical context. But creating an open space is different than study, even if it may be informed by study.[17] It focuses directly on granting God the freedom to communicate with those gathered and granting each person the freedom to receive the particular word God has to offer. Finally, there are a variety of ways to create an open space in small groups, as noted at the beginning of this section. This is important to reiterate because some small group leaders are familiar with only one way of conducting small groups. They may know the three basic steps of inductive Bible study or the repetitive reading of Scripture in *lectio divina*. But one size does not fit all. Different groups need different ways of engaging Scripture, depending on the purpose of the group. It is important for the leaders of small groups to become familiar with a variety of ways Scripture can be engaged in small groups.

Exploring the Stories of Congregations

In the remainder of this chapter, we explore the stories of two types of small groups. One is a small group Bible study, and the other is a small group in which spiritual direction is offered. As you read these stories, try to discern the core elements of small group spiritual companioning as described in the previous section. We will pause at the end of each story and review together what might be learned.

Spiritual Companioning in a Small Group Bible Study

Jim Revery is the associate pastor of adult education at New Hope Church, a nondenominational congregation of about 1,400 members on the West Coast. The church has seven classes for adults on Sunday morning and two regular Bible studies designed to help new Christians learn the basics of the Bible: Bible for Beginners and A One-Year Trip through the Bible. Jim has been quite successful in starting and maintaining a strong small group ministry in the church. He estimates that around 70 percent of the congregation participates in a small group at some point during the year, if you include the short-term family fellowship groups in the four weeks before Easter.

Jim loves to lead small groups, and one of the most effective strategies he has developed over the years is to invite potential small group leaders to participate in the groups he leads. This participation lasts for two months,

17. Martin, *Reading Scripture*, part 1.

and then he encourages the participants to start their own groups. They are asked to pray about this. If they think God is calling them to this ministry, he helps new leaders recruit a small group and stays in close contact throughout their first experience of leadership. He encourages them to ask people to make a six- to eight-week commitment and then to give group members the opportunity to review their covenant and decide if they want to keep meeting, disband, or invite new members. If things go well during this first experience, then Jim gradually pulls back and tells the leaders to contact him if they run into problems. He also checks in by phone with each small group leader he has trained this way at least three times during the leader's first eighteen months of leading a group.

When asked to reflect on the small group ministry as a source of spiritual formation, Jim responds: "I think it is definitely one of the key ways disciple-ship formation takes place in this church. We even organize all new-member classes as small groups. We want everybody to have a positive experience of what this is like. In the years I have been here, we've developed what you might call a culture of small groups in the church. Our members think of the church as a place where they are known and supported in their daily walk with Jesus. They get help with their problems in their small groups. They make friends. They feel connected to the church through their groups."

Jim was asked to share what a typical small group meeting looks like. "They don't all look the same because we've got so many different types of groups." He was then asked to describe one of the training groups he leads. "I always use the inductive Bible study approach in these groups. You know, it involves three basic steps: observation, interpretation, and application. We always begin with a brief time of checking in: how their week's been, what's been going on in their lives. I pray for Christ to be with us through the Holy Spirit and remind the group that as we read and hear the passage, we should be open to the Spirit's guidance. I read the passage we're looking at out loud and ask them to follow it in their Bibles. I then ask them to read it to them-selves silently. Finally, I ask them to close their eyes as I read the passage out loud again, listening for a word or phrase that captures their attention. They then look back at the text in silence and focus on that word or phrase. We then start our discussion of the passage. Our first question is, what does it say? We key off the words or phrases that struck them. Earlier this week, I was leading a group that's been studying Galatians. It was our third meeting. We were focusing on verses eleven through fourteen of chapter two, where Paul shares the story of his confrontation of Peter in Antioch."

Jim continued, "At first, in the observation phase, we just tried to clarify what Paul was writing in these verses. What is the circumcision party? How did they impact Peter's behavior? Who else was influenced by them? What did Paul have in mind when he described Peter as living like a gentile? We shared what we remembered from our other meetings—what was going on in the first part of the letter. We also shared what else we knew from other parts of the Bible about Paul's conflict with the circumcision party, his relationship to Barnabas, and things like that. We then moved to the second part of inductive Bible study: What does it mean?"

When asked to describe this, Jim continued to talk about the group studying Galatians. "The group kept coming back to what Paul wrote right at the beginning of the letter," Jim said, "that the Galatians were turning to a different gospel and that they were being led astray by other leaders in the church. For Peter and even Barnabas to go along with these people must have been a big blow to Paul. The group could see why it made him mad. But they also saw this as a righteous anger. He was standing up for the gospel. He had to confront them. We talked about things like that."

Jim was asked what happened next. He responded, "Well, we moved to the third part of inductive Bible study: application. Here we focus on the question, what does the passage mean for my life? I always try to leave at least half of the meeting for this and our time of prayer, when we pray for ourselves and one another. In the group studying Galatians, I made the shift to this part by asking them to pause for a minute and to think about whom they most identified with at this point in their lives—Peter or Barnabas or Paul—and why. I gave them five minutes of silence and asked them to write down words or phrases or names that expressed their answer. We then began to share. It was a really good discussion. People got pretty personal. One guy who said he identified with Peter even shared that he'd been having thoughts and feelings about a woman at work and that he felt like he needed to be confronted. He didn't want to go there. She's married and so is he. That was pretty personal, but I've stopped being surprised when this kind of stuff happens in these groups. I think it is the Holy Spirit helping people make connections between the Bible and their lives. Other people identified with Barnabas, feeling like they've let down friends. A couple of folks identified with Paul. They felt they needed the courage to stand up to friends who were headed in the wrong direction."

How did the meeting close? "We prayed about all these things. I asked each person to pray for the person on their left and to continue to pray for that person during the week. I also told them that our check-in next meeting would give them a chance to share how they followed up on what we talked about today."

Let's pause and reflect on this example of small group Bible study in light of our understanding of the core elements of spiritual companioning in small groups. While he did not mention it in this interview, Jim Revery shares a group covenant as he recruits each person to participate. He uses the covenant to talk about what the group is like and the commitment that is expected. Jim's covenant is fairly brief. It reads: "I promise to come to each of the eight meetings of our group unless I am out of town or an emergency arises. I will do my best to open my life to God as we study the Bible together and will share what I hear God saying to me. I will keep in strict confidence what other group members share. I will pray for myself and others in the group when we meet and between meetings." The covenant is discussed briefly at the beginning of the first meeting, and everyone is asked to sign a copy that is passed from person to person.

The level of sharing present in the group by their third meeting likely indicates that its members trust Jim and feel relatively safe in the boundaries of the group, especially their commitment to confidentiality. Obviously, prayer is present and the very purpose of the group is to engage Scripture. Jim does a particularly nice job of helping people begin to connect the text to their own particular life circumstances, slowing the group down as each person considers which character in the passage he or she most identifies with.

There is no explicit attention to listening to one another prayerfully or to ministry beyond the group. Yet both are implicitly present in this group. Jim asks the group members to pray for the person on their left and to continue to pray for him or her during the coming week. This requires each person to listen carefully to others in the group. It would not take much to teach them what it means to listen to others prayerfully. Also, Jim is inviting people to participate in the group in order to give them a chance to decide if they would like to become a small group leader, an important ministry in the church. Moreover, as individuals make connections between Galatians and their particular lives, it is possible they will discern ways of serving God in their relationships with others during the coming week.

We can learn many things from this story, and here we highlight only three insights. First, do you want to learn how to lead small group Bible studies to support spiritual companioning in your church? By far, the best way to start is to follow the path Jim uses in recruiting potential leaders. Participate in a small group Bible study yourself. Nothing you can read in a book or online can substitute for the actual experience of being part of a group. If you can find someone like Jim who is very experienced and willing to mentor you, so much the better.

Second, learn one approach to small group Bible study well, and then work at expanding your repertoire. Jim uses the three-step method of inductive Bible study. It is clear in the story that he is quite creative in the way he implements this—by inviting people to identify with different characters in the Galatians passage, for example. But it is important to gradually expand your repertoire of teaching. Here reading can help, for there are many good books introducing different ways of teaching the Bible in small groups. The most important skill set to learn is leading a discussion.[18] This involves learning how to ask good questions and build on the responses people give, while simultaneously involving others in the discussion. Concentrate on this. There are several guidelines at the end of the chapter to help you get started.

Third, and most important, keep in mind the primary purpose of this kind of small group Bible study: spiritual companioning. It is not building up knowledge of Scripture, as important as this may be. It is not psychological healing or friendship. Rather, it is creating an opportunity for people to enter into a deeper relationship with God through their sharing and interaction with one another.

Spiritual Companioning in a Spiritual Direction Group for Women

Liz Ford is a professor in a small liberal arts college in the Midwest. Her field is theology and literature in the English department, and she is a very popular teacher. Liz is actively involved in the Presbyterian church right across from the college campus. Several years ago, she entered a training program in spiritual direction. "I guess I did this mostly for myself," she shared. "I was starting to feel restless. It must have been midlife. [Laughs.] Here I was a single woman who had just hit forty-five. I loved my teaching and my students. But I'd been doing that for over fifteen years, ever since I got my PhD. I got into spiritual direction training because I wanted to see if God had more in store for me. I was restless."

The training program lasted two years, and after she completed it, the associate pastor of her church asked if she would be willing to run a small group offering spiritual direction for women. Most of Liz's training had focused on one-with-one spiritual direction, but she had read several books about this way of offering spiritual direction and attended a workshop by Rose Mary Dougherty, a leader in small group spiritual direction. So Liz decided to give it a try. The associate pastor already had a number of women in mind and invited them to join the group and make an initial commitment of ten months. The associate pastor wanted to participate as well, so the group had a total of eight women. At the end of ten months, one woman dropped out, but the rest were eager to continue. The group has continued to meet for several years.

When asked about the format of the group, Liz responded: "We meet every other week for an hour and fifteen minutes. Sometimes, we go a little longer. We begin with a time of *lectio divina*. I read a very short passage—only three

18. Osmer, *Teaching for Faith*, chap. 4.

or four verses—three times, and after each reading the group moves into silence. They are asked to share a word or phrase that caught their attention.
This is our way of stepping away from the rest of our lives and turning our
attention and focus to God. We always keep an empty chair in the circle for
Christ and have this running joke about remembering who's with us. It is
pretty common for things mentioned briefly during *lectio* to come up later.
This happens a lot."

Liz continued: "When the group first began to meet, I would spend a short
time—about five minutes—talking to them about what's involved in spiritual
direction. I'd talk about things like not giving advice, how to listen for God
when we're together, how to notice God's presence in everyday life, and other
topics. One of the most important things I talked about—and we've kept
coming back to this—is learning how to put aside your own needs and give
your attention totally to the person who is sharing. None of these women had
ever experienced direction before, and I wanted to provide them with a little
teaching about this. Sometimes I'd return to things we'd talked about during
this time, like 'I think we're getting into advice here.' After a while, I stopped
doing this teaching because they were doing the spiritual direction process
successfully together. I began to use this time to ask: Is there anything that
arose in a previous meeting that you'd like to mention? This gave them the
chance to update the group. For example, one of the group members, Martha,
had talked about an issue she was dealing with at work. She's a social worker,
and one of her clients was dying of cancer, a young mother who is divorced.
The mother was in total denial and refused to participate in any planning for
her kids' future. Martha talked about this one week, discussing her struggle
to figure out her role. Several weeks later she updated us during this time."

Liz continued by describing what comes next: "We then move into the heart
of group spiritual direction. Two women share at each meeting. This means
that everyone gets to be the 'focus person' every two months. The group spends
twenty-five minutes on each person. One person talks for ten minutes and then
the group asks questions and reflects back to the person what they're hearing. We end by praying for the person. We repeat the process with the second
person. I took the lead during the first few months in asking questions and
reflecting back. I asked the group to let me do this, and they respected that.
Gradually, I invited them to do this with me, and now everyone participates,
though I probably still ask more questions than anyone else.

"As I think about this part of our meeting, it took us a while to learn how
to ask 'God questions.' What I mean by that is noticing how God was present in the stories they were sharing. They'd talk about relationships or an
event or some issue but didn't make many connections with God. Gradually

our questions helped them learn how to notice God in their lives and to feel comfortable talking about this. They also tended to share stories that were filled with pain. Almost all of these women had dealt with tough issues in their lives; some of them were really painful, like the death of a child. At one meeting, a woman was sharing, and she started off by saying, 'You know, I don't have anything hard to talk about today. I just feel grateful, and I want to share that.' I reinforced this, telling them that we want to share the grace and joy in our lives as well as the hard things.

"Another thing that we had to learn to do was to feel comfortable with silence. I talked about this in one of my teaching times near the beginning and mentioned it several other times in the group. 'It is okay for us to be together in silence,' I shared. 'God is with us, and we're listening for God.' I think learning to be together in silence was a big part of our growth as a group. It was a new level of intimacy and trust. It meant we were comfortable being together with God."

Liz then described the final portion of their time together: "The last part of our group meeting is a time to reflect on what people have noticed about how God was present in our meeting. Sometimes they talk about what was going on in their own hearts. Sometimes they notice how God was present when the group comforted a person or laughed together or how God seemed to be very close in the quiet. We end by reminding ourselves who is going to share the next time we meet."

Liz was asked if there were special times of deep sharing that stand out. After pausing for a moment, she said, "One woman in our group shared the story of her daughter's death. In her early teens, her daughter was involved in an accident, and she died instantly. This woman had been holding her pain inside for a long time. When she shared the story of her daughter's death, we didn't focus only on her pain. We also asked about her relationship with God. What happens when she prays about it? She began to talk about the ways this has affected her relationship with God. She couldn't really pray anymore. She believed that her daughter went to be with God, and she remained active in the church, but her own relationship with God seemed distant and dark. She said something like: 'I guess in my heart, I can't feel close to God. I always trusted God to take care of my children, and then this happened. I really can't pray.'

"The group listened to her, drew her out, and then prayed for her. They also promised to pray for her after each meeting. She embraced that. Gradually, she became increasingly engaged in the group, and she reported that her prayer life began to change. We also noticed how compassionate she was with other group members. I think we all believe that the group has been a small part of God's healing work in her life. A change seems to be taking place in her relationship with God."

Liz also talked about another member of the group: "She returned to school late in life to start a seminary degree, taking classes with young adults nearly half her age. The second time she was the focus person, she shared how conflicted she felt about going back to school: 'Don't get me wrong, I love studying Scripture and theology, learning so much about things I've always wondered about. But I question whether I should spend my time doing this. Maybe I should be taking care of my grandchildren.' Probably the most important thing the group has done for her is to affirm her passion, to validate what she's doing, and to recognize it as a genuine call. She preached in church one Sunday, and several of us came around her afterward to express our appreciation. It was a really special moment for group members and for her."

When we stand back from this story, we can see all of the core elements of spiritual companioning in small groups. Sharing, prayer, prayerful listening, and engaging Scripture as a way of listening for God's Word are readily apparent. Liz never had the group articulate a group covenant, but she did spend some time in the first months clarifying the expectations of group spiritual direction. She also made a very important point in our interview: "You know, in the end, it's the actual experience of the group that keeps people coming. It is not a sense of obligation. They want to come. The group is very important to each of them." She also noted that the group helps each woman work out her "calling" in her own particular situation and to act on it.

Two final insights from Liz are also worth sharing. The group has not led the women to form relationships with each other beyond their meetings. They don't get together as couples or friends. Yet members have arrived at an incredibly deep level of intimacy. She also noted that she is not sure that this kind of group spiritual direction would be right for everyone. "All of these women brought a readiness for spiritual intimacy that was tied up with their pain and longing," she shared. "I guess the particular combination of things that brought this group together is part of the mystery of God's Spirit. I can imagine that group spiritual direction might look different in other groups, and I hope to experience that someday in the future."

Small groups are an important way Protestant congregations have supported spiritual companioning in the past and present. The two examples we have just examined could be multiplied many times over. Spiritual companioning will look different in a divorce recovery group, a small group Bible study, or a ministry team, but many of the core elements we have identified are likely to be present. Christ desires to be our companion, and we open ourselves to his companioning as we companion one another. Something special happens in the sharing, responding, and noticing of small groups. The community is gathered around the Word, and Christ uses the words and relationships of a concrete group of people to speak the grace and truth of the gospel into the particular lives of those gathered.

Exercising Our Companionship: Facilitating a Discussion

Here are some basic techniques for facilitating a discussion:

1. *Ask open-ended questions.* Discussion is not facilitated by questions that require a simple yes or no. Some questions ask for facts or information. (What happened on the seventh day of creation?) Open-ended questions invite group members to share their thoughts and insights. Such questions usually do not have one right answer. (What does it mean for us to rest or practice Sabbath today? Why is this important?)

2. *Affirm people's responses.* This signals to group members that they have been heard and their responses valued. (Thanks for that insight.) This can be done nonverbally by nodding.

3. *Avoid mini-lectures.* While it is helpful to share background information in relevant ways, long-winded statements can derail the participation of others and turn the group leader into the expert.

4. *Ask prompting questions.* When no one comes up with an answer, do *not* panic and give the answer or quickly ask three new questions. Provide clues that help the group members. (Look at v. 19. What does the word "engage" mean?)

5. *Ask probing questions.* These questions invite people to go deeper than their initial response. Often this involves building on the answer that is given and inviting the respondent to say more. (Could you unpack that for us? That's really interesting; say more.)

6. *Redirect the discussion for greater participation.* Shift the discussion away from the answer given by one person and invite others to respond. (Does anyone want to add to Paula's response? What do the rest of you think?)

7. *Give "qualifying instructions" as the flow of the discussion is redirected.* You can control the type of discussion that takes place by "framing" what you are looking for. Sometimes you want the group to work in a collaborative fashion. (Let's build on Jane's insight. Where does this take

us?) You might want the group to debate the topic. (Do any of you see things differently?) You might want to elicit a wide range of responses, before focusing on one theme. (In popcorn fashion, very quickly, let's put as many ideas on the table as possible. *After the group has done so*: Which one of these do you find most interesting? Let's focus on it.)

8. *Become comfortable with silence.* Too often, small group leaders are threatened when they ask a question and no one responds. Sometimes the silence is shorter than we think. People may be pondering, and it is important to give them time to do so. Also, some questions are risky, inviting personal self-disclosure or sharing uncomfortable information. Think of your role as creating an "open space" for God's Spirit to work with people and give time for this to occur. Obviously, we sometimes ask questions that people cannot answer or do not understand. In this case, we may need to rephrase the *same* question or say something like: "I must not have been clear. Could someone take a stab at stating what he or she thinks I was asking?"

For Further Reading

Benner, David. *Sacred Companions: The Gift of Friendship and Direction*. Downers Grove, IL: InterVarsity, 2002. A theologically rich overview of spiritual friendship, with a special chapter on small groups.

Bunton, Peter. *Cell Groups and House Churches: What History Teaches Us*. Lititz, PA: House to House, 2001. A brief but excellent overview of the history of small groups in the Protestant tradition.

Dougherty, Rose Mary. *Group Spiritual Direction: Community for Discernment*. Mahwah, NJ: Paulist Press, 1995. An ecumenical discussion of small group spiritual direction, with special attention given to discernment.

Hestenes, Roberta. *Using the Bible in Groups*. Philadelphia: Westminster Press, 1983. A classic introduction to small group Bible study that addresses group dynamics, teaching methods, and organizational strategies.

Johnson, David, and Frank Johnson. *Joining Together: Group Theory and Group Skills*. 11th ed. Essex, England: Pearson Education, 2014. A basic introduction to small groups, covering group dynamics, leadership, power, and different types of groups.

Martin, George. *Reading Scripture as the Word of God: Practical Approaches and Attitudes*. 4th ed. Ann Arbor, MI: Servant Books, 1998. A classic introduction to the spiritual reading of Scripture, suitable for both Roman Catholics and Protestants.

Vest, Norvene. *Gathered in the Word: Praying the Scripture in Small Groups*. Nashville: Upper Room, 1996. An introduction to *lectio divina* as a way of praying Scripture in small groups.

5

Spiritual Companioning
in Everyday Life

More than two decades ago, I (Angela) was faced with my first solo decision as an emerging adult. The final year of high school was upon me, and I had yet to determine what should come next. The opportunity to make my own decisions felt like a weighty freedom, something I both relished and feared. At the same time, my desire for God was deepening, and I was learning to pray for God's presence and guidance. I went about this diligently, hoping God had some kind of purpose for me that I could identify well enough to take a step in the "right" direction. While I could not have defined the term "spiritual discernment," this is essentially what I was fumbling around with. I was watching and hoping for signs that God had something to communicate to me personally.

There were a few brief, encouraging moments of clarity that I will never forget: a joy-filled experience of preaching in my own congregation, feeling grasped by a biblical passage about the lack of workers in God's plentiful harvest, and having an insight while on retreat that God had not called me to preach to cattle. This final clarifying moment may seem obscure, but it made perfect sense to me since I was deciding whether my future would be tied to the family farm. I prayed about these things and began to talk with my parents and congregational youth leaders about experimenting with full-time ministry through a short-term mission and service organization. This would require delaying college for a year, but it seemed like the perfect time and opportunity to address my inner yearnings.

High school graduation came and went, and I started working as a camp counselor for the summer. For some unknown reason and quite out of character for me, I was slow to complete the mission board's applications. No matter how much I prayed for God to show the way, I could not muster any specific clarity or passion for this direction that once seemed so promising. Instead, I felt a growing apprehension within that I fought to press down. In a few honest moments, I wondered if there was something wrong with me that kept me from knowing God's will. Surely God would want to make it clear if he had a purpose for my life rather than hide it just out of sight. This seemed too cruel and completely unlike the God I believed in. Outwardly, I did not like to appear less than confident or capable, so I kept these feelings to myself. But it must have been obvious to my parents that I was not making much progress.

One Saturday I came home to an empty house and a note on the table. Most of our family notes consisted of grocery lists or housekeeping reminders, but this one was addressed only to me, and it was far from ordinary. My mother wrote that she was increasingly uneasy about my plans for the next year. While they would support me in whatever decision I made, she needed to let me know of her concern.

As I paused to think this over, I imagined how she must have prayed about the note and wrestled within herself over writing it. Many mothers are quick to offer advice to their almost-grown children, but not mine. She encouraged us to make our own decisions and never pressured us to pursue one direction over another. She tended to wait and watch over her children rather than push or prod. After getting over the initial shock of finding the note, I breathed a sigh of relief. Someone else put into words what I myself was feeling. This confirmation gave me the courage to turn in a new direction.

In the days that followed, I recognized that I was learning something very important about hearing from God. Personal decision making does not mean that we must seek God alone. In a culture that values individual freedom above almost all else, the way of the spiritual life often includes submitting ourselves to the wisdom of others who pray for us and companion us. In this situation, the discerning activity of another enabled me to be honest with God and with myself. The note also reflected the changing nature of the relationship I shared with my mother. She might not direct my steps into the future, but she would still seek God on my behalf and be a source of great support. I needed human community in my connection with God to strengthen and enrich my own personal prayer life. With these thoughts, I knew more freedom and less weight.

Many others have companioned me since then, including a spiritual director I met with regularly during my first pregnancy and into early motherhood. She invited me to broaden the process of discernment beyond overarching concerns about work, ministry, and character formation. While I knew that I could share with God in the simple things of everyday life, I had much to learn about practicing God's presence in the manner of Brother Lawrence, through washed dishes and swept floors.[1] This was especially important at the time because I had seen the exhausted faces of new parents, and I was concerned about losing touch with God in a new phase of life. My director invited me to reflect on God's pleasure in every small act of care I offered to my infant child. I could discern God's presence in those moments just as I had in solitude and study. Once again, I grew in my journey with God through engagement with a spiritual companion whom I trusted to challenge me to view life experiences from another perspective.

Understanding the Cultural Context

The desire to seek out the prayerful discernment of others is rooted in a fundamental yearning to hear a word from the Lord. This topic has always been important to God's people. From the stories of Abraham and Moses to the Acts of the Apostles and beyond, we can see that the people of God have given significant attention to recognizing God's voice. It is interesting to note how many call stories figure prominently in Scripture. Over the centuries, spiritual leaders have written extensively about their call narratives and other encounters with God, perhaps because those experiences were life altering, and these leaders believed the stories and teachings would support the education and formation of God's people.

Recognizing the Sacred in the Mundane

Discovering the presence of the sacred continues to be important to many Americans, whether or not they participate in organized religion. This was confirmed by Nancy Ammerman in a recent study on religion and spirituality in everyday life. Ammerman's research team invited a representative group of Americans from diverse backgrounds to record their stories of spiritual engagement over a period of several months. The team found that activities in the realms of work, home, and community all figured as important sources for encountering the sacred.

Ammerman's work challenges a commonly held assumption about American spirituality. Given our cultural commitments to personal independence and

1. See Lawrence, *Practice of the Presence of God.*

the freedom we have to choose our own faith, we may get the idea that the spiritual life is fundamentally an individual endeavor. Ammerman suggests that having a strong "faith in myself" is a flagship notion that dominates American culture. As Ammerman writes, "the solitary, contemplating person has become the icon of American spirituality, and this sort of spiritual experience the essence of authentic religiosity."[2] Our independence can extend to a belief in spiritual autonomy that may hide our interconnectedness with each other and devalue institutions that are actually critical for human flourishing. While our culture romanticizes the image of the lone ranger, there is no place for this way of living according to Christian theology.

What we actually find when we look more deeply at Ammerman's research, which seems to ring true from experience, is that the spiritual journey we live in everyday life is deeply impacted by the connections we share with God, with other human beings, and ultimately with all creation. A few of Ammerman's findings are especially helpful for understanding spiritual companioning in the course of daily life. First, the majority of people described prayer as communication with a divine Presence. Their inner worlds include ongoing conversations with someone who is beyond themselves. They do not pray about ideas or abstractions, but for health, well-being, and safety for themselves and their families.[3] Prayer is not a one-way conversation. Those who tend to be more "spiritually engaged," according to Ammerman, tend to listen for responses from God as a critical part of this relational process. Several participants say that they tend to speak to God in prayer and hear from God through Scripture.

Second, human community serves as a source for awareness of spiritual things. Participants talk about becoming aware of God through nature, the inner self, a meaningful calling, and "the bonds of human connection." The reference to human connections seems especially important for our purposes. Some suggest that they are able to hear from God through the words and actions of others. A number talked about experiencing the sacred through their own acts of service, such as caring for the needs of another. It is clear that human interaction, both giving and receiving, is recognized as part of God's communication with and to us.[4]

Third, religious communities have a profound effect on our interpretation of life from a spiritual perspective. In Ammerman's view, there is a strong connection between active participation in a religious community and regular personal spiritual practices, such as daily prayer. This is especially true for those

2. Ammerman, *Sacred Stories*, 45.
3. Ibid., 63–64.
4. Ibid., 291–92.

who routinely turn to their religious leaders for guidance and support and are involved in a faith community's life beyond weekly worship services. Not surprisingly, those who attended religious services regularly were more likely to have a language for describing everyday life in spiritual terms. Even more, relationships emerge within the larger fellowship that allow people to put into words how God is present in life experiences, to frame life in terms of theological commitments, which often leads naturally to choices and actions lived out. In fact, shared spiritual stories tend to empower us. "Life narratives always provide direction to action, supplying the plots for what is envisioned as possible. Accounts are never merely accounts; they also shape reality."[5] This is facilitated by compassionate listeners who find it a privilege to hear others tell their stories. Though people will come to a congregation for its worship or theology, this kind of relationship becomes the core reason that many choose to stay.[6]

Ammerman's study suggests that there is no boundary line between what is spiritual and what is mundane. She challenges the notion that the sacred is set apart from the rest of life, and whatever boundaries we may construct are permeable. People experience a blending of the ordinary and the extraordinary, of the natural order and the mysteries we interpret as God's in-breaking into our lives. When people build relationships in a faith community, they tend to pay more attention to how God may be calling them in the rest of life, and they are more committed to living out the implications of that calling in what they do. Perhaps this is what the New Testament writers meant when they talked about the importance of encouraging one another toward right living.

In a sense, the community of faith points to the spiritual and the mundane and then enables participants to build a bridge between the two through the ministries of the larger community, including corporate worship and educational classes, and through personal companionship, including pastoral conversations, small groups, and spiritual friendships. These findings encourage us to stay the course in congregational ministry and, even more, to create intentional spaces for exploring personal narratives about God's presence and activity in daily life.

Misconceptions about Hearing God

Part of making connections between the spiritual and the mundane in companioning relationships is the process of discerning how God actually communicates with us. Hearing from God and responding are dimensions of the Christian spiritual journey that most believers have prayed and thought

5. Ibid., 292.
6. Ibid., 105–6.

about. Noticing God with us in our daily living can be delightful and exciting. Many of us recall moments when we have felt certain God was speaking to us somehow. We knew there was a Presence beyond ourselves that was interested in us and wanted to see us heal, have purpose, and flourish. Sometimes our sense of God's communication seems as clear as the bright green road signs pointing the way on a sunny day.

At other times, seeking God's help and guidance feels more challenging, like inching forward through a fog. Our prayers seem to return to us void, and we are not sure why. Does God actually offer personal guidance, and if so, to what degree? Is it more specific than the general guidance available to us through the Scriptures? When I believe God is speaking to me, how do I know it is really God and not my own wishful thinking? The apostle Paul talks about the journey toward Christlike formation with the Corinthian believers. He does not mince words when he states that they have to start with spiritual milk before graduating to solid food (1 Cor. 3:2). We may enjoy a crunchy apple or a bite of steak, but these tasty foods would be dangerous to an infant without the teeth to chew them. We do not first come to faith with full-blown Christian maturity, and this includes our skills for discerning God's presence and guidance.

Because our brokenness distorts and damages the relationship with God, we may develop some misconceptions along the way. Many believe that the ability to hear a specific word from the Lord is a sign of closeness with God. This idea sounds right on the surface, but it can have a troubling underbelly. If we lack a clear word from the Lord, we think it must be because we have done something wrong or have strayed outside of his perfect will for us. We respond by confessing every possible sin and diligently practicing spiritual disciplines so that we won't miss a chance to hear what God is saying. These efforts may be built upon the notion that God has one specific will for each of us whom God has chosen: one career, one marriage partner, one educational path, and so on.

What is especially dangerous is the notion that accurate decision making depends on finding out what God's will is for each individual circumstance and then following it exactly. This involves considerable time, effort, and not a little anxiety. In a sense we are treating God as a master who must be followed precisely. We are striving to be like the faithful servants who receive additional talents in the kingdom (Matt. 25:14–30), but we believe the master does not really trust us with those talents. The relationship with God becomes only about what we *do* for God rather than who we *are* with God.

Ironically, the opposite of this way of thinking is also common. We may assume that only specific people like Isaiah or Paul or the pastors, priests, and missionaries in our time have a calling, or vocation, to discern God's guidance and need to develop the skills to hear from God. The rest of us take what we find in Scripture and other resources of the church and try to live a moral life in whatever context we find ourselves in.

The content and focus of our discernment is also a challenging matter. What exactly are we trying to discern? We hear this question in our opening narrative. Like many young adults, I (Angela) spent considerable energy discerning major life decisions and with time came to appreciate a much broader view of discernment, including the deep richness of watching for God's presence in what is commonplace, from the colors of the sunrise to a kind word of affirmation. For all of us, discernment can become a self-focused endeavor, in which we are especially concerned for the future, specifically safety and security for ourselves and our loved ones.

Theologians and philosophers have long been aware that personal spirituality tends toward bargaining with a divine power for protection and safety, blessing and salvation, and help for overcoming crises.[7] In his book *Hearing God*, Dallas Willard suggests that focusing only on securing our own comfort, safety, and righteousness makes it impossible for us to receive God's guidance.[8] While God certainly cares about these things, he cannot build life-giving communication upon a foundation centered only in the self. This is not the way of Christ's kingdom.

The false impressions we hold can extend to our ideas about who God really is. If we doubt that God's character is completely loving and just, how can we trust God with the longings of our hearts? How will we recognize God's voice if our images of God have been distorted? Psychologist Ana-Maria Rizzuto suggests that children form some kind of representation of God in their early years, and they typically impose images and characteristics of their parents onto God.[9] In our experience, this holds true. These images develop and change over time, but they continue to carry influence beyond childhood. Over the years, we have observed countless seminary students with a wide range of images of God. While most are capable of saying the "right" things about God, naming God's unconditional love and grace, some find that they actually hold deep-seated images of God that are significantly different.

We have heard students unpack their honest impressions of a God who is judgmental or unavailable. Some feel God has impossibly high expectations or doubt that they can honestly express true feelings before God, especially

7. Ibid., 291.
8. Willard, *Hearing God*, 27–28.
9. Rizzuto, *Birth of the Living God*, 52, 200.

anger. The variations are endless. With a little more digging, it is not uncommon to find that they remember a primary caregiver responding to them in similar ways. This is not always the case, but it is common enough. Even when the impression of God does not reflect what we believe theologically, it is still a challenge to change responses to God that are guided by long-held images. Misconceptions about God's character create distance between us and God, making it difficult for us to trust that God is really on our side. Sometimes we find it hard to believe it is really God speaking words of affirmation and encouragement through the voice of another or in our own inner reflection. Distorted representations also distort our hearing of God's voice.

Revealing the Misconceptions

Any marriage counselor will tell you that forming a loving relationship built upon effective communication takes time and plenty of conversation. One of the counselor's most important roles is helping the couple to hear each other clearly. Having an outside resource person who listens well for what each partner tries to say can make an extraordinary difference in the building of relationship. Obviously a marriage is fundamentally different from the kind of relationship we share with God, yet there are several biblical references that point to the relationships between God and Israel or Christ and the church as analogous to marriage (e.g., Isa. 54:5; Jer. 3:20; Hosea 1:2; Eph. 5:21–33; Rev. 19:7–9). The form of companionship may be different, but some of the principles are similar. We learn to hear God well as we open up to relationship over time, tending it from our side and creating a freshly groomed vine ready for the Spirit's fruit to flourish (John 15:1–7). Like a marriage counselor, the spiritual companion supports this process, helping us to listen well and to recognize God's voice. Sometimes this means identifying any distortions of God's voice that we may not notice, or offering a word of encouragement, or simply being a prayerful presence in Christ's name.

As we grow ever more deeply into communion with God, abiding in the relationship, Jesus is confident that God hears and grants our requests. He offers a picture of a God wishing to be close to us and communicate with us, not a presence working against us or trying to hide just out of sight. The images of God we find in Scripture suggest both committed kinship and an invitation to friendship. And this relationship is not for the individual and God alone; Jesus's metaphor about the vine and the branches extends to abiding with one another in love and friendship (John 15:12–17). Not only did Jesus teach about friendship with God and one another; he also practiced it. We can learn a great deal about spiritual companionship from Jesus's own commitment to journey with others as they learned to recognize God's presence and calling. No one has ever done it better, and it is to his example that we now turn.

Listening to Scripture

From the very beginning of the book of Matthew, even before Jesus's birth is reported, we get the message that a new thing is coming in the way God interacts with humanity. The Hebrews had such an exalted concept of God that they did not even say God's name aloud or make any kind of image of God. Now this same mysterious God is coming in person to live alongside people in extraordinarily humble conditions. The angel advises that this person is to be named Emmanuel, God-with-us. God's in-breaking in human history is an essential claim that Protestants hold dear and that sets the stage for all that God will do in Jesus Christ. God did not come to live among people because it benefited God in any way. God's presence was solely for the sake of others. Jesus became a hands-on spiritual companion to human beings as he lived right along *with* them.

What we discover in Jesus as God-with-us is God's willingness to be present with people in celebration and sorrow, in work and play, in human faithfulness and human sin. What we see in Jesus and the Holy Spirit, whom Jesus calls the Advocate (John 14:26; also translated Counselor, Helper, and Comforter), is God's desire for us to know who he is and what he is like, his desire to communicate with us and support us. Jesus also teaches us something about how to companion one another as we discern God's presence in the activities of life.

This is a radical shift from the experiences of Moses and Elijah, who had to cover their faces for that brief moment when the wind of God's presence blew by. Matthew announces that God will, in fact, live with and love people in a way that no human being could ever have imagined. God knows our deeply relational nature, our need to watch and learn from a human being, to be mentored by another, to be listened to and taught, to be served and to receive compassion. What Jesus offers in the remaining pages of the Gospels is a ministry of *presence*, a kind of relationship rooted in many qualities, including *patient attention* and the invitation to explore a *God's-eye view* of the circumstances.

Companionship on the Way to Emmaus

We see Jesus, the one who is truly present with others, in various ways. This is particularly true in the relationships he shared with disciples and followers. Jesus was living and working among a mixed group of people from varied backgrounds with unique strengths and personalities. This is not so different from the contemporary congregation. On several occasions, we see Jesus making efforts to train his followers by modeling for them what he is about. The encounter with disciples on the way to Emmaus (Luke 24:13–35) is one example of Jesus demonstrating *presence* as a spiritual companion. After a terrible loss, these two Jesus followers are walking along and reflecting on the events of the past days when a fellow traveler joins them. Somehow they do not recognize that Jesus is the traveler, and he makes the decision not to enlighten them. In the very next story of Luke, Jesus handles the encounter with other disciples very differently. He immediately reveals his identity: "It is I myself," he reassures them, inviting them to touch him and see his scars. Why, then, the lack of candor on the way to Emmaus?

Instead of identifying himself, Jesus lets the pair feel their sorrow. Rather than offering immediate revelation, Jesus asks a question: what are they discussing? He does not interrupt their thoughtful reflections with divine revelation; he lets them talk, considering their experiences. Empowered by the Father through the Spirit, Jesus has just capped off a one-of-a-kind life of ministry with a most miraculous act, but he holds back his own news to meet his followers exactly where they are. He wants to know *their* thoughts before explaining *his*. He walks with them, literally and figuratively, giving them his time and patient attention before he says a word about what he knows to be true. Jesus was such a master at listening that he reached beyond the protective façade to the true fears and questions for the disciples bound for Emmaus, the rich young ruler, the woman at the well, and so many others.

Jesus models for us another side to seeking God's guidance: the spiritual companion's discernment about when to speak and when to listen. He allows these followers on the way to Emmaus time to reflect and express their pain even though he already knows the answers to their questions. A spiritual companion learns to attend to others in every context, from text message to casual chatter to serious one-with-one conversations. We set aside our own thoughts and experiences to go deeper into those of another; we put aside our own inner need to be effective helpers and resist the urge to offer quick advice, something that goes against the grain in social media and most face-to-face conversations. Jesus listened well and caught a glimpse of the deeper anxieties, something these two felt comfortable enough to share with a stranger in a time when many of Jesus's followers were hiding away in fear for their lives.

Another look at the Emmaus Road narrative reveals that Jesus does more than listen attentively. He challenges these hope-drained disciples in a way that seems rather unexpected and ill suited to the character of a patient and compassionate spiritual companion. Jesus calls them "foolish" and "slow of heart." This is not the kind of response we might normally think appropriate to offer someone gripped with sorrow and immersed in a deep, inner struggle. This is certainly not one of the approaches to spiritual direction that we have recommended! Perhaps it is a moment when the resurrected Jesus, who has complete knowledge of the mysteries of God, may take a little more license than we would ourselves.

The Way of Discernment

When we see beyond the surprising response, we notice Jesus does something here that is critical for effective spiritual companionship. The disciples have interpreted the events of the previous week from a particular viewpoint. They are rooted in a background and culture that has given them specific ideas about who the Messiah will be. Based upon their own life experiences rooted in first-century Judaism under Roman rule, these disciples are puzzling over the events and feeling despair. They had hoped Jesus would free Israel, and now that hope seems lost. They may have an immediate destination in mind on the way to Emmaus, but the deeper reality is that they have lost direction. What seemed to them to be God's purpose is not working out.

From our privileged position many centuries down the road, we can also understand why Jesus appears frustrated. After all the time he has already invested in them, revealing who God is and what God cares about through his own life and teachings, they still need to broaden their horizons. His response to their interpretation of events is remarkable. He will stretch their skills for discernment and push them to see a bigger picture, something they simply have not recognized and understood before. As a spiritual companion, Jesus helps them to consider an alternate interpretation of the events, pushing them back into the Scriptures and showing them the Messiah's path through suffering into glory. The meaning of Jesus as Messiah and Redeemer of Israel is much greater than they could have imagined. He urges them to step back and attend to what God is doing in this situation. They can begin to discern these purposes by drawing upon Scripture, a source of interpretive authority on God's interactions with humanity.

In a sense, the disciples are encouraged to open their minds to a God's-eye view of things. Just as a bird soaring through the air can take in a broad perspective of trees, water, buildings, and open land beyond what we can see from our own front step, so a God's-eye view considers God's active efforts toward redemption beyond the immediate circumstances these disciples find themselves in. What seems true from our vantage point does not take into account the larger view God has for human history. We can never fully gain a God's-eye view of events, but God's choices to reveal some of his purposes allow us to catch a glimpse of what God has in mind for the world. For the disciples, Jesus's death and his return to life become a paradigm, a way of understanding everything else Jesus has said and done in ministry. We can see in the record of the Gospels, especially Matthew, that it even becomes a reinterpretation of the entire Hebrew Scriptures.

In his resurrected body, Jesus offers a new kind of ministry of presence and points to what God had in mind all along. Acting as a spiritual companion, Jesus listens to the traveling disciples' interpretation of events and helps them discern how God is alive and at work in the challenging circumstances they face. While they may not fully grasp everything Jesus explains to them, there is a glimpse of God's purposes as they begin to see how Jesus's death and resurrection can be interpreted as a necessary part of the greater story of God's interaction with humanity.

After Jesus leaves, the disciples do two things that most of us have done ourselves while trying to understand a life experience in terms of our spiritual and theological convictions. They turn to one another to tell the story about what has just happened. They look to human spiritual companions to sort through what has just happened, first with each other and then with the other disciples. By the time they reach Jesus's other followers, they have clearly determined that Jesus is alive. In the coming days, they will also discover that Jesus's ministry of companionship requires an active response of believing and living in light of who he says he is. As in all discernment processes, we do not always understand things fully right away. Apparently hindsight is 20/20, and there is some truth to this in our experiences of God's presence in life events. The glimpse of a God's-eye view that Jesus has given the disciples will become clearer and clearer over time. Ultimately, this view of the story has filtered down through thousands of years.

The two disciples also do the important work of checking their own internal responses to the event. They describe how their hearts burned within. Over the centuries, many people have reported sensing a confirmation from God through a kind of inner burning or passion at the very core. Fire is one of the most stunning biblical images we have of the Holy Spirit's presence. This inner burning that witnesses to the Spirit's presence is coupled with the observation of activity they have seen Jesus do many times before. Sometimes the memory of previous occasions when God has seemed especially near helps to interpret the present moment. Turning to the support of community, narrating events in terms of our theology and life experiences, and confirming what we sense within are all important components of discerning God's activity in life events.

As we look back over this story within the larger Gospel accounts, we are left with a few curious questions. Why, at this point in the narrative of Jesus's life, does he bother to meet up with these two followers and walk with them? When there are so many other things he could be doing, why is this a priority? We could speculate at length about these things, but for our purposes it seems clear that Jesus loves these followers, and he is wholeheartedly committed to companioning them into a knowledge of God and God's purposes for them and for the world. God wants them to hear his voice, and God is clearly *for* them. Jesus takes the time to walk alongside and tend to the relationship he has with them, which is just what God does with Adam and Eve in the garden. The Scriptures witness to the unchanging character of a loving God who invites us into intimate relationship.

Jesus companions his followers in many other stories as they consider their callings (e.g., inviting Thomas to believe), their images of God (e.g., helping them recognize that God is like Jesus), their communication with God (e.g., teaching them how to pray), and their values (e.g., challenging social norms). While Jesus's role is obviously unique in human history, his followers also learn something from him about becoming discerning support for one another in the days that follow.

Mining the Protestant Tradition

Ever since that time, Jesus's followers have been learning to companion one another in the process of discerning God's presence. In recent decades, denominational boundaries have become increasingly permeable, and Protestants are undertaking a rediscovery of spiritual writings on discernment from various traditions. As the interest grows, we can also take another look at the stories and writings from across the spectrum of Protestant leaders and laypeople who have explored these same issues.

Spiritual Companioning at Home

One of the most remarkable families to exemplify and write about the breadth and depth of discerning God's voice is well known to many of us. John and Charles Wesley were founders of a movement concerned with the nature of Christian spirituality. Above all, they sought to practice the presence of God and to receive and give God's perfect love. Close companionship with God and spiritual friendships in the church became hallmarks of the communities they served. Their training in the spiritual life began long before the first formative small groups they organized. John and Charles were the sons of a minister and his wife, Samuel and Susanna, and they spent most of their upbringing in a remote English community.

In the context of near constant poverty and hardship, Susanna birthed nineteen children, ten of whom survived into adulthood. She took on the primary responsibility of educating the children and training them in the Christian faith. They were expected to follow a rigid routine that required respect for rules and adherence to ongoing devotional practices. In the middle of numerous pregnancies, infant deaths, and the responsibilities of a sizeable household, Susanna managed to give significant attention to her children's personal spiritual growth. She companioned each child by creating a space for them to encounter God and to reflect on those encounters.

Several key qualities of Susanna's companionship stand out. She regularly led the children in family worship, Scripture lessons, and prayer. Her methodical approach to prayer and other spiritual disciplines deeply influenced John and Charles, who would later incorporate this kind of discipline into their own ministry. Susanna also encouraged her children in their moral development, requiring them to respect each other's belongings and practice confession and forgiveness. She served her local community and educated others about overseas mission work. When her husband left for an extended absence, she welcomed a few hundred people into her home for evening prayers and readings about foreign missionaries.

Perhaps one of the most astounding things about Susanna's mothering was her commitment to weekly spiritual conversations with each child, individually or in pairs, from early childhood until adulthood. She continued to provide spiritual counsel, words of encouragement, and the promise of constant intercessory prayer in her letters to John and Charles. Susanna believed in the value of modeling a relationship with God by sharing her own joys and challenges in the life of faith. As she trained her children to interpret life through the lenses of prayer, theological convictions, and responsive action, she gave them a worldview and a language for recognizing the spiritual in the ordinary.

Susanna's life reminds us that no matter what our sense of call or lack thereof, all of us have a vocation from God that we can live out. Richard Foster suggests that Susanna Wesley can be identified with the incarnational tradition of Christian spirituality. She viewed her home and neighborhood as the place where God is present and active, and she understood family relationships to be worthy of intentional spiritual companionship. While she did not have a traditional profession, she did have a *vocation* in the biblical sense, a calling far greater than any one particular job. Susanna lived her faith in a way that focused on "making present and visible the realm of the invisible spirit."[10]

---

10. Foster, *Streams of Living Water*, 272. Susanna's story is discussed on pp. 237–72.

When we approach spirituality in this way, we make space for God to act, even if our daily work seems completely ordinary. As Susanna put it, "Help me, Lord, to remember that religion is not to be confined to the church, or closet, nor exercised only in prayer and meditation, but that everywhere I am in Thy presence. . . . May all things instruct me and afford me the opportunity of exercising some virtue and daily learning and growing toward Thy likeness. . . . Amen."[11] Susanna's life reminds us that companioning begins in the home, and we explore practices for companioning in families below.

Wesleyan Models of Companionship

Susanna modeled for her sons the value of habitual spiritual practices shared in community, including practices of worship, confession, and other spiritual conversation. They understood the importance of an inward spiritual life but, after their mother's example, also recognized the need for personal formation through conversation and accountability. In our chapter on small groups, we explored briefly how John Wesley set up a network of different groupings for communal formation. It is helpful to reflect on one type of group in greater depth. Wesley's *bands* required the highest degree of mutual accountability. They gathered weekly and committed to significant levels of vulnerability with one another for the purpose of spiritual growth toward holiness. Before individuals could join a band, they were asked some very difficult questions. For example:

- Have you peace with God, through our Lord Jesus Christ?
- Is the love of God shed abroad in your heart?
- Do you desire to be told of your faults?
- Do you desire that every one of us should tell you, from time to time, whatsoever is in his heart concerning you?
- Do you desire that, in doing this, we should come close as possible, that we should cut to the quick, and search your heart to the bottom?[12]

Most people today would not be interested in a group that requires answers to these questions before even joining. Alcoholics Anonymous gatherings and the 12-step process may be the closest common example we have for this level of transparency. Many alcoholics come to a group and a personal sponsor desperate for help to change because they have tried everything else. They are

11. Kline, *Susanna Wesley*, 42.
12. Outler, *John Wesley*, 180–81.

willing to do the painful work of revealing their shadow sides to others. What makes the process effective is the shared experience of pain and growth. Sadly, most of us never become this desperate about our sinfulness or so determined to do what it takes to grow in faith and holy maturity.

In their relationships with one another, believers were encouraged by Wesley to engage in a particular kind of conversation that he called "Christian Conferences." This form of interaction created space for reflection on significant moments with God. As we are learning from sociologists such as Nancy Ammerman, telling our stories of the extraordinary in the ordinary allows us to interpret our life experiences in light of our spiritual convictions. Wesley drew from the teachings of the Anglican Church that God's self-revelation is rooted in Scripture first, then also in the traditions of the church and the human ability to reason. What he added was the role of experience in discerning God's presence and will. John himself reported having significant personal experiences of inner calling that he attributed to the presence of the Holy Spirit. He believed that an inner stirring of conscience is actually the beginning of the spiritual life. The experiences of God, even extraordinary revelations and gifts, may come to any Christian. They are not required for salvation but should be welcomed by the believer. Wesley's small groups provided spaces for exploring the experiences of God in daily life.

Conferences were also serious conversations about righteousness. They were intended to help each person grow through direct discussion about the presence and absence of growth in holiness. Participants were asked direct questions about their spiritual disciplines and personal actions in daily life. Wesley believed that the Holy Spirit would be present to offer promptings, nudgings, and even warnings. With the community gathered, the potential for revelation multiplied. These conversations were meant to be "seasoned with salt" and couched in prayer beforehand and afterward.[13] They were not used for the purpose of chastising or tearing down. If this had been the case, the gatherings would not have lasted any length of time. Instead, they were considered a form of one-anothering emerging through the grace of Christ out of mutual love and under the guidance of the Holy Spirit.

Reclaiming Accountability

Wesley believed that opportunities for accountability are a necessary element of spiritual formation. One of our concerns about typical small groups, spiritual friendships, and intentional spiritual direction relationships is the lack of consistent attention to accountability. It is much easier to invite another to

13. Watson, *Covenant Discipleship*, 39, 47, 92.

talk about the significance of God's presence in everyday life than to ask about areas of personal struggle and brokenness. We avoid holding one another accountable for our lack of spiritual disciplines, moral actions, or acts of service.

Recognizing God's calling in everyday life sometimes means sensing an invitation to repent and change. Like the disciples on the road to Emmaus, we all need to hear Christ tell us that we have been foolish and slow of heart at times. The compassionate presence of others we trust can help us see these matters more clearly. Unfortunately, most of our congregations do not have a mechanism or structure that naturally supports accountability. Wesley's approach to spiritual companioning provides a vision for recovering accountability in a way that we can grow into and find encouraging.

Practicing Spiritual Companioning

It is easy to appreciate the value of hearing from God in our daily lives. Congregations and their members generally want to be more attentive to the voice of God and know the counsel of the Holy Spirit in tangible ways. Yet even if we are convinced by this kind of companioning, we still face the challenge of creating supportive guidelines and tools for discernment. One of the key ways to develop opportunities for discernment is by sharing together in intentional spiritual practices.

Companioning in the Home

We have already described the importance of the "good enough" parents for health and well-being and the implications of caregiving relationships for our images of God. We must not underestimate the importance of the home environment for spiritual formation. Even though our focus tends to be on the younger ones among us, all family members need to attend to God in the midst of such everyday activities as preparing for the day, eating meals, running errands, and relaxing. Family members also benefit from intentional time given to special practices. One meaningful practice is to follow the *church year* together, reading Scriptures and offering prayers connected to the seasons. Families may give focused attention to Lent and Advent by doing weekly devotionals together. When adults encourage young children to anticipate these "special" family moments, they frequently look forward to them. Older children and teens can be encouraged to participate in leadership. Practices such as lighting Advent candles and displaying a wreath are meaningful reminders in the Christmas season of God's presence at home. Many resources are available that provide helpful suggestions.

Another way of tending to God's presence in everyday life is to serve together. Families who volunteer to support others learn to watch for God not only in their own inner responses to acts of service but also in the world around them. Congregations and communities are often looking for individuals to serve. While there are fewer opportunities for young children, certain organizations welcome whole families to volunteer. Delivering meals to shut-ins, filling the shelves of a food bank, or buying school supplies for a child halfway around the world reminds us that God cares not just for us but for others too. Serving together has value in itself, but serving and then reflecting on the meaning and experience of our actions helps us to become more aware of God's invitations in our lives. In any kind of spiritual practice or service, we may find that our greatest accountability partners are the youngest among us. If we share these experiences with them joyfully, and they catch our delight, they will be quick to remind us to participate again.

One of the most helpful ways of learning to communicate with one another about the presence and activity of God is through informal storytelling. We might start by telling our own "little girl" or "little boy" stories to young children before they go to bed at night. They may enjoy staying up those few extra minutes and hearing about moments in our lives long before they were born. At times, we can incorporate our own stories of noticing God, participating in congregational life, or living out our faith. These stories communicate the spiritual values that we share, and they prepare children to appreciate the importance of interpreting their own life events through Christian commitments.

A particularly meaningful practice for families with children and adults of any age is the *daily examen*. The examen is a method of prayer discussed by Ignatius of Loyola in *The Spiritual Exercises*, and it has been a rich resource for believers over the centuries. Ignatius expected that God would speak through our deepest feelings, specifically what he called "consolation" and "desolation." Very simply, consolation might be understood as whatever seems to draw us toward God and make us more aware of God's presence in ourselves, in others, and in the world around us. Desolation is whatever seems to draw us away from God or causes us to be unaware of God's presence in and around us. The beauty of the practice for families is that it focuses very simply on everyday life—it is a way of sharing our days with one another with a specific focus on watching for the Spirit.

When we practice the examen together, we acknowledge that the Spirit's work of revelation is not over. God is still revealing himself to us, and he invites us to share this in our most intimate forms of community. The practice can be done in various ways, allowing for as much or as little silence and reflection as we need. Young children will need us to talk through each step.

We begin here with questions about thankfulness, knowing that we tend to be most thankful in moments of consolation and least thankful in moments of desolation. We also recognize theologically that every good gift comes from God and is worthy of our thanks (James 1:17). As children grow, they may be able to reflect on questions that take a more abstract format and have the sound of spiritual direction, such as "When did I most notice God?" and "When did I least notice God?"

- Light a candle (*optional*).
- Offer a brief prayer and focus on God's loving presence.
- Review the events, experiences, and thoughts of the last twenty-four hours.
- Consider two questions:
  What moment am I most thankful for?
  What moment am I least thankful for?
- Share any insights with family members.
- Give thanks to God and offer any prayers of confession or petition that arise.

Companioning through Accountability

As we have already noted, relationships that encourage honest account-ability may be difficult to find in congregations, but there are pathways toward facilitating change. Several things are needed to develop opportunities for accountability: (1) companions who desire to grow in holiness and extend the grace of God to one another; (2) a recognition that the God who knows and loves us just as we are is at the center of our gatherings; (3) a willingness to trust those we will be accountable to; and (4) a structure for intentional conversation that gives participants permission to address their personal and communal covenant commitments.

David Watson has studied John Wesley's bands and class meetings for decades and developed a useful structure for recovering Wesley's vision of accountability.[14] He suggests that Wesley's general rule of discipleship covers four intersecting areas: acts of compassion, acts of worship, acts of justice, and acts of devotion. Each area is important and reflects Wesley's holistic understanding of Christian spirituality. First and foremost, a covenant is made with God, reflecting the special relationship we share with our Creator. The covenant is founded upon God's love and grace. The work of developing and

---

14. Watson, *Covenant Discipleship*.

revisiting the covenant must be bathed in the presence of the Holy Spirit, with each companion prayerfully discerning the content. The companions must agree to each of the tasks, or disciplines, listed in the covenant, and each of Wesley's four areas of discipleship should be represented. A few items in each category are sufficient, such as a daily prayer practice, weekly participation in communal worship, a daily act of kindness for a coworker or family member, or monthly commitment to voluntary service. It helps to be somewhat specific, and each item becomes part of a carefully constructed framework for growing in discipleship. The framework is flexible and can be altered, but it also must be taken seriously.

The spiritual companions gather weekly or biweekly and report to one another briefly on each covenant item. The leader invites everyone to respond to each item in turn. Wesley himself suggested that meetings should be rather short, about an hour in length. In our experience, this method for accountability can also be altered so that companions hold one another accountable for their own individual covenants. This process is a regular part of spiritual formation training in one of our seminaries.

Praying with the Scriptures

Lectio divina, or "divine reading," is another important practice that has been recovered by many Protestant congregations in recent decades. This one practice alone has transformed the spiritual lives of many individuals and the experiences of spiritual companioning in countless small groups. The process includes *lectio* (reading), *meditatio* (meditation), *oratio* (prayer), and *contemplatio* (contemplation). The practice naturally encourages reading for formation rather than information. This is a challenge for many of us who have been taught to analyze anything we read critically and to approach Scripture with an eye toward issues like cultural context and accurate translation. The beauty of *lectio divina* is the inclusion of silence for listening to God. In our experience, many groups that practice *lectio divina* will often discuss invitations from God that relate to issues in everyday life. We offer one approach to the practice later in this chapter.

A lesser-known form of praying with the Scriptures comes from the Protestant Reformer Martin Luther. Given his monastic background, it is not surprising to find that he was well acquainted with solitary and communal prayer practices. In a booklet titled *A Simple Way to Pray, for Master Peter the Barber*, he responds to a request from his friend, Peter Beskendorf, for suggestions concerning prayer. In the text, Luther presents prayer as a discipline and draws upon the barbering profession for an eye-opening metaphor.

"A good and attentive barber keeps his thoughts, attention, and eyes on the razor and hair and does not forget how far he has gotten with his shaving or cutting." Luther warns that if the barber lets his mind wander, "he is likely to cut his customer's mouth, nose, or even his throat. Thus, if anything is to be done well, it requires the full attention of all one's senses."[15]

Luther goes on to suggest a practical plan for prayer that he himself uses. He chooses a small passage of Scripture and prays through it as if it is a garland of four strands. He follows four steps in his meditation on the passage: instruction, thanksgiving, confession, and prayer. Luther's plan for praying with the Scriptures is a valuable and simple resource worth recovering. Much like traditional *lectio divina*, it allows us to relate the passage to the events of our lives and respond in prayer. Spiritual companions who want to experiment with Luther's plan could create a simple process for communal reflection, reading the text four times, pausing each time to focus on one step. Silence and communal reflection might be included along with verbal prayer.

Exploring the Stories of Congregations

Many stories could be told about congregations and their members who have found the church to be a place for attending to God's voice. One particular narrative stands out to us, especially as it holds up the Scriptures as the most important source for discernment. (*Sola scriptura* was a foundational principle for the Protestant Reformers and continues to be for most Protestant denominations.)

Having grown up in Germany in the 1950s and '60s, Kurt had an approach to faith that was typical for his generation. He went to religious education classes and was confirmed in a Protestant church, but the experience meant little to him. He developed a strong aversion to institutional religion through his teenage years. Kurt's parents insisted that they were not antireligious, but they rarely attended worship services. He and his family viewed the Christian faith and all of its trappings as something to hold at arm's length, an institution that had little to do with everyday life.

As Kurt entered his thirties and forties, this view of religion was no longer enough. He began to turn his keen intellectual gifts toward the things of God. He desired much more than a passing acquaintance with God and faith; he yearned to *know*. Around this time, he met and married an American, and they moved to her hometown. Kurt joined Emmanuel Fellowship, a church with a number of highly educated people, and continued his intellectual search.

15. Tappert, *Luther*, 128.

He began to feed his appetite for knowledge in the Scriptures, developing a habit of personal and small group Bible study. Kurt cherished the riches of the biblical heritage he was coming to understand and embraced them in a way that he had failed to in his youth.

When the pastors at Emmanuel announced the beginning of spiritual discovery groups, Kurt was interested. He expected to find another Bible study group, something that would be a good fit for him. What he encountered in the group was a complete surprise. Instead of sharing ideas about the cultural background or inherent meaning of a biblical text, the group invited Kurt to listen in silence. He discovered that simple meditation and even awareness of his own emotional responses could enrich and deepen his knowledge of Scripture and his understanding of God. This new experience was so much more than the intellectual search he expected. Kurt also shared something significant with members of this group, who came from all walks of life. "It was a precious intimacy," he says, "that feeling that I can be all me." This was a remarkable discovery for an immigrant who had never quite felt at home in this small-town church.

Kurt observes that the group grows through personal sharing of everyday experiences of God, but the foundation of the meeting is the *lectio divina.* He describes the experience as a process of listening to a biblical passage or other text without "the constant endeavor to try to understand it or, what is even worse, so I can say something smart about it." This is an act of attending to Scripture that puts one's own ego aside, "stripping yourself to be able to listen in that specific way."

The group members are providing spiritual companionship for each other as they read Scripture prayerfully and listen to one another tell about God's presence in their lives. Kurt's pastor notices group participants beginning to trust that the Scriptures have something to say to them in the here and now, something that connects with everyday living. They grow to trust that the Scriptures are somehow *for them.* There is a deepened love and appreciation for the Word of God. The purpose of drawing on a biblical text is not to analyze the text and figure out some kind of mystery, the type of thing Kurt might do most naturally. Instead, participants listen to individual stories within the group and understand that the Spirit speaks through the Scriptures to meet them personally. Often the Scripture discussed in the beginning of a session is later woven into the sharing. Insights or images from the chosen text will bubble up again to inform a particular aspect of someone's story. Participants make two-year commitments to these groups because they are hungry for a word from the Lord. Kurt is one among many who find that their own story is a part of the Great Story of God's participation with humanity.

Exercising Our Companionship: Praying the Scriptures

The following suggestions for practicing *lectio divina* or "praying the Scriptures" are based upon Norvene Vest's excellent process in *Gathered in the Word: Praying the Scripture in Small Groups.* The process may be adapted for many communal and individual settings.

1. Welcoming one another

2. Attending to God's presence

    (*Comments are optional; use your own words.*) We close our eyes and relax into our chairs. In these moments, we remember that God is here with us. Take some deep breaths. As we breathe in, we remember that our life depends on God. As we breathe out, we release to God any anxieties or concerns we brought with us today.

3. Praying the Scriptures

    The leader reads the Scripture through four times, pausing for two to three minutes between readings.

    • First Reading
      (*silent reflection*)
      Ask: What word or phrase attracts your attention?

    • Second Reading
      (*silent reflection*)
      Ask: How does this passage touch your life today?

    • Third Reading
      (*silent reflection*)
      Ask: Is there an invitation here for you? *Or*, what may God be calling you to do or to be?

    • Fourth Reading
      (*silent reflection*)
      Say: Take a few moments to respond to God silently.
      (*pause*)
      Say: Amen.

4. Sharing in community

    Within the group, share any insights you have gained. You are always free to remain silent if you choose to do so.

5. Interceding for one another

    Pray for each other and for any other requests that have been named. (Optional: Each person prays a sentence or two for the person sitting to his or her right.)

Note: This is one approach to bringing together Scripture, silence, prayer, and communal sharing. Feel free to make changes to timing and content. Texts should be brief and offer images and ideas that capture the imagination. Often a few verses are enough.

For Further Reading

Ammerman, Nancy Tatom. *Sacred Stories, Spiritual Tribes: Finding Religion in Everyday Life*. New York: Oxford University Press, 2013. A fascinating book that describes findings of research on the experience and understanding of spirituality in daily life.

Lawrence, Brother. *The Practice of the Presence of God*. New abridged ed. New Kensington, PA: Whitaker House, 1982. A classic text drawing upon the wisdom of Brother Lawrence, a seventeenth-century Carmelite monk who described his experiences of growing in daily communication with God.

Palmer, Parker J. *Let Your Life Speak: Listening for the Voice of Vocation*. San Francisco: Jossey-Bass, 1999. A book that is rooted in Quaker theology and invites readers to attend to the inner voice guiding them in the discernment of meaningful purpose through calling and vocation.

Vest, Norvene. *Gathered in the Word: Praying the Scripture in Small Groups*. Nashville: Upper Room, 1996. An introduction to the practice of *lectio divina* that is useful for many types of small groups.

Watson, David Lowes. *Covenant Discipleship: Christian Formation through Mutual Accountability*. Eugene, OR: Wipf & Stock, 2002. A text that is focused on accountability and Wesley's "general rule" and provides guidelines and helpful details for covenant discipleship groups.

Willard, Dallas. *Hearing God: Developing a Conversational Relationship with God*. Downers Grove, IL: InterVarsity, 2012. A book that offers significant practical and theological wisdom for recognizing God's voice and developing personal communication and partnership with him.

Wright, Wendy. *Seasons of a Family's Life: Cultivating the Contemplative Spirit at Home*. San Francisco: Jossey-Bass, 2009. A book that explores the process of developing a prayerful awareness of God in the midst of the busy realities of family life.

Yust, Karen Marie. *Real Kids, Real Faith: Practices for Nurturing Children's Spiritual Lives*. San Francisco: Jossey-Bass, 2004. A helpful resource rooted in extensive research that offers many useful spiritual practices appropriate for all ages.

6

Spiritual Companioning and the Journey of Life

Spiritual companioning gives priority to individuals' current experiences of God. Yet all people have a story. They may have grown up on a farm in the Midwest or in a large city in the Northeast. They may have experienced traumatic events while serving in Iraq during young adulthood or passed these years as a carefree student in college. We don't really know people until we have some understanding of the story of their journey. Telling and receiving stories has long been a part of spiritual companioning in the Protestant tradition. We begin with the stories of Carmen Cutler and John Davidson, with whom we will travel over the course of this chapter.

Carmen Cutler is sixty-one and recently began spiritual direction with a staff member of a retreat center located near her home in the mountains of western North Carolina. As she shared in an interview with one of the authors, "I told him that I'm restless. I have this sense that God still has something for me to do with my life. But I don't know what it is. I really love my church. You can't even believe how much it has helped me over the years. But at this point in my life, I want to talk to someone outside the church." As Carmen enters a spiritual companioning relationship, it will be very helpful for her guide to gather her story.

Carmen joined Trinity Chapel nine years ago, after her marriage of seventeen years broke up. Trinity is a church of eight hundred members, known for its strong support of families and youth, as well as its thriving small group ministry. Carmen joined the church because one of her friends was a member. She invited Carmen to become a part of her small group right after Carmen's marriage broke up. "For several years, this group was my lifeline," Carmen shares. "I was a mess after my divorce. My husband ran off with a younger woman, and it shook the very fabric of my life. My small group loved me back to life. They listened to my sad tale, but most of all, they helped me find God at a very dark time of my life. I hadn't been involved in the church since I was a teenager. But my divorce, along with these wonderful women, brought me back to God."

Carmen seeks one-with-one spiritual companioning out of a sense of restlessness in her life, a feeling that God has something more for her to do as she enters older adulthood. Likely, this is where her spiritual guide will begin. But as their relationship unfolds, it will be helpful if Carmen's guide gathers more of her story, placing the present chapter of her life in the longer journey she has taken.

John Davidson is thirty-three. He has recently become involved in the singles ministry of a large congregation in the Chicago area, Church of the Redeemer. As John puts it: "I started coming to Redeemer's singles program because I was looking for a community and friends. To be honest, I also was hoping to find some good women. [Laughs.] The singles scene in Chicago is pretty brutal. I'm really sick of the bars and all the game-playing. I'm ready to meet someone who wants more than fun and casual sex. I was raised in the church, and when I heard about the singles program at Redeemer, I decided to stick my toe in the water and see if was right for me."

Redeemer's singles ministry puts a lot of emphasis on fun and fellowship. Around 120 people participate regularly. It has a recreational volleyball program every Wednesday evening, followed by a late supper. It also sponsors special outings to sports events and dance clubs. It has its own church school class that meets on Sunday mornings. It supports several small groups that meet at five o'clock on Saturday afternoons and join together afterward for some kind of outing.

Kristen Johnson is the staff member who oversees this program. She is a single young adult who came to this position directly out of seminary. During her early years at Redeemer, she entered a two-year program in spiritual direction, which focuses primarily on one-with-one companioning. "I really love what I do," she shares. "There is a lot of administration. I'm the one who keeps things going so everyone else can get to know each other and have fun. But I think the most important thing I do is to help people in our program develop spiritual friendships. I try to set the tone for this by getting together with everybody who comes to our program. I know all of the regulars so it is easy for me to spot the newcomers. I usually meet with them over lunch or dinner and get them to tell me their story. I even have a budget for this."

What will Kristen find out about John Davidson when they get together? Here is what he shared of his story in an interview with one of the authors of this book. He began by talking about his current job. John graduated from college with a math major and then pursued a master's degree in computer science. He has been running the technology department of a small college in the Chicago area since he was twenty-five. "I love my job," he says. "I love the people and the work. It's the best part of my life right now."

As the conversation continued, John talked about his parents' divorce when he was a child. "I was ten when my Dad moved out. He owned his own car company and was pretty successful. He and Mom just couldn't get along. They fought about everything—money, discipline, friends—everything! Some of it was stupid stuff, like which movie to see. I saw my Dad pretty much the first few years after the divorce, but then he remarried. I didn't really like his new wife's kids so I stopped spending much time at Dad's place. We keep in touch, but it's not very deep."

Gathering John Davidson's story is an important part of Kristen Johnson's ministry at Redeemer. It signals to people like John that Redeemer is not only a place for fun but also a place to build relationships in which people get to know each other. John is not seeking spiritual companioning in a one-with-one relationship or a small group at this point. But Kristen's willingness to invest the time in gathering his story may be the beginning of a process that gradually leads him in this direction.

In this chapter, we develop two perspectives on the stories people share. One is theological; the other draws on contemporary social science. The theological perspective explores the ways the Bible tells the story of the redemptive actions of God in history, which culminate in the life, death, and resurrection of Jesus Christ. Conversion, spiritual growth, worship, and the life of discipleship are part of a process in which we allow our stories to be shaped and transformed by the story Scripture tells. The divine actors in the biblical narrative are not confined to the past; the Triune God is actively involved in our lives and world today. As our stories are shaped and transformed by the story Scripture tells, Christ becomes our companion, and the Holy Spirit, our guide. Our journey through life becomes a spiritual journey under the lordship of Christ and the ministering work of the Spirit. This biblical and theological perspective is one we have developed throughout this book.

The second perspective is *life course* theory. This is a theory about human growth and development based on the research of sociologists, like Glen

Elder Jr., Janet Giele, and many others.[1] It is important not to confuse this with *life cycle* theory. Life cycle theories focus on the predictable crises people face at different points in their lives. Erik Erikson is perhaps the best-known proponent of life cycle theory.[2] He portrays adolescence, for example, as a time of the identity crisis, a psychological moratorium in which young people "pause" to explore themselves, their values, and their possible careers. Similarly, he characterizes people at midlife as facing the crisis of generativity, the psychological need to feel that they are contributing to the next generation through parenting, mentoring, or work. Daniel Levinson and Gail Sheehy also are well-known proponents of life cycle theory.[3] Sheehy's popular book *Passages* is subtitled *Predictable Crises of Adult Life*, which expresses nicely the basic assumption of life cycle theory: human growth and development are characterized by predictable crises as people move through life.

The proponents of life course theory are critical of life cycle theory precisely at this point. Drawing on many sociological studies, they conclude that human growth and development do not follow a common pattern characterized by predictable crises. Rather, they are shaped by two factors: (1) the particular events of a person's life, and (2) the patterns and historical events of the social context in which people grow up and live.

Does it really make sense to speak of a midlife crisis, for example, when the average life expectancy of individuals in certain social groups is only forty-seven years—as it is in Sierra Leone, Somalia, and other parts of Africa?[4] The mid- to late forties is supposedly the time of a midlife crisis. Social contexts matter. So do the particular events of an individual's life. Suppose an African American male, raised in very difficult economic circumstances, chooses to escape poverty by entering the military immediately after high school. After basic training, he is shipped off to Iraq for several tours of duty. Does it make sense to characterize this person as facing an "identity crisis" during this period? It is doubtful that his experience can be characterized as a psychological moratorium in which self-exploration is primary. This particular individual may face an identity crisis of some sort when he leaves the military and transitions to civilian work. Or he may find a job that allows him to draw on the discipline and skills he gained in the military. Particular events will shape the course of his life. Growth, development, and change are not as predictable as life cycle theory would have us believe.

Throughout this book, we draw on various psychological and sociological theories like life course theory. Why should we even bother with this kind

1. Elder, *Children of the Great Depression*; Elder and Giele, *Craft of Life Course Research*.
2. Erikson, *Childhood and Society*.
3. Levinson, *Seasons of a Man's Life*; Sheehy, *Passages*.
4. World Health Organization, "Life Expectancy."

of material in a book on spiritual companioning? Perhaps the best way to answer this question is with an analogy.[5] When medical missionaries travel overseas, they bring with them all the knowledge and skills they have gained as doctors or nurses. Ultimately, their goal is to improve the lives of people in the name of Jesus Christ as a way of bearing witness to the gospel. But what they know about modern medicine—about nutrition, vaccinations, surgery, and so forth—will help them greatly in their work as missionaries. Analogously, the social sciences are helpful tools that assist us in achieving our primary goal: strengthening the practices of spiritual companioning in contemporary congregations. Just as we hope that medical missionaries will have the best knowledge available to doctors and nurses, so too we hope that people practicing spiritual companioning will be informed by the best knowledge available on small groups, human growth, the contemporary context, and other matters relevant to this ministry.

Understanding the Cultural Context

Carmen Cutler and John Davidson grew up in different generations and circumstances. It is important for spiritual guides to understand the journeys people have traveled. What would we think of a doctor who practiced medicine in the following way? A person comes to him with a broken toe. His response: "Take two aspirins and go to bed." Another comes with pneumonia. His response: "Take two aspirins and go to bed." Still a third person comes with lung cancer. His response: "Take two aspirins and go to bed." Obviously, this doctor is no doctor at all! We expect doctors to treat persons differently, according to their needs.

The same is true of spiritual guides, especially guides who have been trained in spiritual companioning. We hope they will work with a *differentiated understanding* of the persons they are companioning. We hope, for example, they will be sensitive to gender differences. Men often have trouble accessing their emotions in spiritual companioning relationships. Women often feel overly responsible for problems in relationships and need support in claiming their own voice. People who are raised in different circumstances often struggle with different kinds of issues. We hope that spiritual guides will do more than tell every person to take two aspirins and go to bed.

It is important, thus, for spiritual guides to gather the stories of the people they are companioning. This provides them with a deeper understanding of

5. For a discussion of different interdisciplinary models, see Osmer, *Practical Theology*, chap. 3.

the journey each has taken and how this impacts the person's present relationship with God. Life course theory provides help in interpreting these stories. It sensitizes spiritual guides to patterns that are present in a person's journey. In recent decades, a number of authors have brought spiritual companioning into dialogue with life cycle theory.[6] While these writings offer many wonderful insights, they rely on the assumption that human growth and change fall into predictable patterns. Life course theory, in contrast, invites us to focus on the particular events of persons' lives and the ways their social context has shaped their stories. There are good reasons to be cautious about life cycle theory today and pay more attention to the kinds of issues lifted up by life course theory.

As our society has become more diverse, we have become aware of the ways cultural and family background, income level, nutrition, education, and access to health care impact the course of life. We also have become aware that individuals respond to the same context in very different ways. Research on Asian American families, for example, reveals very high expectations and involvement of parents in the educational achievement of their children.[7] Overall, Asian Americans do, in fact, make better grades and go further in education than other children raised in comparable economic circumstances. But this is not the case for all Asian Americans. The Hmong, who immigrated to the United States from southeast Asia, often struggle in American schools.[8] Even Asian American families with children who are highly successful in school sometimes have a child who rebels during adolescence or does extremely well throughout high school but then suffers a kind of identity crisis when leaving home for college and does poorly in this setting. In our diverse world today, it is very important not to impose a common, supposedly universal pattern of growth and development on the persons we companion.

Central Concepts of Life Course Theory

Life course theory invites us to pay attention to the particularity of each person's story while also being sensitive to the ways diverse social contexts may shape a person's growth and development in different directions. It uses five central concepts to help us think about these issues: cohorts, life stories and turning points, the timing of lives, social convoys, and the dynamic relationship between persons and communities.[9]

6. Fischer, *Winter Grace* and *Autumn Gospel*; Guenther, *Toward Holy Ground*.
7. Li, *Cultural Foundations of Learning*.
8. Walker-Moffat, *Other Side*.
9. For an excellent introduction to life course theory, see Hutchison, *Dimensions of Human Behavior*.

COHORTS

Life course theorists refer to the members of a society who grow up during a particular historical period as cohorts. Cohorts experience important historical events and social trends that mark them off from previous generations and give them a shared identity. The GI generation, for example, grew up during the hardship of the Great Depression and came of age as World War II began. The baby boomers, in contrast, came of age during the 1960s and '70s, a period of prosperity and cultural change in American history. The life experiences of these two cohorts were very different, with long-lasting implications for their adult lives.

LIFE STORIES AND TURNING POINTS

Life course theory also pays attention to the particular life stories of individuals, using narrative research methods. This theory is especially helpful to spiritual companioning in the way it examines the stories of individuals in terms of *life events* and *turning points*. A life event is a significant occurrence that marks a person's life. It includes such things as moving, being accepted into college or law school, getting married, starting a successful small business, or receiving an unexpected inheritance from a long-lost aunt. Turning points are major events that lead to a new direction in a person's life story. These include a conversion experience, the death of a parent or child, losing a job, or getting divorced. In the chapter on small groups, for example, we encountered the painful story of a woman whose teenage daughter was killed in a car accident. This turning point shaped her life for many years. Life stories are not as predictable as developmental and life cycle psychology might lead us to believe. They are filled with discontinuities, sudden changes, and significant events that are turning points.

THE TIMING OF LIVES

All societies are organized, in part, around age. They have shared expectations about when it is appropriate to make the transition from one stage of life to another. When is it time to start school, to start dating, to leave home, get married, start working, or have children? Often, these expectations vary from one social group to another. Life course theorists classify these transitions in the life of an individual as "on-time" or "off-time," according to whether they are in or out of sync with the expectations of a particular community. In the United States, for example, most people believe that it is off-time for a girl of twelve to have a baby or for a fourteen-year-old boy to be the primary breadwinner for his family. They also believe that something is not quite right when a person refuses to "grow up," a kind of Peter Pan who flits from one job and relationship to another well into his or her forties.[10]

SOCIAL CONVOYS

Life course theorists portray human lives as linked and interdependent. Some use the term "social convoys" to capture the dynamic quality of linked lives.[11] People do not travel through life by themselves, as solitary individuals. They travel with others, like trucks driving down a highway in a convoy. The family is one of the most important social convoys. Families move through life together in relationships that are constantly changing. Children are born, enter school, and leave home. If a parent gets cancer or loses a job, this reverberates through the entire family convoy. People also travel through life in other social convoys: friends at church, peer groups during adolescence, coworkers, and social friends. Typically, these kinds of relationships are more loosely linked than families. Yet they can have a major impact on the life course of individuals. At-risk behaviors during adolescence, for example, are often rooted in peer group convoys. Long-term friendships at church are closely related to members' involvement and satisfaction with their congregations.

THE DYNAMIC RELATIONSHIP BETWEEN PERSONS AND COMMUNITIES

In life course theory, personal agency and social influences are both viewed as important. Individuals are not completely determined by their social contexts. Their life course is influenced by the choices they make and the kind of life they live. At the same time, persons are not viewed as completely free, unencumbered by the particular events of their lives, their relationships, and the social conditions around them. People who grew up during the Depression, in the 1930s, were impacted in real and lasting ways by experiences of economic hardship. Yet families and individuals responded to the events of this era in different ways. Life course theory seeks to understand the ways personal agency and social constraints interact to shape persons' lives.

Life Course Theory and Carmen Cutler

Let us pause at this point and look at the story of Carmen Cutler through the lens of life course theory. Carmen was born in 1954 and came of age during

10. Research indicates that these expectations have become more flexible and diverse in many societies today. The timing of important transitions like marriage, childbirth, and retirement is more tied to the expectations of a particular cohort than to social expectations that are handed down from one generation to another.
11. Moen and Hernandez, "Social Convoys."

the late 1960s and early '70s. She was born in Richmond, Virginia, the third daughter of two lawyers who worked full time throughout her childhood. "My mother called me her 'Wild Child' as long as I can remember," Carmen says. "My two sisters were raised to be modern southern ladies—smart, pretty, and groomed in all the social graces. I just wasn't made from the same cloth. They were debutantes; I refused to even consider it. They went through confirmation classes and joined Second Church; I went through the classes but refused to be confirmed. They were really good at tennis and golf; I loved music and painting. I just didn't do things the way my sisters did."

One of Carmen's sisters attended the University of Virginia, and the other, Dartmouth. "I got into Princeton but refused to go," Carmen says. "I had my heart set on Western Carolina because it had a good program in the arts and crafts. I wanted to be a potter at that point. Once I got there, I decided I wanted to be a painter and then a musician. I dropped out midway through and lived in an artist colony. What can I say? I was young! My whole life was ahead of me. And the guy I was living with at the time was so handsome and so much fun. I didn't think at all about making money. Of course my parents were appalled. But my sisters gave them enough of the 'good and dutiful' daughter stuff. Evelyn married a doctor, and Gracie, a lawyer. So they let me be."

What sorts of insights emerge by reflecting on Carmen's story with the concepts of life course theory? Does it help her spiritual guide to better understand the sense of "restlessness" she shared in their first meeting? We are struck by her statement that she is not made of "the same cloth" as her sisters and is called "my Wild Child" by her mother. Within Carmen's family convoy, it was clear very early that she was not going to follow the same script as her sisters or fulfill her parents' expectations that she become a "modern southern lady." She was determined to forge a different path in her life. This is reflected in many choices over the course of her journey: refusing to be confirmed or a debutante, investing in music and painting, deciding not to attend Princeton, dropping out of Western Carolina after changing her major several times, and cohabiting with a man in an artist colony.

In earlier generations, these decisions would likely have been viewed as "off-time" by parents and peers. But Carmen came of age during the late 1960s and early '70s as part of the baby boomer cohort.[12] This generation experienced the civil rights movement, the counterculture, and the second wave of feminism. It also was an era of unprecedented prosperity, driven by the expansion of the American economy and higher education following World War II. Many young people in this cohort gradually developed beliefs

12. For an overview of this period, see Putnam and Campbell, *American Grace*.

quite different from earlier generations about premarital sex, the value of work, and gender roles. Long-established expectations about the timing of life transitions began to change. In this context, many of Carmen's peers would not have viewed her decisions as off-time. Instead, they likely saw them as an expression of personal freedom during a time of social change.

We will return to Carmen's story later in the chapter. At this point, we simply raise several questions that Carmen's spiritual guide may wish to consider. How does Carmen currently think about the journey she took during adolescence and young adulthood? Does she view this part of her story with regret, appreciation, or ambivalence? Even though she left the church during this period, does she see God as involved in this part of her journey when she looks back at it today? Are there any connections between her many decisions to forge her own path and the feelings of restlessness she is experiencing as she enters older adulthood?

We don't know the answers to these questions, but they may be important for Carmen's spiritual guide to explore as their relationship unfolds. Let us be clear: we do *not* believe that spiritual guides offer "therapy lite," helping individuals solve their personal problems. This is not the purpose of spiritual companioning. It helps people attend to their present experiences of God. But we *do* believe that spiritual companioning is enriched when guides gather the stories of the people with whom they are working and reflect on these stories with the help of perspectives like life course theory. The importance of gathering stories becomes even clearer when we turn to Scripture and explore the Protestant tradition.

Listening to Scripture

The Bible tells a story. Indeed, it offers a metanarrative: "a story about the meaning of reality as a whole . . . [that encompasses] all the immense diversity of human stories in a single, overall story which integrates them into a single meaning."[13] Scripture invites us to discover and renarrate our stories within this larger story. It offers us the "clue" to the meaning of human and cosmic history, as well as our personal lives.[14] It invites us to remember the story of God's actions in the past so we can discern God's activity in our lives and world in the present.

Scripture itself bears witness to the importance of remembering the story of God's redemptive actions in history. This remembering lay at the heart of

13. Bauckham, *Bible and Mission*, 4. Cf. Bartholomew and Goheen, *Drama of Scripture*; Hauerwas and Jones, *Why Narrative?*; Stroup, *Promise of Narrative Theology*; Placher, *Jesus the Savior*.
14. Newbigin, *Finality of Christ*, 65–87.

Israel's worship. Deuteronomy, for example, instructs Israel to recall the key events of its story when it brings the firstfruits of the harvest to God:

> You shall make this response before the LORD your God: "A wandering Aramean was my ancestor; he went down into Egypt and lived there as an alien, few in number, and there he became a great nation, mighty and populous. When the Egyptians treated us harshly and afflicted us, by imposing hard labor on us, we cried to the LORD. . . . The LORD brought us out of Egypt with a mighty hand and an outstretched arm . . . and he brought us into this place and gave us this land, a land flowing with milk and honey." (Deut. 26:5–9)

These short summaries, or credos, of Israel's story are found throughout the Old Testament. In a covenant renewal ceremony, for example, Joshua leads Israel in recalling the key events of its story (Josh. 24:2–13). Likewise, the Psalms repeatedly recall the story of God's past actions in the context of worship and prayer (e.g., Pss. 105 and 136).

In these examples, Israel worships God by recalling the redemptive actions of the past as *their* story: Abraham is *my* ancestor; God rescued *us* from Pharaoh and brought *us* into the promised land. The events of the past shape Israel's identity in the present. Parents are instructed to "recite them to your children" and "write them on the doorposts of your house" (Deut. 6:7, 9). Israel is told that it forgets this story at its own peril:

> We will tell to the coming generation
> the glorious deeds of the LORD . . . ,
>   so that they should set their hope in God,
> and not forget the works of God,
>   but keep his commandments;
> and that they should not be like their ancestors,
>   a stubborn and rebellious generation,
> a generation whose heart was not steadfast,
>   whose spirit was not faithful to God.
> (Ps. 78:4, 7–8)

Israel's identity as a community was shaped by recalling God's redemptive actions in the past. This recalling was part of the formation of the community. But even more was involved. As Don Saliers points out, "biblical remembering" offered Israel a way of discerning God's involvement in its present experience.[15] There was a dynamic relationship between "Israel remembers" and "God remembers." As Saliers puts it: "There had to be

15. Saliers, *Worship and Spirituality,* 9–10.

a contemporary encounter, a vivid recognition on the basis of what was remembered, that God was now encountering Israel anew in the present experience—in the very exile or suffering, or in whatever time and place forced them to remember."[16] This is especially evident in the Psalms, where Israel calls upon God to remember them as they lament or give thanks. Over and over, the psalmists pray to God: "Remember your congregation, . . . / which you redeemed" (Ps. 74:2; cf. Pss. 25; 51; 74; 79). In remembering the story of God's redemptive actions in the past, Israel discerns how this same God is acting in its present circumstances today.

The same is true in the New Testament. The Gospels tell the story of Jesus Christ, and the book of Acts and the Epistles, the story of the Holy Spirit's work among early Christian communities. Here too, recalling the story of God's redemptive actions in the past reminds readers that this same God still remembers the Christian community in the present. We might call this the *kerygmatic* purpose of the New Testament stories.[17] As the Gospels narrate the past events of God's salvation of the world in Jesus Christ, these narratives invite readers to discern the meaning of the gospel for their present lives. As Acts and the Epistles narrate the past events of the Spirit's work in the early Christian mission, they challenge readers to discern the ways the Spirit is still at work in the mission of their own Christian communities. To put it simply, the New Testament narrates the story of the gospel so readers can find their own stories within the story Scripture tells.

Let us see how this takes place in the Gospel of Mark, following the interpretation of Richard Peace. Peace believes that Mark is telling the story of the twelve disciples' gradual conversion.[18] Unlike Paul, whose conversion took place in a dramatic moment on the road to Damascus, the twelve disciples only gradually recognize Jesus as the Messiah and the Son of God. As readers follow the Twelve on this spiritual journey, they are challenged to take this same journey of conversion and spiritual growth themselves.

During the first part of Mark's story, the disciples view Jesus as a great teacher and prophet. These culturally determined ways of understanding Jesus—as a rabbi and a miracle-working prophet—were familiar in the disciples' cultural context. Large crowds of people flock to Jesus's ministry. But

16. Ibid., 9.

17. Recognition of the *kerygmatic* purpose of the New Testament is part of a much broader shift in recent biblical scholarship to the theological interpretation of Scripture. For an overview, see Treier, *Introducing Theological Interpretation*. Within this discussion, see especially Fee, *Paul*; Dunn, *Theology of Paul*; and Wright, *New Testament*. In this chapter, the emphasis of these authors on historical, as well as literary, approaches to Scripture is followed.

18. Peace, *Conversion in the New Testament*. Throughout this section, I follow Peace's interpretation of Mark.

it is not until Peter's confession at Caesarea Philippi that the disciples finally realize that Jesus is God's Messiah. Even here, Peter and the disciples do not really comprehend the kind of Messiah Jesus is. Peter protests when Jesus tells them he must suffer and die. Jesus immediately tells the crowd (and the readers) that his followers must "deny themselves and take up their cross and follow me" (Mark 8:27–34). Moving beyond familiar, culturally determined ways of understanding Jesus is not an easy process. The second half of Mark's story follows the disciples as they gradually realize the kind of Messiah Jesus is and who they must become as his disciples.

Three titles for Jesus provide clues to the spiritual journey of the disciples during the second part of Mark's story. In 8:31–10:45, Jesus tells the disciples four times that the *Son of Man* must suffer and die (8:31; 9:12, 31; 10:33–34). A suffering Messiah is foreign to the common expectations of Israel, and the disciples struggle to understand what Jesus is telling them. So he teaches them why this must take place (a "ransom for many," 10:45) and what it means for his followers (servanthood, 10:42–44).

In 10:46–13:37, the title "Son of David" is prominent. Jesus is the long-expected king who will judge those who were left in charge of his kingdom and who have corrupted their calling (10:46–52; 11:1–10; 12:35–37). The kingship of Jesus, the Son of David, is different from the rule of the religious leaders of Israel. He rules through his loving care of the outcasts and vulnerable, people like blind Bartimaeus, who addresses Jesus as David's son (10:46–52). In sharp contrast, the hatred of Israel's leaders toward Jesus grows during this part of the story. They begin to hatch schemes to kill Jesus. Their hardness of heart keeps them from recognizing who Jesus is. The disciples have already been warned that they too show signs of this same hardness of heart (6:52; 8:17–21). They are at risk.

In the final part of Mark's story, 14:1–15:39, the title "Son of God" is prominent. It culminates in the declaration of the centurion: "Truly this man was God's Son!" (15:39). Throughout this section, the disciples' failure is prominent. They fall asleep when Jesus asks them to keep watch; Judas betrays him; they all desert him as he travels to the cross; Peter denies him. The disciples have reached bottom. Then Jesus is crucified and buried. The disciples hide in fear and grief. But to their utter surprise and amazement, Jesus is raised from the dead. The angel at the empty tomb tells them to go to Galilee, where Jesus will meet them. Jesus appears and tells them: "Go into all the world and proclaim the good news to the whole creation" (16:15).

Only here, at the end of their long journey with Jesus, do the disciples finally realize that he is God's Messiah, who must suffer as a ransom for all, and God's Son, who lives and reigns as their Lord and the King of all. Their conversion is complete. But their story is not over. Mark's ending clearly indicates that the disciples must now embark on a new journey of Christian discipleship.

The Gospel of Mark is written with a kerygmatic purpose. It invites readers to encounter the gospel in their present lives as they follow the story of the disciples' journey with Jesus. They too must move beyond cultural stereotypes of Jesus. They too must learn that Jesus is a different kind of Messiah, One who suffers and dies to ransom humanity from sin and death. They too must learn what it means to take up their cross and follow him. And like the disciples, readers are directed to their own Galilee, where they finally realize that Jesus is God's Messiah and Son. In faith and obedience, they must then venture forth on the new journey of Christian discipleship in which they share the gospel with all creation.

Mining the Protestant Tradition

In light of the importance of Scripture in the Protestant tradition, it is no accident that the Bible has figured prominently in many of that tradition's practices of spiritual companioning. In these practices, people are given the opportunity to renarrate their stories within the story Scripture tells. In what follows we point to several practices in which this takes place.

One of the most prominent is the practice of *testimony*, in which individuals share the story of their conversion or an important episode in their spiritual journey: a crisis, a special moment of joy, or a time of darkness in which God is found anew. This often takes place in the context of worship or an informal gathering of believers. Testimony also is a way that Christians share their faith with persons outside the church or with lapsed Christians in the context of a personal relationship.

Among English and colonial Puritans, sharing one's conversion narrative was common. It sometimes was even required as a condition of full membership in the church.[19] Among Methodists, the Wesleyan Holiness movement, and Baptists, testimony was a way of sharing the story of an individual's journey to Jesus, laced with biblical references and characters, which helped to interpret the person's experience.[20] Today, testimonial narratives are found on blog posts and websites.[21]

Recent research underscores the power of testimony. Drawing on her study of contemporary adolescent testimony, Amanda Drury gives attention to

19. Caldwell, *Puritan Conversion Narrative*. Cf. Morgan, *Visible Saints*.
20. Drury, *Saying Is Believing*. Cf. Florence, *Preaching as Testimony*; Long, *Testimony*.
21. See, e.g., http://www.iamsecond.com/.

the contribution of this practice to the spiritual formation of congregations. Testimony is a vivid reminder that the God of whom Scripture speaks continues to act in the lives of persons today.[22] Drury's research also points to the influence of testimony on the one who testifies. The activity of articulating one's faith—bringing one's story to expression in testimony—shapes the identity of the one who testifies. This is especially true when testimony is offered in public settings and involves thoughtful preparation and mentoring in advance.

Recent research also reveals the importance of testimony in evangelism.[23] Rather than presenting a prepared formula of spiritual laws or doctrinal beliefs, which culminate in the sinner's prayer, evangelism is more effective in a relationship in which care is offered and trust is built over time. In the context of this relationship, sharing the story of God's redemptive presence in one's life has credibility in communicating the gospel. This sort of testimony in evangelism is a form of spiritual companioning.

Thomas Long notes that many Christians feel anxious about finding the words to describe their faith experiences, especially in public. It is easier to leave it to the professional talkers, the preachers and evangelists.[24] They fear others will not appreciate God experiences that sound mystical or seem to have no clear explanation. Often people speak of intimate encounters with God almost apologetically, as if doubting that their listeners will give them any credence.

It is important to remember other practices in the Protestant tradition that have made it possible for persons to bring their stories into dialogue with the story Scripture tells, often in a circle of trusted friends. The *spiritual autobiography* is one such practice, which tells the story of a person's spiritual journey from his or her earliest days to the present. This genre became especially important to Protestants in the seventeenth century. John Bunyan, for example, wrote *Grace Abounding to the Chief of Sinners* to describe his own life with God, including God's expectations and Bunyan's own spiritual experiences, temptations, and mentoring relationships, as well as his recognition of a divine calling and his growth in prayer.

These same concerns continue to be valuable points of reflection for us today, and naming them before others, as Bunyan did, creates opportunities for genuine companionship. In our time, retreat settings, church staff meetings, congregational committees, small groups, and individual friendships where

22. Drury, *Saying Is Believing*, chap. 3.
23. Reese, *Unbinding the Gospel*; Peace, *Holy Conversation*.
24. Long, *Testimony*, 4.

trust is present are excellent places to practice sharing our spiritual narratives. We have included a sample practice for developing a spiritual autobiography at the end of this chapter.

Writing diaries and journals has also been an important spiritual practice in the Protestant tradition. Mark Knights offers a helpful overview of the significance of this practice:

> The most common reason for keeping a diary in the seventeenth century was to keep an account of providence or God's ordering of the world and of individual lives. Ralph Josselin called the diary he kept between 1641 and 1683 "a thankfull observation of divine providence and goodness towards me and a summary view of my life." . . . Diaries also allowed their authors to meditate regularly on personal failings—a type of written confession in a protestant world that had rejected the need for a catholic priest to mediate sins. Or the diarist could count his blessings, and give thanks for births or marriages or seek consolation for illness and death.[25]

Jonathan Edwards and John Wesley kept journals for most of their adult lives. This practice became widespread among Protestants as paper became less expensive and the population more literate. It helped people discern the spiritual meaning of their lives, weaving the biblical story of God's providential care into their interpretation of everyday events.[26] Their stories were now seen as a part of God's story as narrated in Scripture.

Reading devotional literature was also widespread in the Protestant tradition. Some of this literature invited readers to view the spiritual life as a journey or pilgrimage. John Bunyan's *The Pilgrim's Progress* became a classic in the Protestant tradition. The book is an allegory of the spiritual life in which Christian, a kind of Protestant everyman, travels from his home, the "City of Destruction," to the "Celestial City" atop Mount Zion. Along his journey, Christian encounters many trials and false paths before reaching his destination. This kind of devotional literature invited Protestants to view the course of life as a spiritual journey and to articulate the meaning of their own experience in story form.

Testimony, spiritual autobiographies, journals, and devotional literature represent the high priority the Protestant tradition has placed on Scripture in the spiritual life. They are practices that help people articulate their stories within the story Scripture tells. Just as God acted to save and guide his people in the past, he continues to do so in the present. As people remember

---

25. Knights, "Diaries of the Seventeenth Century."
26. Cf. Botonaki, "Seventeenth-Century Englishwomen's Spiritual Diaries."

the biblical story of God's redemptive actions, they learn to trust that God still remembers them today.

Practicing Spiritual Companioning

In this chapter, we have explored some of the ways companioning in the Protestant tradition is shaped by viewing the course of life as a spiritual journey. Three basic points have emerged:

1. Spiritual guides are encouraged to gather the stories of people involved in spiritual companioning. This helps them understand some of the ways individuals' present experiences of God are shaped by their spiritual journeys.
2. Spiritual guides are encouraged to reflect on these stories with perspectives like life course theory. This is especially important for those who have received training in spiritual companioning.
3. Spiritual guides are encouraged to follow the lead of Scripture and help people find their stories within the story of God's redemptive actions in the past. As people encounter the story Scripture tells, they realize that God remembers them today and is still involved in their lives and world.

Let us return to the story of John Davidson and consider some of the practical issues involved in integrating these three emphases into spiritual companioning. We can recall that John is thirty-three and has recently become a part of the singles ministry at Church of the Redeemer in the Chicago area. Kristen Johnson is the associate pastor in charge of this ministry. She begins to gather the story of all newcomers while treating them to a meal.

Kristen hopes the singles ministry will be a place where people develop spiritual friendships. While she expends a lot of energy administering the program, she also supports spiritual companioning in intentional ways. She leads several small groups for singles. One is a small group Bible study on Saturday afternoon. Another offers small group spiritual direction for women, which meets for eight weeks every spring. She occasionally enters into one-with-one relationships with people in the singles ministry, as well as church youth. How might Kristen gather the stories of people in these settings?

In one-with-one spiritual companioning, guides handle this in different ways. Some allow snippets of a person's story to emerge naturally as their relationship unfolds. If John were to mention, for example, that his parents divorced when he was a child, Kristen might invite him to share more about this turning point in his life. Other guides begin their companioning by inviting people to share their stories in a special session, taking notes that can be reviewed later. The guide tells the person that this is *not* the way they normally will spend their time together, but it is helpful to understand his or her story as they begin their relationship.

In small groups, guides use similar strategies. Some invite people to share more of their stories as important life events emerge naturally in the sharing of the group. In a small group Bible study, for example, the guide might invite people to recall a time in their past when they have experienced God's healing as they study one of Jesus's healings in a Gospel. In this sort of spontaneous gathering of stories, an important rule of thumb is to put aside the lesson plan when deep sharing begins to emerge. It is less important to cover every part of a plan than to be fully present to one another when a moment of vulnerability or self-disclosure occurs.

In contrast, some leaders of small groups set aside time in the initial sessions for all participants to share key events of their spiritual journeys. Usually, the group members know in advance they will have only ten to fifteen minutes to share and are asked to choose the most important events. The sharing and gathering of stories is a powerful way of beginning small group spiritual companioning. A feeling of community is built as people share and receive the stories of one another.

Kristen Johnson received formal training in spiritual direction. Likely, this included some attention to psychological theories that will help her reflect on the journeys of people she companions. These kinds of theories sensitize guides to gender differences and to the kinds of issues people face at different points in their lives. Only rarely, however, does this training introduce people to life course theory. This is one of the reasons we have given it special attention in this chapter. How might this perspective provide Kristen with insight into John's spiritual journey and the issues he faces today?

John Davidson and the other members of the singles ministry are part of the millennial generation. Unlike earlier cohorts, millennials grew up with the new communication technologies of the digital revolution. John's story is typical. Even as the only child of a single mother living in a small town in Missouri, John had access at a very early age to a desktop computer and a Game Boy handheld video game device. "My mom worked," he says, "and she knew that I was more comfortable at home after school if I wasn't alone. So I always had friends over. Mom was pretty strict about the video games we played, but she was okay with playing. Cheaper than a babysitter I guess. [Laughs.]"

As a cohort, millennials are comfortable with the new, digital media. They use them to communicate with friends and parents and to gain instant access to information. They build and maintain relationships through social media. They are adept at interacting simultaneously across a variety of media platforms, working on a school project on a laptop while watching television and sending text messages to friends. They do not like being passive consumers of knowledge, as in sermons or lectures. They are used to being actively involved in finding and constructing knowledge. It is not surprising that John, like many millennials, finds traditional worship "very, very boring," in his words. He attends worship only when he is meeting friends from the singles ministry to go out to lunch.

Far more central to John's involvement at Redeemer is his hunger for meaningful relationships. Like many in his cohort, John is a child of divorce. While he longs for relationships, he also is deeply conflicted about relationships, especially with women. This is known as the "sleeper effect" among the children of divorce.[27] It is an ambivalence that often emerges when young adults leave their family convoy and begin to explore commitments and relationships that might become long term. John describes this sort of ambivalence in his relationships: "I spent most of my twenties moving in and out of relationships with women. I've always had a steady circle of guy friends. But when it comes to women, I want to get close, but then I draw back. Is this really the one? I don't want to make the same mistake my parents did."

It is noteworthy that John, like many millennials, did not experience any support from his religious community when his parents divorced. When asked if his church was helpful during his parents' divorce, John gave a common answer: "Nope. Not a bit. It was like everybody was too embarrassed to talk about it. Mom started going to another church after she and Dad finally split. Nobody talked to me about it there either." In a national study of divorce, Elizabeth Marquardt found that two-thirds of young adults whose parents divorced during childhood report that *no one* from their religious community reached out to them—not a clergyperson or member of their congregation.[28] As a result, the children of divorce are less likely than their peers to become involved in organized religion as they make the transition into young adulthood.[29] The church offered John no spiritual companioning at this turning point in his life. It will have to earn his trust as he begins to reengage Christianity.

This presents a challenge to Kristen Johnson. How can she help John and other millennials find meaning in their lives by encountering the story

27. Marquardt, *Between Two Worlds*, 10.
28. Ibid., 155.
29. Ibid., 139.

Scripture tells? She cannot assume that John will automatically grant Scripture special authority. Like many millennials, he is skeptical and even distrustful of institutional authorities. Scripture will become authoritative only when it is experienced as life-giving and is integrated into spiritual companioning in meaningful ways. If John were to participate in one of Kristen's small groups or enter into one-with-one companioning with her, how might Kristen's understanding of John's story influence the ways she draws on Scripture?

One place for Kristen to start is to reflect on the turning points in John's story. There are many indications that John's experience of his parents' divorce remains important. The absence of spiritual companioning when this occurred during childhood contributed to his dropping out of the church as a young adult. He now has returned at thirty-three, tired of the singles scene and looking for deeper relationships. It may be that he will need to revisit this painful time in his life in the context of one of Kristen's small groups or a one-with-one relationship. In this sort of spiritual companioning, Kristen might have the opportunity to encourage John to invite God into his memories of this period.

It is possible these memories include feelings of anger, guilt, or helplessness. Kristen might teach John how to pray Psalms that articulate these kinds of feelings as a way of encouraging him to build a relationship with God that is more open and trusting. It also is possible that John will need to forgive his parents for the pain they brought into his life. There are many stories in the New Testament in which Jesus's healing and forgiveness are prominent. Kristen might teach John how to pray Scripture imaginatively, reading these stories and then asking the Holy Spirit to place him in the story. What does Jesus say to him? What does he want to share with Jesus? What actions occur? Can he ask his parents to join him in the story? What does he tell them? What does Jesus say to them?

These are just a few of the ways that Kristen might draw on her understanding of John's journey to bring his story into dialogue with the story of Scripture. She cannot force John to do this kind of spiritual work. She must trust that the Holy Spirit will deepen his longing for spiritual growth and renewal. But Kristen can gently encourage John to move in this direction. She might talk to him about organizing an eight-week small group for singles who experienced divorce as children. She might draw him out around this part of his life over lunch. Gathering the stories of others is an important part of spiritual companioning in congregations. It allows guides to make connections between individuals' life stories and the story Scripture tells.

Exploring the Stories of Congregations

We conclude this chapter by returning to the story of Carmen Cutler. Carmen's story is a vivid reminder that people may need different types of spiritual companioning at different points on their journeys. It also tells the story of a congregation that prepares its members to share the stories of their own spiritual journeys as a form of evangelism. When we left Carmen's story, she had dropped out of Western Carolina and was living with a man in an artist colony. By the time she reached her thirties, Carmen began to feel a kind of emptiness and loneliness in her life. She had lived with several men by that point, but none of these relationships had become permanent.

Carmen also began to wish she had a degree and a skill set that would allow her to get a decent job. So the "Wild Child" returned to Western Carolina as a thirty-year-old and completed her degree—majoring in business, not art. She settled in the mountains of North Carolina, working as a secretary and accountant for a law firm while painting and making pottery on the side. At thirty-five, she married one of the lawyers in the firm. "Kind of ironic, isn't it?" she says. "Me, marrying a lawyer like my parents? But Paul was very good to me. It was his second marriage, and he really wanted to make it work. He made enough money for me to quit my job and pursue my art full time. I 'painted and pottered,' as I liked to put it. I even helped start a cooperative on Main Street for local artists so they could sell their work without a middleman."

Carmen also became involved in local politics. "I was always something of a feminist," she shares. "And it really bothered me to see the way women were treated around here. They didn't have the chance to go to college. A lot of them were afraid of their husbands. They'd take the back of their hand to their wives without thinking twice. And the women would take it and just keep going. But they were afraid." She ran successfully for town council and, over time, was able to persuade the council to support programs for the victims of domestic violence. "I was their token feminist liberal," she says. "But even the men on the council began to see that domestic violence was a real problem and cost a lot of money. Men end up in jail, and, you know, it costs a lot to prosecute someone and keep him in jail. And their families would end up on welfare. We needed to find ways to intervene before it reached that point."

Like many baby boomers, Carmen settled into a relatively stable life after a prolonged period of exploration during young adulthood that defied the expectations of her parents' generation. She remained on the liberal end of the political and cultural spectrum and did not feel any need for religion. As she put it, "My art was my spirituality. And the way I saw it, religion was part of the problem, not the solution. Most of the churches around here are so conservative. They use religion to keep women in their place. They fought against everything I was doing about domestic violence. I remember one pastor telling me, 'What you're doing is just going to lead to more divorce. God wants families to stay together.' He even quoted some passage about women being subordinate to their husbands. I asked him, 'Even if they hit them and beat them up?' He told me that Jesus could fix any problem."

What kind of spiritual companioning might have been meaningful to Carmen during this part of her life? Often, books on midlife spirituality for women focus on the opportunities that emerge when children leave home. But the particular events of Carmen's life did not make this a relevant issue for her. She had no children. More promising are forms of spirituality emerging in the context of shelters and counseling centers for the victims of domestic violence. As a leader on the issue of domestic violence in a part of the country that was politically and religiously conservative, Carmen might have resonated with forms of spiritual companioning that help women break free from patterns of abuse.[30] Unfortunately, not a single church in her area partnered with the centers providing services to the victims of domestic violence. As far as Carmen was concerned, Christian spirituality was part of the problem, not the solution. So she remained outside of the church.

It was not until her marriage fell apart that Carmen began a journey that eventually led her back to the church. As she put it, "When Paul left me for a younger woman, it blew up the foundation of my life. It was like everything I trusted and believed in was flushed down the toilet. I was too old to start over. I was fifty-two! I hadn't worked in years. But most of all, it was the trust thing. The one person I really trusted betrayed me." For several years after her divorce, Carmen struggled with depression and began to drink too much at night. "I was lonely, and I was angry," she says. "But the more I drank, the worse I felt. I began to put on a lot of weight too."

At this very dark moment in Carmen's life, Betsey Leatherwood reached out to her. Betsey was a neighbor, but she and Carmen grew close only after Carmen's divorce. Betsey consistently and persistently invited her out to eat, called her to see how she was doing, and included her in family events during the holidays. It was in the context of this relationship of care that Carmen

---

30. For an overview of research on the contribution of religious communities and spirituality to women who are survivors of domestic violence, see Gillum, Sullivan, and Bybee, "Importance of Spirituality."

was willing to trust her friend's invitation to come to her small group Bible study of eight women. Gradually, Carmen became more involved in Trinity. She began to attend worship regularly and later became involved in several of the ministries of the congregation.

Trinity Chapel is a wonderful example of a church that builds deep connections between spiritual companioning within the congregation and evangelistic outreach outside the congregation.[31] The church supports spiritual companioning in a variety of ways. It has a strong small group ministry. It has a care team that regularly visits people in the hospital and elderly members who need help getting to the grocery store. It offers classes on prayer and journaling. Its youth group, church staff, and lay leaders regularly go on retreats that devote significant time to praying together and sharing what is going on in their spiritual lives.

In all of these activities, Trinity encourages its members to share with one another the stories of God's involvement in their lives. After every mission trip, for example, youth and adults offer testimony in worship. They are asked to talk about how God showed up on the trip and what this means for their lives back home. Carmen comments on this ethos: "This is what attracted me to the church in the end—this sharing of personal stories. And they aren't always bright and happy. I remember hearing a woman sharing her struggle with alcoholism in a Sunday school class. She had fallen off the wagon but was trying to get back up. And the people accepted her and prayed for her. I never experienced that kind of honesty in the church where I was raised. It really made me wonder what I had missed all those years."

It is no accident that Betsey Leatherwood was comfortable inviting Carmen to her small group and sharing the story of her own spiritual journey with Carmen. Trinity encourages its members to articulate their stories to one another and to share them with people beyond the church. The minister talks about this in his preaching, and it is a part of the training of the care team and church leaders. The church staff tries to model this. Spiritual companioning and evangelism go hand in hand at Trinity. The upbuilding of the fellowship of the church equips members for outreach in which they offer genuine care to others and share the story of God's involvement in their lives in the context of a relationship. This is a fitting way to bring this chapter to a close. The church does not exist for itself. It exists to serve God and participate in God's mission to the world. Spiritual companioning is one of the ways the church is equipped to carry out its missionary task.

31. For further discussion of the relationship between evangelism and spiritual companioning, see Johnson, *Speaking of God.*

Exercising Our Companionship: Gathering and Telling Our Stories

Spiritual Autobiography

The purpose of this exercise is to get you thinking about your own spiritual journey.[32] Understanding how you have been formed spiritually up to this point is critical for developing a vision for ongoing formation. One helpful way to approach the spiritual autobiography is to begin with a symbolic image. For example, a river is a very meaningful symbol in many cultures, and most people find it quite natural to think about their own lives in terms of a river. The following exercise is useful as a way of stimulating personal reflection, leading to greater self-knowledge and awareness of God's presence and guidance (or the apparent absence of God's presence) in one's life. It is a way of discovering how personal formation has taken place along the flow of your life, and in particular, how spiritual development has been a part of that journey.

In a quiet place, ask God to be present with you and begin to reflect on your life as a river's journey. Notice its source, its tributaries, its flow, its changes, its depth, its obstacles and shorelines. After some time, begin to respond with the activities below:

1. Draw a river to represent your life, beginning with your birth and continuing to the present. Include all parts of your life, paying special attention to your spiritual formation over time. Use different colors to express your experience of various events and circumstances, and include descriptive labels. Take note of the following:
   - Quiet, peaceful times (calm river, deep pools)
   - Painful, stormy, and turbulent periods (rapids, waterfalls, barriers in the river)
   - Times of excitement and rapid growth (fast-moving waters)
   - Major influences contributing to your growth, such as people and events (tributaries, streams, and springs flowing into the river that may be toxic or life-giving)
2. Ask: where and how has God been active and moving?
3. Ask: where is the church in relation to the river?

Other questions to keep in mind as you reflect on the river:

- Where did you first become aware of God?
- What role has your family of origin played in your spiritual formation?

32. This exercise was adapted from course materials developed by Wendy Miller and Kevin Clark at Eastern Mennonite Seminary, Harrisonburg, Virginia.

- Who has been important in helping you recognize God? Why? What has that person or persons said or done?
- What has been your experience with the church?
- What events or practices have been spiritually formative?
- How have you come to describe God?
- How do you see spiritual formation happening in your life?

Three Keys to Gathering and Sharing Stories

INVITATION

Gathering stories begins with an invitation by one person to another to share some part of his or her story. Obviously, common sense about when and where this invitation is offered is important. People usually feel more comfortable sharing their story with others whom they know, at least a little bit, and in a setting with one or two people. You might be surprised how powerful it is just to ask people to share some part of their story. People today are very busy and often relate to one another in terms of tasks they need to accomplish. So don't underestimate the power of inviting people to share their stories. This can be the first step toward spiritual friendship or sharing your faith with a person outside the church. Gathering stories is especially important in spiritual companioning, where understanding the journey people have traveled is essential.

ACTIVE LISTENING

Inviting people to share their stories implies that you are genuinely interested in what they have to say. Active listening is important. This involves being fully present to another person, putting aside other matters that might distract you from listening, such as thoughts about some task you need to accomplish or looking at other people who are walking by. Your focus needs to be on the person who is sharing. Active listening also involves paying attention to nonverbal communication—to feelings and gestures that accompany the words. Sometimes, people share a lot about themselves in the way they talk about their life and not just in what they say.

MUTUAL SHARING

Mutuality in sharing stories is not found in all forms of spiritual companioning. In spiritual friendships, the sharing of stories is usually mutual. In small groups, it is generally assumed that everyone will share part of his or her story at some point. In one-with-one companioning, however, the focus is on the directee's story and the spiritual guide does not share in the same way.

Congregations that support the sharing and receiving of stories in a variety of ways are likely to be places where spiritual companioning occurs through informal friendships and in intentional ways. This is, perhaps, the best training ground for relational evangelism, in which ordinary Christians share their faith with others. Here, mutual sharing is important. If you ask someone to share his or her story with you and listen attentively, then the person often asks you to share in turn. You have the opportunity to share God's involvement in your own story in a way that is natural to the relationship and conversation. The mutual sharing of stories, thus, is important not only within the church but also in the ways its members share the gospel with others.

For Further Reading

Bauckham, Richard. *The Bible and Mission: Christian Witness in a Postmodern World*. Grand Rapids: Baker Academic, 2003. An exploration, based on Bauckham's presentations for the Easneye Lectures, of the metanarrative of Scripture as the foundation of Christian witness and mission.

Drury, Amanda Hontz. *Saying Is Believing: The Necessity of Testimony in Adolescent Spiritual Development*. Downers Grove, IL: InterVarsity, 2015. An excellent overview of the power of testimony, including recent research on testimony as a practice of faith sharing and spiritual formation.

Hauerwas, Stanley, and L. Gregory Jones, eds. *Why Narrative? Readings in Narrative Theology*. Eugene, OR: Wipf & Stock, 1997. A collection of important writings on narrative in theology and human life.

Hutchison, Elizabeth. *Dimensions of Human Behavior: The Changing Life Course*. 4th ed. Thousand Oaks, CA: Sage Publications, 2011. A clear and well-written introduction to life course theory.

Peace, Richard. *Conversion in the New Testament: Paul and the Twelve*. Grand Rapids: Eerdmans, 1999. A thought-provoking introduction to the biblical basis of evangelism that compares Paul's conversion and the twelve disciples' journey with Jesus.

Reese, Martha Grace. *Unbinding the Gospel: Real Life Evangelism*. St. Louis: Chalice, 2008. A nontechnical introduction to Reese's research on evangelism that is suitable for a lay audience and builds connections between spiritual companioning and sharing the faith.

Saliers, Don. *Worship and Spirituality*. 2nd ed. Maryville, TN: OSL, 1996. A short but rich introduction to the relationship between worship and spirituality that is grounded in both the Bible and theology.

Stroup, George. *The Promise of Narrative Theology: Recovering the Gospel in the Church*. Atlanta: John Knox, 1981. An older book that offers one of the best available introductions to narrative as a key to Christian identity.

7

Spiritual Companioning for Leaders

Recently a group of pastors gathered to talk about the ministry of spiritual companionship. In preparation for the meeting, they read about the historic practice of spiritual direction, and each one kept a journal to record personal reflections. A fruitful conversation developed about church leaders who serve as spiritual guides in their congregations and nurture these kinds of relationships. Mason, a seasoned pastor in his thirties, was one of the participants in the discussion. He had been rather quiet throughout the evening, but near the end of the conversation his words stopped the rest of the group in their tracks. Mason acknowledged the importance of providing spiritual guidance for others, but this is not what caught his attention in the readings and in the conversation. After a decade of ministry, Mason could not remember one person in his life who regularly put aside his or her own agenda and served as a spiritual guide to *him*. He longed for someone who would offer the attention and space to let him talk about his own spiritual life.

Mason felt a deep hunger for a relationship of spiritual companionship through which he could be honest about his own joys and failures. He shared with the group these thoughts that he had recorded in his journal:

> What I need the most is a spiritual director for myself. . . . My struggle with finding a spiritual director is: who in the world has time for me? Other pastors are just as worn out as I am. . . . I have pastor friends in the area, but I struggle

finding the time to meet with them because of the demands of pastoral ministry in a large church. Recently, I wrote this text message to a pastor friend: "I only have a few short years that my girls want to run up to me for hugs and kisses, and tonight I yelled at them for it because I was in a deacons' meeting when they did. I suck as a dad. I want that moment back so bad I want to cry. . . . I am looking at pictures of my sweet little girls on my wall. What if one day [my girls] hate church and hate God because they took away their daddy, and then they hate their daddy as well because he allowed himself to be taken?" . . . [My pastor friend] never wrote me back.

Even as Mason shared these anguished words, he acknowledged that the friend he texted was struggling with a family illness while leading his own large congregation. He did not blame his friend for the lack of response, and he recognized that a text message alone would not provide the spiritual guidance he needed. Yet the experience confirmed just how difficult it is for leaders to find the kind of spiritual care they give to others. Mason was reaching out to a friend and colleague who he hoped could be a source of accountability. He wanted to confess and be heard by someone he could trust, someone who was also walking the journey with God and who might respond with compassion in the face of guilt. Mason did not want, in his words, "to cry alone."

Understanding the Cultural Context

When we think of Mason's experience, we are reminded that our lives are meant to be lived in community, not isolation. As we have already noted, we believe in "God-with-us," not "God-with-me." Spiritual leaders in churches, parachurch organizations, educational institutions, and many other contexts need human spiritual companionship just like everyone else, the feeling that another person is truly present to them—listening and caring. Ironically, those with a calling to companion others often find that they lack companionship for themselves. In our years of teaching and providing spiritual care for ministers, we have observed that Mason's experience is not unique. Some time ago, a large group of pastors and denominational leaders gathered to discuss issues of health and wellness in ministry. The speaker asked people to raise their hands if they could honestly say that they had a best friend. Only a few hands went up.

What we have heard from spiritual leaders about the lack of companionship aligns closely with larger studies on health and well-being in ministry. Through a major research project titled Pulpit & Pew, Dean Hoge and Jacqueline Wenger contacted over a thousand former Protestant ministers from five denominations to explore their motivations for leaving local church ministry. The researchers suggested twelve possible reasons for these transitions, and the ministers noted those they felt were most or somewhat important. Two reasons were named most often: (1) a feeling of being drained by the demands placed upon them (58%), and (2) a feeling of loneliness or isolation (51%). Among the other reasons, ministers also noted a lack of support by denominational leaders (43%) and marital or personal relationship problems (27%).[1] While the study dealt specifically with those who left congregational ministry, other research suggests that these struggles are shared by many who continue in ministry.

Each of these particular motivations has something to do with relationships and expectations. Ministers generally have strong gifts for social interaction and communication—this is a major part of what makes them suitable for the work—yet somehow they still find themselves struggling to establish the kind of supportive fellowship they need. As we have already noted, there is a general trend toward isolation in our culture. All of us battle the challenges of disintegration in our communities; very few are immune. Yet there seem to be some specific aspects of spiritual leadership that cause spiritual caregivers to feel alone.

A Place on a Pedestal

Sometimes the greatest challenge a minister faces is simply an absence of meaningful human connections that reach to the level of soul. The inner circle of close friends is much too small or does not exist at all. There may be many reasons for this, but one of the most significant is the notion that a spiritual leader, and potentially the leader's family, is placed on a pedestal before others. One of the most common purposes for a pedestal is to feature a special item that we want to look at and admire. We use it to separate out and raise up what is worthy of observation. Our culture places people in various roles on metaphorical pedestals—everyone from government officials to rock stars—and many acknowledge that it is a lonely place to be.

Spiritual leaders are set apart in a particular way in that they are expected to set an example for others in their words and actions. The apostle Paul himself took on this responsibility of leadership, inviting others to imitate him (1 Cor. 4:16; Phil. 3:17; 2 Thess. 3:9). The New Testament urges the church to choose leaders who display the qualities of hospitality, goodness, self-control, and dedication to God; they should not be greedy, arrogant, or

1. Hoge and Wenger, *Pastors in Transition*, 36–37.

quick tempered. Quite simply, leaders ought to be blameless before God and others (Titus 1:5–9).

These are certainly high ideals worth emulating, but they can also leave ministers facing subtle pressures to live up to standards of excellence without any room for weakness or failure. Leaders may sense that community members evaluate them with a kind of moral measuring stick rooted in the congregation's understanding of holiness. Many times people come to view their spiritual leaders as somehow separate or "more holy" than they are.

We need only pay attention to the media to see that this is true. Somehow the personal moral failure of a spiritual leader is newsworthy even though that same failure may not be reported about an average church member. What makes it a news story is that someone who is supposed to stand for what is loving and good and right failed miserably. What the news does not account for is how spiritual leaders face human temptations just like everyone else.

We have spoken with many spiritual leaders who describe the experience of feeling set apart and treated differently than others. One young pastor talked about gathering socially with his peers in the church. When he was invited, there was no alcohol, but on many other occasions these same church members drank socially with each other. The pastor was not particularly bothered by this, but it caused him to reflect upon the fact that his role does not really allow him to become "just another one of the guys." He is expected to live by a different standard of conduct. Another minister described the painful process of telling her congregation that she and her husband were experiencing marital difficulties. Though the congregation had always been supportive and encouraging, she wondered how they would respond to this kind of news. The pastor admits that she was truly surprised to receive more acceptance than judgment.

As spiritual leaders perceive that others place them on pedestals, they usually want to live up to these expectations and hate to disappoint anyone with a dose of honesty about their weaknesses. Over time, they may become convinced that God shares these expectations of perfection, and that they ought to be without any significant spiritual doubts or major struggles. One pastor noted that he began to focus intently on his role as the guy who represents God in his community and is charged with the responsibility of being Christ to others. The impression grew within him subtly over time to the point that he focused so much on being an unfailing witness for Christ that his weaknesses nearly overwhelmed him.

In this kind of context, it is especially difficult to wisely discern how much to share about personal struggles and temptations for fear that others do not want to know or to see the image on the pedestal become tarnished. On occasion, this knowledge in the hands of others may even put a minister's position at risk. There are valid reasons for caution, but there are also dangers in hiding too much. One pastor who offers spiritual direction to other ministers suggests that they have a tendency to become lone rangers. He describes it this way: "I see a lot of pastors just succumbing to and yielding to the pressures . . . , pastors who feel like they're the lone dog, the lone ranger, [like] they can't reveal their cracks or their warts, their shortcomings. . . . I get ready for work the same way everyone else does and I'm subject to the same temptations they are. . . . Some [pastors] need a reality check that they are not God."[2] From up on the pedestal, it may be hard to remember that God—and many people as well—readily accepts and loves them as they truly are.

Interacting with Peers

Over the course of their study, Hoge and Wenger asked former congregational ministers for any words of wisdom they might want to offer other pastors and denominational leaders. The most common recommendation was this: ministers must have ongoing, supportive relationships both in everyday life and during crises. There is a great need for relationships among peers in which ministers can get beyond positive surface camaraderie to real life experiences. Far too often, ministers actually feel competitive toward one another, and so they hesitate to share their problems with each other. The minister to whom you acknowledged your weakness may someday take another role in your professional life and perhaps even have authority over you.[3]

Relatively few spiritual leaders have Mason's courage and are willing to name a personal struggle or feeling of guilt before a group of peers. Perhaps this is why Mason's confession caught his listeners by surprise. Quite frankly, we can think of only a handful of times ourselves when we have seen this happen so poignantly. When courageous leaders do share about their own struggles, they tend to choose issues they have already overcome. It is easier to talk about the problem or temptation they have mastery over than the one they are dealing with now. Ministers generally want to show by example that God has the power to transform every aspect of a person's life. Most also want to appear competent and successful in both their personal lives and their ministry contexts. If competition is truly a factor, as ministers have suggested, it is not surprising that they are not forthcoming about their struggles.

2. Reed, *Quest for Spiritual Community*, 55.
3. Hoge and Wenger, *Pastors in Transition*, 199, 207.

Competing Expectations

Spiritual leaders who find themselves on a pedestal also feel external pressure to meet the expectations or demands of others within their circles of relationship. These expectations seem to come from many directions at once, including family members and friends, congregational members, colleagues in ministry, and even God, depending upon what they believe God requires of them. How leaders respond to the variety of expectations or demands depends, in part, on how much they believe their role is to please others and meet everyone's needs. Quite often it is the minister's own need to be needed that magnifies the inner tension she or he feels over competing expectations.

Like Mason, many ministers feel the strain between availability to the congregation and availability to family and friends. Those who regularly offer an empathic presence in situations of painful crisis or joy-filled energy may find that they give their best selves at work and are too exhausted to listen well and actively engage in their most significant relationships. Opportunities to spend an evening with a good friend, visit a parent, or join a spouse for a date may take second place to the unexpected call from a grieving family or the youth who just wants to talk. Problems arise when relationships fall out of balance—when the energy for interpersonal connecting is directed outside the most important reciprocal relationships in the minister's life. The boundaries between ministry and personal life are often difficult to place, and the problem is only magnified when ministers do not have time to develop and sustain relationships outside the congregation.

Conflict is another issue that often taxes relationships. When ministers in Hoge and Wenger's study described feeling drained by demands or isolated and lonely, they often named conflicts in the congregation or with denominational leaders as leading causes. In some cases, family problems increased their sense of being in conflict. We have observed this frequently. One associate minister described a difficult situation that led her to feel anxious and alone. A layperson in church leadership suggested that the congregation use a new pay scale for all ministers that would result in greater income disparity among the staff. The associate minister's spouse believed the decision was unjust and became upset by it. The minister herself was not sure what to think about the change; all she knew for certain was that she felt caught in the middle and her relationships on both sides seemed to suffer.

Leaders are often drawn into conflicts in congregations, whether or not they want to be. Even if they know the value of healthy conflict resolution in theory, ministers often react as if conflict is something "bad" that they cannot easily reconcile with a gospel of peace. Avoidance seems like a better option, which ultimately does nothing to deepen and enrich relationships. It is not surprising that Hoge and Wenger found that ministers associated conflict with feelings of loneliness and isolation.[4]

Self-Care Is Not Selfish

With all of these expectations and complex relationships to hold together, ministers will frequently set aside their own needs for the sake of others. In some denominations, the image of the "servant leader" is especially prominent, sending the message that Christlike ministers ought to put their own needs toward the end of their to-do lists. Activities of self-care, including regular times for retreat or spiritual companionship, seem indulgent and even selfish. The minister's need for spiritual companionship is something to attend to during "free" time. Of course, the servant always finds additional ways to help others, so this kind of time may be hard to find. Add to this the emotional energy spiritual companioning requires—opening up to the Spirit's inner work on the soul is profoundly enriching but also demanding—and servant leaders are often unable to commit to spiritual companionship for themselves. Parker Palmer has written extensively on the spiritual journey and vocation, and he challenges the notion that attending to one's own needs is optional: "Self-care is never a selfish act—it is simply good stewardship of the only gift I have, the gift I was put on earth to offer to others."[5]

Even when ministers make the commitment to seek companionship and are prepared to risk opening up to a peer or colleague, they may hesitate to ask for support. As Mason aptly noted, "Who in the world has time for me?" Most gifted spiritual caregivers already seem to have their hands full. Since ministers understand what that is like, they hesitate to burden others for more than a few brief moments of deeper personal reflection—a quick text message, for example. Unfortunately, this does little to resolve the deeper desire to sense God's loving care in and alongside the gift of a companion's undivided attention.

Taking Stock

In spite of the demanding and sometimes lonely workload, spiritual leaders hold tightly to the sense of call that brought them into ministry in the first place. They willingly overlook the isolating difficulties because they believe they are doing important work in the world, God's work. Yet over time, that

4. Ibid., 36–37.
5. Palmer, *Let Your Life Speak*, 25.

vision can be distorted just enough so that what was meant to be a life-giving invitation to ministry instead becomes an increasingly discouraging and lonely journey. Even though seasons of loneliness will come to nearly everyone, this is not God's design for leadership.

All of us benefit from following Mason's lead by taking an honest look at our relationships or lack thereof. Certainly we are not the only ones in our culture who feel isolated, but how can we teach about discipleship and Christian community when we ourselves do not pursue intentional spiritual companionship? We can begin to take stock of our circumstances by prayerfully considering a few simple questions:

- What do my regular patterns and habits say about my priorities in relationships? Which relationships get my "best self" most often?
- Where does my God-given need for spiritual companionship fall on my to-do list?
- Does anyone regularly companion me in my own spiritual life? How may God be inviting me to meet this need?

What we hope to communicate in this chapter essentially comes down to a few key concerns. First, if leaders do not address their own need for spiritual companionship, guidance, and accountability, it will be nearly impossible for them to be effective spiritual companions to others. We cannot join people on a path that we are unwilling or unable to take ourselves. If we are vulnerable with no one, how can we expect to understand and care for others in their vulnerability?

Before we fall into the trap of pursuing companionship for ourselves because it will strengthen our ministries, we must keep a second concern in mind: *leaders need spiritual companions because God wants a relationship with them too*. This may seem obvious, but it is a truth that is easily overlooked in daily living. When we meet with another person who holds us accountable and asks good questions about our own spiritual lives, we are reminded that God loves us not for what we *accomplish* for him but for who we *are* to him: dearly beloved children with a relationship to our Father. Even if we never complete another act of service for God, he cherishes us the same. This truth is worth investing in, and it sustains us through all of the other challenges we face.

Listening to Scripture

Fortunately, Scripture is full of marvelous stories of people who have given and received spiritual companionship. We have explored a few examples throughout the book, but there is more to say, especially when it comes to God's priorities for companioning in leadership. Each brief account is a kind of snapshot that helps us understand more fully what God wills for those who guide God's people. We begin with one of the most telling stories: Elijah's journey up Mount Horeb.

Supporting Leaders in Crisis

Spiritual leaders who know about risking conflict and personal loss for the sake of God's call must certainly wince when they read about Elijah's journey in 1 Kings 19. This is not the mantle of leadership most of us would look forward to donning. Elijah has just accomplished the unimaginable task of facing down a crowd and calling on God to perform a fiery miracle. Under God's guidance and by his power, Elijah is wildly successful and even manages to root out the spiritual leaders who have taken God's people down the wrong path. What should be a new season of peace for the embattled prophet turns into a lonely journey when Jezebel sends a message that she will avenge these losses. The prophet who has just seen the wonder of God's power is truly afraid and flees into the wilderness.

Elijah is completely and utterly alone. Serving as a spiritual leader for the one true God has isolated him, and he feels it keenly. In a moment of sincere honesty, he complains to God that he is the only one left who is passionately committed to Yahweh, and this commitment could very well lead to his imminent death. The ongoing conflict has worn him down, and he cannot see any supporters who are taking his side. He is ready for God to intervene again and take his life. When Elijah evaluates his circumstances, he does not see the point of going on to fight for God alone (v. 4).

The wisdom of God's response must not be understated. God might have chastised Elijah, reminding him of the powerful works he has just performed. He might have taken Jezebel out, stricken her with an illness or accomplished some other act against her. God could have shown his power again in any number of ways. Instead God is revealed in gentle, companionable whispers. Like a spiritual director himself, God invites Elijah to reflect upon the problems he is facing, and then God offers hope through human community. Elijah will not be proceeding in the mission alone. God is calling out many others who will come alongside. In fact, several thousand are with Elijah in spirit (v. 18). For Elijah's personal need, the most important of all is a new spiritual companion who will accompany him on his journeys. Elisha responds to the invitation energetically (vv. 20–21). He becomes a successor and proves himself to be an enthusiastic student and caring servant (2 Kings 3:11).

God recognizes Elijah's need for human community and fills it faithfully. What Elijah the spiritual leader needs in a time of crisis is quite similar to what the pastors in Hoge and Wenger's study needed. Leaders often find conflict debilitating and isolating, and they consider walking away from it all—some do because they believe God is calling them to, and others do because they are pushed out or cannot take it anymore. Spiritual companions who come alongside in times of crisis can make the difference between the leader who *chooses to stay* in the wilderness and the one who comes down from the mountain *back into the thick of ministry*. Companionship provides an additional source of support and discernment in a critical time.

God places Elisha in Elijah's life at a critical time. Elisha serves as a reminder of God's presence and purposes in this moment of intense need and through everyday life over the rest of Elijah's career. In God's community, companionship may arise from unexpected places, in this case a young farmer who will be mentored into spiritual leadership for the sake of a nation. Through a task of ministry—providing leadership training—God prepares Elisha and also meets Elijah's needs.

Calling Out New Leaders

Another remarkable snapshot of leadership comes through the story of two Jews in a foreign land: Esther and her adoptive father, Mordecai. This is one of the most profound stories in Scripture about the power of trusted spiritual companionship to accomplish a truly daring task. We know that they care very much for each other. Mordecai visits the palace daily, a protective presence checking on Esther's welfare (Esther 2:11). Esther is equally committed to him, obedient since childhood and concerned for him when he is obviously in deep distress (2:20; 4:4). Through the challenging circumstances of Esther's youth and emerging adulthood, the two have been faithful to one another. Mordecai chooses to companion her at every stage, even into the unexpected turn of events that brings Esther into the royal family.

Mordecai's companionship takes on a particular focus after the announcement that all Jews in the kingdom will be destroyed. He sends a message that Esther should approach the king and entreat him on behalf of herself and her people. Her hesitation is certainly understandable—she risks death if the king chooses not to welcome her and hear her request. Women were expected to serve and do the will of their husbands. The previous queen had been removed from her position over exactly this issue (1:10–22). Mordecai is certainly aware of the risks of his request, but he challenges Esther to stand up for what is right. He holds her accountable to what may be her greater purpose as queen. In his words, "Who knows? Perhaps you have come to royal dignity for just such a time as this" (4:14). Esther's social position, both her gender and lineage, limit her power in this ancient Near Eastern culture, but Mordecai looks past these factors and believes in who she is and what she is capable of. She may become a leader with the power to benefit her family and her larger community. Mordecai exemplifies the notion that companions nurture and protect, but they also call out those they are charged to walk with, urging them to discern and fulfill their divine purposes even if it means doing the hard thing. We can imagine that the story might have unfolded much differently if not for Mordecai's guidance at critical moments.

The narrative also gives us an insight into the kind of preparation Esther has received for this unplanned leadership opportunity. When she accepts her potential calling, she responds out of the foundations of her tradition. Before acting, she commits to the spiritual practice of fasting. In Jewish tradition, the fast would have incorporated prayers of petition, a process of seeking God's guidance and intervention in the situation. Esther draws upon the spiritual roots passed on to her by Mordecai, who raised her, and by others from her spiritual community. She knows just how to respond in this situation, and Mordecai's decision to act according to her wishes signifies his agreement with her judgment. As a spiritual companion, he has trained her to turn toward God and seek his power and direction. Effective spiritual companionship in everyday life in the contexts of family and worshiping community are critical preparation for opportunities to lead with humility before God.

As the story unfolds, Esther and Mordecai increasingly support and strengthen each other. In essence, the roles begin to shift from parent/child companioning to a shared form of connection and support. Mordecai calls Esther to take on an important role through her position as queen, and Esther creates opportunities for Mordecai, recognizing him before the king for his courageous acts and giving him charge over the house of their enemy Haman that the king has awarded to her (2:20; 8:2). We can imagine that Esther's support strengthened Mordecai's ability to rise in government, and they ultimately instituted Purim together, a new sacred event of remembrance incorporating both fasting and feasting.

The child who was adopted and raised by Mordecai as a daughter becomes his co-laborer for the benefit of the Jewish people. They model the possibilities for parents who have offered leadership and guidance to their children, but who in turn receive their offspring's support and wisdom as time passes. Sometimes it is difficult for parents, pastors, mentors, and other older members to recognize the importance of moving to shared forms of companionship that allow for hearing God's guidance through younger generations. Mordecai knows when to follow the orders of the girl he raised (4:17), and he welcomes the opportunity to share in leadership with her. True companionship transcends official title, gender, and even age in families and faith communities. God can speak and act through whomever he chooses.

Inviting Leaders to Heal

One of the most important tasks of those who companion leaders is to offer reassurance, hope, and occasionally a reminder of God's forgiveness. Many leaders feel the weightiness of living on pedestals, knowing that their words and actions have repercussions beyond themselves. Acknowledging and accepting personal sin and brokenness can be especially difficult if they believe that they have failed not only themselves and God but also those they lead. Scripture tells the stories of numerous leaders, from King David to the apostle Paul, who learned to accept past mistakes and move on with purpose. Simon Peter is one leader whose story of failure and forgiveness is especially compelling; we encounter several of his foibles in the New Testament and many details of his growth into leadership. Jesus companions Peter through the early years of his development. The unique relationship they share gives us a glimpse into what it means for spiritual companions to offer grace when leaders fail.

By the time Peter reconnects with Jesus on the seashore after the resurrection (John 21), he has been through several significant highs and terrible lows in their shared journey. One of the finest moments was Jesus's announcement that Simon, the fisherman, would now be called Peter, the rock, a strong foundation for the church (Matt. 16:18). The darkest moment was certainly Peter's public denial that he knew Jesus at all or had been following him. Peter wept bitterly over this moment of fear-filled betrayal, and we can imagine that the guilt was not easily assuaged (26:69–75). Now as Jesus returns again to a handful of his followers, he has a few choice questions for the one who will lead his church. Peter will soon be preaching the name of Jesus before thousands, but of course he does not know it yet. Before this can occur, Jesus has a conversation with him one-with-one, offering spiritual companionship at a pivotal moment.

One of the first striking elements of this encounter is Peter's urgency to come to Jesus. He does not hang back or hesitate to encounter Jesus. Many of us would probably be nervous, unable to fully forgive ourselves or let go of the pain. We know what it means to make a big mistake and then have a difficult time letting it go. Like Adam and Eve in the garden of Eden, we hide the truth of our failure, unsure how to overcome it in our own minds and hearts. Though Peter has already seen Jesus and rejoiced that he is alive, we have no indication that there was any personal resolution between Peter and Jesus before this moment. Yet when Jesus is recognized, Peter does the opposite of what we might expect. He leaps into the water, just like the Peter of old, pressing forward toward the shore. He is willing to come face-to-face with the one he has betrayed. Peter knows God's nature in the personhood of Jesus, and he appears confident that he will be received and accepted. When leaders deal with guilt, one of the first things they need to hear from their companions is a reminder of who God is; God's love has not changed, and they need not hang back.

We also notice that Jesus, the spiritual companion, initiates a conversation with Peter that cannot have been easy for either of them. Three times Jesus asks Peter if he loves him, and every time he calls him "Simon." Jesus chooses not to use the name associated with Peter's new leadership calling, which surely must have stung. By the time Jesus asks a third time, "Simon, son of John, do you love me?" Peter is genuinely hurt. Just as he denied Christ three times, so now he must affirm his love three times. This Peter once boasted that he would certainly be more faithful to Jesus than any others (Matt. 26:33). Now he must do the honest inner work that Jesus requires, and his response is humble before the One who is Lord over his life. Peter reaffirms his love a third time and acknowledges that Jesus sees his innermost self: "Lord, you know everything; you know that I love you."

Assuming that Jesus is not being vindictive here, we can imagine that he has a purpose in causing Peter this pain. The kind of forgiveness and acceptance that enables true release from guilt sometimes requires deeper probing and reflection, opening up to the purification of character that God deems necessary. In this case, verbal affirmations of commitment seem especially important. This honest reflection is absolutely critical for those who have felt others set them apart as more "spiritual" or "holy." The type of leader Jesus is looking for often has wonderful gifts for the work—Peter certainly does—but, even more, has character, a willingness to continually grow and be formed in the innermost places where others cannot see. Well-chosen companions can be very helpful in illuminating what is needed along the way.

Even as Jesus invites Peter to take a deeper look at himself, he also accepts the confession of Peter's love and offers him the opportunity to reclaim his calling: a very particular kind of leadership involving the feeding and shepherding of God's people. After sin is acknowledged and the brokenness understood, God offers a word of grace and reaffirmation of the call. The spiritual companioning relationship becomes a safe place to confirm God's forgiveness and invitation to healing.

It is a beautiful thing to watch the narrative of Peter's journey unfold from the witness of the Gospels to Acts and the letters attributed to him. Even though Peter seems to be called out in a special way to be a foundation for the church, there are always others who share in leadership, companioning one another through a variety of life experiences together. Jesus creates a community of leaders who will continue to companion one another after he moves on; in nearly every scriptural account there are at least two people teaching or eating or traveling or engaging in any number of other activities together. Peter may be the rock, but he prays, discerns, and acts together with others. This is a natural process of mutual spiritual companionship with those who share Peter's love for Jesus (Acts 1:12–26; 6:2–4). God clearly has a purpose for calling out several disciples and apostles rather than just one. The most effective kind of leadership is shared, especially when this sharing incorporates genuine companionship enriched by prayer.

Mining the Protestant Tradition

In other chapters, we have explored a few key companioning relationships, such as Dietrich Bonhoeffer with Eberhard Bethge, but frankly it is difficult to know much about how Protestant leaders have sought and benefited from spiritual companionship. These stories have rarely been recorded at length; this was not the topic most Protestant writers were concerned about communicating to their lay readers. The notion that spiritual companionship might actually be studied and discussed as a part of a minister's "self-care" is a relatively recent phenomenon that accompanies the rise of an entire field of literature dedicated to pastoral care and counseling. Having said this, we can still uncover considerable theological and practical wisdom from the Protestant past. One tradition actually began by challenging the notion of leadership as a role set apart, and it continues to be prophetic on this score today; it is the Society of Friends, the Quakers.[6]

Challenging Leadership Roles

In the mid-seventeenth century, a shepherd and leather worker in Britain with minimal formal education embarked on a personal spiritual quest. George Fox pursued institutional religion and sought out numerous

---

6. Some Friends might balk at the suggestion that they are fully in the Protestant camp, even as some Anabaptists do. They understand and practice corporate polity, sacraments, and gatherings for worship and business very differently than other Protestant traditions. Yet they share many theological foundations with the larger Protestant community and offer a particular challenge to the notions of leadership that may challenge us.

professional ministers but was unable to encounter God in the ways that he longed to. One minister suggested taking tobacco and singing psalms, not much help to someone who disliked tobacco and could not sing well. Fox sought out spiritual counsel and companionship from those the church viewed as experts, but he could not find an answer for the temptations and inner turmoil that plagued him. Finally he experienced a series of mystical moments that seemed to meet the need in profound ways. He recorded his thoughts in a journal:

> But as I had forsaken all the priests, so I left the separate preachers also, and those called the most experienced people; for I saw there was none among them all that could speak to my condition. And when all my hopes in them and in all men were gone, so that I had nothing outwardly to help me, nor could tell what to do, then, Oh then, I heard a voice which said, "There is one, even Christ Jesus, that can speak to thy condition," and when I heard it my heart did leap for joy. Then the Lord did let me see why there was none upon the earth that could speak to my condition, namely, that I might give him all the glory; for all are concluded under sin, and shut up in unbelief as I had been, that Jesus Christ might have the preeminence, who enlightens, and gives grace, and faith and power. Thus, when God doth work who shall let [prevent] it? And this I know experimentally [i.e., experientially].[7]

Fox experienced personal transformation and a new focus in life. He became part of a gathering of seekers longing for fresh and authentic ways of knowing Christ personally and living faithfully out of this relationship. They developed a community of friendship, sharing together in the experience of Christ within them, so that they might "know each other in that which is eternal."[8] They set aside the seeming infallibility of the institutionalized church and its hired leaders to seek God for themselves. Fox expressed concern that clergy ought to be more responsible for their congregations and value a rich spiritual life for themselves. Academic qualifications alone are not sufficient for leadership.

Fox wanted to remove heavy theological verbiage and extensive quarreling over doctrines and creeds in exchange for gatherings that created space for the "tendering" of the indwelling Christ. Feeling called to share about their encounters with God, several Friends paired up and traveled the countryside. Fox spoke openly about his convictions and, not surprisingly, quickly fell afoul of church leaders and members, who attacked him. Ultimately, the entire movement faced severe persecution.[9]

7. Steere, *Quaker Spirituality*, 7, 65–66.
8. Ibid., 12.
9. Ibid., 12–13.

A Priesthood of All Believers

Perhaps more than any other group arising out of Protestant history, the Society of Friends has lived intentionally according to a theology of a priesthood of all believers. Friends believe that the Spirit is present to all and that the structure of silence and prayer makes it possible for any to hear a word from the Lord. The more intimately people become connected to Christ within, the more he draws them together, so that the community often comes to unity of voice and action. No one person is placed on a pedestal and/or expected to have supreme wisdom. While some Friends have more experience and knowledge along the spiritual journey, they are not set apart as somehow different or unique. In the Friends community, all have a responsibility to help the gathered meeting become a conduit for the Holy Spirit's presence.

The Inner Light

This priesthood of all believers works only when it is rooted in a theological conviction that God is constantly present to all who open up to him. In his classic text, *A Testament of Devotion*, Quaker professor Thomas Kelly offers more than a dozen metaphors for the presence of God, including the "Light Within," "Shekinah of the Soul," "Eternal Internal," and (one of the most creative) the "Whole-Wheat Bread of Life." Quakers draw upon the Gospel of John to lay out a theology of Christ as the Light who initiates connection with us and reveals any darkness, including the dark places within. Christ invites us to respond with continual communication so that we may be "prayed through" and calls us to go the whole way in obedience, surrendering and opening to God.[10]

In the Friends tradition, all are called to attend to the guidance and teaching of the Light Within in personal prayer and a devotional life. Personal practices of silence are critical for managing a busy life if we are to have any hope of hearing from God.[11] Private worship nurtures personal commitment to humility and transformation; clarity in community depends on this. When the community meets, everyone is invited to silently wait with expectation for the Spirit and to offer vocal ministry, perhaps a word of wisdom or a passage of Scripture, but only as they feel compelled to do so. The collection of wisdom is gathered up to provide a sense of how the Spirit was moving in the meeting.

Gatherings for business extend this prayerful listening to discernment of God's will for the community through consensus. This process becomes an

10. Kelly, *Testament of Devotion*, 18, 27.
11. Steere, *Quaker Spirituality*, 28.

organic form of companionship so that even those who tend toward roles of leadership, including the clerk of the business meeting, know that they can be ministered to by others in the community. They can also share their callings for service in the world and find support for discernment. The Clearness Committee is one such process through which an individual can invite other, wise Friends to join in a time of hearing from God for a specific decision. They ask the focus person questions about the decision to be made, not unlike the questions raised in spiritual direction. This is another context in which leaders are often involved but are not responsible to offer the sole word of advice. They participate by providing the gift of spiritual companionship together with others. Fox's vision of a community that learns to listen for God together, essentially practicing key features of spiritual companionship, continues to flow in and through Quaker gatherings today.

Most Protestant congregations remain committed to the notion of well-trained, ordained clergy (a practice some Friends communities also embrace today). What the Quaker witness urges us to consider, however, is the purpose and shape of this spiritual leadership. Is it possible to reimagine the notion of the priesthood of all believers so that more laypeople are welcome to speak a word from the Lord, are called to tend to those who are sick and in crisis, and are charged with the tasks of leading business meetings according to a model of silent waiting upon God? Can ministers begin to come off the pedestal so they feel less isolation and more companionship in the spiritual journey? Might spiritual leaders also learn to listen to God more deeply, considering silence and meditation to be central to their calling so that they can better discern Christ's nudgings within themselves and the community as a whole?

Practicing Spiritual Companioning

As we have explored the contemporary context and the witness of God's people, it is clear that struggles in ministry are often rooted in relationship. In the 1970s, psychologist Herbert Freudenberger coined the term "burnout" to talk about the consequences of significant stress related especially to the helping professions. He used the shocking image of a building that is utterly devastated, burned from the inside out. Freudenberger found that an overemphasis on relationships of caregiving that maintain a certain professional distance can cause burnout over time. He also discovered that well-being comes through the opposite: *closeness* in relationship. While relationships can cause challenges, they are a necessary part of the healing. Freudenberger argues that we must achieve closeness with ourselves and with others to be healthy over time.[12] We believe these observations hold true for ministers today.

As we consider Freudenberger's discoveries, it is important for ministers to keep a few issues in mind. Impending or full-blown burnout is a serious matter that requires decisive action. Cynicism, exhaustion, and a general lack of hope may be signs that we ought to give this issue some attention. When these signs are present, seeking psychological counseling can be a life-giving step toward restoring balance and health. In addition, many books and resources address the topic of burnout more fully than we are able to here, including one that is listed at the end of this chapter. To be clear, though, our purpose in giving greater attention to our relational needs is never to focus so much on ourselves and our challenges or the high expectations of our ministries that we become resentful martyrs. Sometimes self-care in ministry can be overemphasized to the point of holding our own unrealistic expectations or becoming inflexible in our work. The best approach is to make an ongoing commitment to receiving spiritual companionship, and possibly psychological counseling, in order to manage the moments and seasons that are more demanding.

Developing a Covenant for Companioning

One effective method for attending to spiritual companioning in leadership is to create a personal covenant for companionship, not unlike the forms of covenant we have discussed in previous chapters. Any relationship can nurture spiritual health or wreak spiritual damage. The covenant allows us to do two things: (1) identify our usual patterns and practices of relating, healthy or not, and (2) choose a few regular practices that will create space for life-giving spiritual companioning.

GETTING STARTED

- Prayerfully consider four essential areas of relationship in your life: relationship with God, yourself, those closest to you, and those you serve in ministry.[13] We offer questions for reflection on each form of relationship in the personal covenant below. As you read the questions, take note of your responses. Do not hurry through this process. Listen for your sense of what the light of Christ within is illuminating and drawing you toward. Some questions may be more significant than others at any given time.

12. Freudenberger, *Burn-Out*, 123–24.
13. For an interesting discussion on developing a rule of life that draws upon four related areas of relationship, see Guenther, *At Home in the World*.

- After reflecting on the questions, go back over every area of relationship, naming a few commitments (perhaps two or three) that you believe may nurture spiritual formation in your own life and in the lives of others around you. Begin with commitments that stretch you slightly but that are essentially similar to things you already have in place. If you tend to sleep until seven most mornings, do not commit to an hour of daily prayer at five. If you have never fasted, don't start by forgoing food for a whole week. These approaches are recipes for disappointment. Do what seems realistic and life-giving, adding, adjusting, and removing practices as you sense God's guidance.

- Take the initiative to form commitments in conversation with those who will be most affected by them. This may include family members who are directly involved, such as spouses and children who have ideas about date nights or family devotional time. Other people can also have a voice in your covenant, including church/ministry staff whom you work with regularly or who are in authority over you. Seek their wisdom and be thoughtful about their responses. Along the way, it may be helpful for church members to understand that pastors are doing their work when they go away on personal retreats a few times a year. If you have the support of others, the process will be significantly more life-giving and create less conflict.

- With the Wesleyan tradition of spiritual companionship in mind, we recommend sharing the covenant with at least one other person or small group regularly (every two to eight weeks, depending on the relationship). This may be incorporated into a time of shared spiritual practice or some form of intentional soul conversation with a spiritual companion.

- You will need to evaluate and revise your covenant at regular intervals, depending on the demands of the season of the year (e.g., summer versus Lent) and other circumstances of life and work.

In one of our seminaries, doctor of ministry students who are leaders in various ministry positions develop and maintain a personal covenant over a period of two years and then report to one another about their progress. They come to campus for a number of weeks each year and meet an hour each day in small groups, sharing their covenants and participating in spiritual practices. At other times of the year, they post personal comments and respond to one another on each area of relationship on a dedicated Facebook page. Many participants have noted that sharing a covenant with peers in ministry has become a lifeline for them. Most come to trust these peers, letting go of their masks and the competitiveness they might otherwise feel. This kind of spiritual companioning is remarkably fruitful. It exemplifies what we believe God intends for us all to experience.

Personal Covenant: Questions for Reflection

- *How are you attending to your relationship with God?* Do you experience God as a friend or spiritual companion? What is your prayer life like? Are you primarily praying or studying Scripture for the sake of ministry, or do you spend time with God just for you? Do you keep a Sabbath day? Do you sense God's presence or God's absence more often right now? Why might that be? Is there a person you trust who can listen while you talk about your relationship with God?

- *How are you attending to your relationship with yourself?* How would you assess your physical, emotional, and psychological well-being? Are you eating well and exercising? Do you need psychological counseling or any other kind of care? Do you have a hobby or regular practice that helps you unwind? Do you have any unhealthy patterns that need attention? If so, what are those patterns doing to you and to those around you?

- *How are you attending to your relationships with those who are closest to you?* Do you listen to your family members? Do you have fun with them? Do you Sabbath with them? Do you have friends—real friends with whom you can be your true self? Who provides you with the spiritual companionship that you need? How do you provide spiritual companionship for those God has given you to love—your spouse, children, parents, or friends?

- *How are you attending to your relationships in ministry?* What about ministry excites you? What do you love to do? Do you have a sense of your own joy meeting the world's needs? How can you provide spiritual companionship through specific tasks of ministry, such as pastoral care, teaching, worship leading, evangelism and service, and so on? Is there anyone God is calling you to companion in a particular way right now? Is God inviting you to companion any of your peers in ministry?

Offering Spiritual Companionship to the Congregation

Working through the last category of relationship raises questions about how ministers become spiritual companions to the community of faith within its programmatic structures. What we have discovered from experience and observation is that the very same things making spiritual direction effective one-with-one can be applied to the tasks of ministry. This means that sermons may draw upon spiritual direction questions for reflection, worship can incorporate brief periods of silence for reflection on discerning God's presence, and interactions in the church parking lot may include a question or two about a person's spiritual well-being. Really any task of ministry is a place for spiritual companioning.

This is an organic process, and each leader will apply the principles and practices we have discussed according to his or her own context and artistry. What is important to remember is the need to begin slowly, introducing new practices and ways of relating carefully so that people understand the purpose. One pastor incorporated what he had learned about spiritual companioning into his ministry by setting aside all meetings and tasks for several weeks (with the support of the congregation) and taking time to have a soul conversation with nearly every member of his church. It was a remarkable, life-giving experience that transformed his knowledge of the people and his ministry to the congregation in the months that followed.

Exploring the Stories of Congregations

Tiana took her first ministry position right out of seminary. She had been interested in church work since her late teens and, with the encouragement of her former pastor, chose to pursue a youth and family ministry degree. After completing an internship at Second Street Church near the seminary, she jumped at the opportunity to join their staff when they officially offered her a position. Tiana had a passion for youth, and it showed. She was soon deeply invested in the lives of students in her congregation, quickly coming to think of them as her community. Between social media and cell phones, Tiana was also available to the kids almost around the clock. She was a great listener, something they came to recognize quickly.

The church members regularly expressed their appreciation for Tiana's dedication and commitment to their youth. Parents sought her out for advice, and she was often invited to family meals, musical performances, and sporting events. While she loved her work, Tiana began to find that her church social calendar was squeezing out other relationships in her life. Visits to her family, who lived about two hours away, were increasingly few and far between. There was always another event to attend or student to visit that kept her in town. College and seminary friendships that had once been so important to her were sliding down her list of priorities. Many of her friends had moved elsewhere, and she found that she barely made the effort to keep up with them beyond a brief phone call or Facebook post. The church provided more than enough social connections, especially for an introvert like Tiana.

After Tiana had been in the position about eighteen months, the senior pastor began to notice that she appeared weary and had become increasingly distant. At a church staff meeting, he took the opportunity to ask her how she was doing, and if she had seen any of her family or friends from home recently. Tiana saw the concern on his face, and she found herself bursting into tears. The rise of emotion embarrassed her; she liked to appear strong and capable before the others, especially since she was the youngest person on staff, but she made a decision in that moment to share what she had been feeling for some time. In her words, "I had to be honest with these people who cared about me. I loved the work I was doing, but I knew that I wouldn't be able to keep going in it if something didn't change. After all those years in seminary, I wasn't about to give up on my dream of working in ministry. Being vulnerable before the others was difficult. I wasn't sure what they would think of me, but I had to take the risk that they would understand what I was going through."

Tiana was able to explain that she felt overwhelmed by the social demands of her position. She described her feelings of loss over relationships that she no longer made time for, and her habit of checking her phone messages and email constantly. She had finally come to accept that she was exhausted when she saw a couple of church youth from a distance at a local restaurant, and she slipped into the bathroom so they wouldn't see her. Tiana felt the warmth and understanding of the other staff members, and the senior pastor suggested that they meet to discuss how they could revise her responsibilities to make the work more manageable. There was another minister at the church in the recent past who had nearly burned out before leaving the congregation, and they did not want to see that happen again.

The senior pastor began to mentor Tiana, helping her think through her schedule and urging her to take a weekly Sabbath when she could leave town to visit family and friends if she chose to, and when she would not be available to the youth in person or by phone. He suggested vacation time and a personal retreat for refreshment and renewal. She also started meeting with a local spiritual director and came to realize that this kind of soul conversation was what she thought ministry was supposed to be about. The conversation quickly moved beyond surface concerns to a deeper discussion of her inner thoughts and feelings and God's presence with her. Tiana felt a passion for ministry begin to rekindle, and she started practicing simple soul conversations with the youth and young adults in her congregation. She began learning about spiritual direction and other spiritual practices. Change did not come easily for Tiana, but she felt more and more like herself as time went on, and she had a renewed sense that God would not abandon her. She could again imagine a life in ministry over the long term and a future serving others as a spiritual companion.

Exercising Our Companionship: Beginning a Ministry of Spiritual Companioning

We offer these guidelines to help congregations and their leaders consider how they might want to begin developing an intentional ministry of spiritual companioning.[14]

Forms of Companionship

1. Spiritual companionship in the congregation may occur in the contexts of intentional one-with-one or group spiritual direction or spiritual friendship interactions.

2. One-with-one spiritual direction provides in-depth engagement between a trained spiritual director and a directee but typically limits the number of persons who can participate due to the time constraints of the director.

3. Group spiritual direction is generally led by a trained spiritual director or, at minimum, someone who has experience with spiritual direction. The group setting allows for participation of several persons and helps build congregational community but provides less privacy and individual time.

4. Spiritual friendship is a peer relationship that involves an intentional reciprocal interaction that encourages mutual conversation with another about one's experience of God. Ideally, participants will have some opportunity to learn about and experiment with the process of listening prayerfully and responding reflectively.

5. Spiritual companionship may also occur more informally in various contexts in the congregation, home, and community, including church staff meetings, retreats, Christian formation or education classes, small groups, age-based gatherings, family life, and so on.

6. Persons interested in becoming spiritual directors will find training opportunities through seminaries and independent institutes. Spiritual Directors International is an interfaith organization that provides helpful resources for locating spiritual directors and training programs.

Leadership and Structures

1. *Denominational organizations* may play a significant role in promoting relationships of spiritual companionship for the support and accountability of all pastors. Leaders may want to consider the following:

14. These guidelines draw upon a document prepared for the Mennonite Church by Marcus Smucker and Marlene Kropf.

a. Having a clear statement of policy concerning spiritual accountability for pastors

b. Creating a list of spiritual directors who are spiritually and theologically compatible with the denominational body and are available to serve

c. Helping to identify appropriate language and resources for developing a culture of spiritual companioning within the denomination

d. Establishing a procedure for recognizing spiritual directors who work within and on behalf of the denomination

2. *Pastors* have a role in providing for the spiritual life of the congregation. This may include the following:

a. Being a spiritual companion and guide for the congregation as a whole

b. Seeking spiritual direction and other forms of companionship for themselves

c. Teaching and preaching about spiritual companioning relationships, including biblical models, theological instruction, and personal experiences

d. Initiating a program of spiritual companioning within the congregation, including one or more forms of companionship

e. Assembling and leading one or two spiritual direction groups that meet regularly for a given length of time (e.g., every other week for two years)

f. Providing one-with-one spiritual direction for a limited number of members with the following considerations:

- Limiting this ministry to two to four members in any given period, depending upon time constraints

- Selecting carefully those whom the pastor can constructively engage in such a relationship

- Limiting the duration of the direction relationship to approximately two years

- Communicating this policy clearly so members will know that the pastor will also be potentially available to others in the congregation

- Being intentional about the transition of members from directees to parishioners

3. *Congregational leaders* have a role in providing for a ministry of spiritual companionship in the structures and programs of the congregation. This may include the following:

a. Supporting a ministry of one-with-one or group spiritual direction provided by the pastoral staff

b. Inviting a trained lay spiritual director to be adjunct to the pastoral care team

c. Inviting and providing space for a lay spiritual director to serve the congregation as an independent practitioner with accountability to a leadership group within the congregation (including the pastor)

d. Preparing a list of recommended spiritual directors for interested congregational members

e. Developing a ministry of spiritual direction as a mission beyond the congregation

Practical Considerations for Congregations

1. *Language*: What terms will be used to define the ministry, such as "companionship," "guidance," "friendship," or "direction"?

2. *Structure*: How will this ministry be lodged within the structure of the congregation? Will it be considered a ministry of pastoral care or Christian education/formation? Who will be responsible for providing access to facilities and other specific needs?

3. *Reporting*: What reporting and accountability will be required? Is the ministry under the authority of a pastor or another leadership group, and do congregational leaders stay in contact with the spiritual director(s)?

4. *Confidentiality*: Will there be times when it is wise or necessary to consult with a pastor concerning situations encountered in spiritual direction?

5. *Fees*: Would lay spiritual directors be collecting a fee or contributing their time as part of their voluntary service?

6. *Supervision*: What would be the congregation's policy regarding the necessity for spiritual direction supervision? If supervision is required or expected, who would pay for it?

7. *Insurance*: Would spiritual directors be covered under the general malpractice insurance of the congregation, or would each director need to get his or her own insurance?

For Further Reading

Guenther, Margaret. *At Home in the World: A Rule of Life for the Rest of Us*. New York: Seabury Books, 2006. A book, written for spiritual leaders and laypeople alike, that discusses the ancient practice of developing a "rule of life" for the contemporary context.

Johnson, Ben, and Andrew Dreitcer. *Beyond the Ordinary: Spirituality for Church Leaders*. Grand Rapids: Eerdmans, 2001. A text that provides a framework for spirituality and spiritual formation in ministry by addressing important concerns, such as ministry roles and metaphors, as well as reflection on prayer, mission, and Scripture.

Northcutt, Kay. *Kindling Desire for God: Preaching as Spiritual Direction*. Minneapolis: Fortress, 2009. A book that develops a practical theological perspective on preaching as spiritual direction and describes specific skills that directors may employ in the process of preparing and delivering sermons.

Oswald, Roy. *Clergy Self-Care: Finding a Balance for Effective Ministry*. Herndon, VA: Alban Institute, 1995. A resource that offers various self-assessment tools, real-life experiences, and self-care strategies in its exploration of the process of nurturing personal health and well-being while also caring for others.

Peterson, Eugene. *The Contemplative Pastor: Returning to the Art of Spiritual Direction*. Grand Rapids: Eerdmans, 1993. A book for church leaders that artfully addresses topics such as the cure of souls, the language of prayer, the ministry of small talk, and the sabbatical.

Rice, Howard. *The Pastor as Spiritual Guide*. Nashville: Upper Room, 1998. A work that focuses on providing spiritual guidance through many tasks of pastoral ministry from preaching to pastoral care to administration.

Stairs, Jean. *Listening for the Soul: Pastoral Care and Spiritual Direction*. Minneapolis: Fortress, 2000. A book that offers helpful principles, resources, and techniques for pastoral care and spiritual direction in the context of various life stages and life events.

Bibliography

Ammerman, Nancy Tatom. *Sacred Stories, Spiritual Tribes: Finding Religion in Everyday Life*. New York: Oxford University Press, 2013.

Baker, Frank. *The Works of John Wesley*. Vol. 25, *Letters I (1721–1739)*. Nashville: Abingdon, 1980.

———. *The Works of John Wesley*. Vol. 26, *Letters II (1740–1755)*. Nashville: Abingdon, 1987.

Bartholomew, Craig, and Michael Goheen. *The Drama of Scripture: Finding Our Place in the Biblical Story*. Grand Rapids: Baker Academic, 2004.

Bauckham, Richard. *The Bible and Mission: Christian Witness in a Postmodern World*. Grand Rapids: Baker Academic, 2003.

Bonhoeffer, Dietrich. *The Cost of Discipleship*. New York: Touchstone, 1995.

———. *Letters and Papers from Prison*. New York: Touchstone, 1997.

———. *Life Together: The Classic Exploration of Faith in Community*. San Francisco: HarperOne, 2009.

Botonaki, Effie. "Seventeenth-Century Englishwomen's Spiritual Diaries: Self-Examination, Covenanting, and Account Keeping." *Sixteenth Century Journal* 30, no. 1 (Spring 1999): 3–21.

Bunton, Peter. *Cell Groups and House Churches: What History Teaches Us*. Lititz, PA: House to House, 2001.

Bunyan, John. *Grace Abounding to the Chief of Sinners: With Other Spiritual Autobiographies*, ed. John Stachniewski. Oxford World Classics Paperback. Oxford: Oxford University Press, 1998. Reprint, 2008.

———. *The Pilgrim's Progress*. Mineola, NY: Dover, 2003. First published 1678.

Caldwell, Patricia. *The Puritan Conversion Narrative: The Beginnings of American Expression*. New York: Cambridge University Press, 1983.

Carr, Nicholas. *The Shallows: What the Internet Is Doing to Our Brains*. New York: Norton, 2011.

Coles, Robert, ed. *Dietrich Bonhoeffer: Writings*. Maryknoll, NY: Orbis Books, 1998.

Drury, Amanda Hontz. *Saying Is Believing: The Necessity of Testimony in Adolescent Spiritual Development*. Downers Grove, IL: InterVarsity, 2015.

Dunn, James. *The Theology of Paul the Apostle*. Grand Rapids: Eerdmans, 1998.

Elder, Glen. *Children of the Great Depression*. Chicago: University of Chicago Press, 1974.

Elder, Glen, and Janet Giele. *The Craft of Life Course Research*. New York: Guilford, 2009.

Entner, Roger. "Under-Aged Texting Usage and Actual Cost." Nielsen Company. "Newswire." January 27, 2010. http://www.nielsen.com/us/en/newswire/2010/under-aged-texting-usage-and-actual-cost.html.

Erikson, Erik. *Childhood and Society*. New York: Norton, 1950.

Fee, Gordon. *Paul, the Spirit, and the People of God*. Peabody, MA: Hendrickson, 1996.

Fischer, Kathleen. *Autumn Gospel: Women in the Second Half of Life*. Mahwah, NJ: Paulist Press, 1995.

———. *Winter Grace: Spirituality and Aging*. Nashville: Upper Room, 1998.

Florence, Anna Carter. *Preaching as Testimony*. Louisville: Westminster John Knox, 2007.

Foster, Richard J. *Streams of Living Water: Essential Practices from the Six Great Traditions of Christian Faith*. New York: HarperSanFrancisco, 1998.

Freudenberger, Herbert J., with Geraldine Richelson. *Burn-Out: The High Cost of High Achievement*. Garden City, NY: Anchor, 1980.

Friedman, Meyer, and Ray Rosenman. *Type A Behavior and Your Heart*. New York: Alfred A. Knopf, 1974.

Gillum, Tameka, Cris Sullivan, and Deborah Bybee. "The Importance of Spirituality in the Lives of Domestic Violence Survivors." *Violence against Women* 12, no. 3 (March 2006): 240–50.

Goodhead, Andrew. *A Crown and a Cross: The Rise, Development, and Decline of the Methodist Class Meeting in Eighteenth-Century England*. Eugene, OR: Wipf & Stock, 2010.

Guenther, Margaret. *At Home in the World: A Rule of Life for the Rest of Us*. New York: Seabury Books, 2006.

———. *Toward Holy Ground: Spiritual Directions for the Second Half of Life*. Cambridge, MA: Cowley, 1995.

Hauerwas, Stanley, and L. Gregory Jones, eds. *Why Narrative? Readings in Narrative Theology*. Eugene, OR: Wipf & Stock, 1997.

Henderson, D. Michael. *John Wesley's Class Meeting—A Model for Making Disciples*. Nappanee, IN: Evangel, 1997.

Hestenes, Roberta. *Using the Bible in Groups*. Philadelphia: Westminster, 1983.

Hoge, Dean R., and Jacqueline E. Wenger. *Pastors in Transition: Why Clergy Leave Local Church Ministry*. Grand Rapids: Eerdmans, 2005.

Hutchison, Elizabeth. *Dimensions of Human Behavior: The Changing Life Course*. 4th ed. Thousand Oaks, CA: Sage Publications, 2011.

Johnson, Ben Campbell. *Speaking of God: Evangelism as Initial Spiritual Guidance*. Louisville: Westminster John Knox, 1991.

Kelly, Thomas R. *A Testament of Devotion*. New York: Harper & Brothers, 1941.

Kline, Donald L. *Susanna Wesley: God's Catalyst for Revival*. Lima, OH: CSS Publishing, 1980.

Knights, Mark. "Diaries of the Seventeenth Century." British Broadcasting Corporation. Last updated February 17, 2011. http://www.bbc.co.uk/history/british/civil_war_revolution/diaries_01.shtml.

Lawrence, Brother. *The Practice of the Presence of God*. New abridged ed. New Kensington, PA: Whitaker House, 1982.

Leech, Kenneth. *Soul Friend: An Invitation to Spiritual Direction*. New York: HarperCollins, 1980.

Levinson, Daniel. *The Seasons of a Man's Life*. New York: Ballantine Books, 1978.

Lewis, C. S. *Mere Christianity*. New York: Macmillan, 1958.

Li, Jin. *Cultural Foundations of Learning: East and West*. Cambridge: Cambridge University Press, 2012.

Long, Thomas. *Testimony: Talking Ourselves into Being Christian*. San Francisco: Jossey-Bass, 2004.

Marquardt, Elizabeth. *Between Two Worlds: The Inner Lives of the Children of Divorce*. New York: Random House, 2005.

Martin, George. *Reading Scripture as the Word of God: Practical Approaches and Attitudes*. 4th ed. Ann Arbor, MI: Servant Books, 1998.

McPherson, Miller, Lynn Smith-Loven, and Matthew Brashears. "Social Isolation in America: Changes in Core Discussion Networks over Two Decades." *American Sociological Review* 71 (2006): 353–75.

Moen, Phyllis, and Elaine Hernandez. "Social Convoys: Studying Linked Lives in Time, Context, and Motion." In *The Craft of Life Course Research*, edited by Glen Elder and Janet Giele, 258–79. New York: Guilford, 2009.

Morgan, Edmund. *Visible Saints: The History of a Puritan Idea*. Ithaca, NY: Cornell University Press, 1963.

Newbigin, Lesslie. *The Finality of Christ*. London: SCM, 1969.

Osmer, Richard R. *Practical Theology: An Introduction*. Grand Rapids: Eerdmans, 2008.

———. *Teaching for Faith: A Guide for Teachers of Adult Classes*. Louisville: Westminster John Knox, 1992.

Outler, Albert C, ed. *John Wesley*. New York: Oxford University Press, 1980.

Palmer, Parker J. *Let Your Life Speak: Listening for the Voice of Vocation*. San Francisco: Jossey-Bass, 1999.

Peace, Richard. *Conversion in the New Testament: Paul and the Twelve*. Grand Rapids: Eerdmans, 1999.

———. *Holy Conversation: Talking about God in Everyday Life*. Downers Grove, IL: InterVarsity, 2006.

Peterson, Eugene. *The Message: The Bible in Contemporary Language*. Colorado Springs: NavPress, 2002.

———."Spirit Quest." *Christianity Today*, November 8, 1993, 27–30.

Placher, William C. *Jesus the Savior: The Meaning of Jesus Christ for Christian Faith*. Louisville: Westminster John Knox, 2001.

Putnam, Robert. *Bowling Alone: The Collapse and Revival of American Community*. New York: Simon & Schuster, 2001.

Putnam, Robert, and David Campbell. *American Grace: How Religion Divides and Unites Us*. New York: Simon & Schuster, 2010.

Rainie, Lee, and Barry Wellman. *Networked: The New Social Operating System*. Cambridge, MA: MIT Press, 2012.

Ranft, Patricia. *A Woman's Way: The Forgotten History of Women Spiritual Directors*. New York: Palgrave, 2001.

Reed, Angela H. *Quest for Spiritual Community: Reclaiming Spiritual Guidance for Contemporary Congregations*. New York: T&T Clark, 2011.

Reese, Martha Grace. *Unbinding the Gospel: Real Life Evangelism*. St. Louis: Chalice, 2008.

Rideout, Victoria J., Ulla G. Foehr, and Donald F. Roberts. "Generation M^2: Media in the Lives of 8- to 18-Year-Olds." Henry J. Kaiser Family Foundation. January 2010. https://kaiserfamilyfoundation.files.wordpress.com/2013/01/8010.pdf.

Rizzuto, Ana-Maria. *The Birth of the Living God: A Psychoanalytic Study*. Chicago: University of Chicago Press, 1981.

Ruffing, Janet. *To Tell the Sacred Tale: Spiritual Direction and Narrative*. New York: Paulist Press, 2011.

Saliers, Don. *Worship and Spirituality*. 2nd ed. Maryville, TN: OSL, 1996.

Sheehy, Gail. *Passages: Predictable Crises of Adult Life*. New York: Ballantine Books, 1976.

Silva, Jennifer M. "Young and Isolated." *New York Times*, June 23, 2013. SR7.

Steere, Douglas, V. *Quaker Spirituality: Selected Writings*. Mahwah, NJ: Paulist Press, 1984.

Stroup, George. *The Promise of Narrative Theology: Recovering the Gospel in the Church*. Atlanta: John Knox, 1981.

Stucky, Nathan. "Disorienting Grace: Sabbath, Youth, and the Potential of a Grace-Rooted Identity." PhD diss., Princeton Theological Seminary, 2015.

Tappert, Theodore G., ed. and trans. *Luther: Letters of Spiritual Counsel*. Vancouver: Regent College Publishing, 2003.

Treier, Daniel. *Introducing Theological Interpretation of Scripture: Recovering a Christian Practice*. Grand Rapids: Baker Academic, 2008.

Turkle, Sherry. *Alone Together: Why We Expect More from Technology and Less from Each Other*. New York: Basic Books, 2011.

Vest, Norvene. *Gathered in the Word: Praying the Scripture in Small Groups*. Nashville: Upper Room, 1996.

Walker-Moffat, Wendy. *The Other Side of the Asian American Success Story*. San Francisco: Jossey-Bass, 1995.

Watson, David Lowes. *Covenant Discipleship: Christian Formation through Mutual Accountability*. Eugene, OR: Wipf & Stock, 2002.

———. *The Early Methodist Class Meeting: Its Origins and Significance*. Nashville: Discipleship Resources, 1985.

Wellman, Barry. *Networks in the Global Village: Life in Contemporary Communities*. Boulder, CO: Westview, 1999.

White, Charles. "Concerning Earnest Christians: A Newly Discovered Letter of Martin Luther." *Currents in Theology and Mission* 10, no. 5 (1983): 273–82.

Willard, Dallas. *Hearing God: Developing a Conversational Relationship with God*. Downers Grove, IL: InterVarsity, 2012.

Winnicott, Donald. *The Maturational Processes and the Facilitating Environment: Studies in the Theory of Emotional Development*. London: Karnac, 1996.

———. *Playing and Reality*. London: Routledge, 2005.

Winseman, Albert L. "Congregational Engagement Ascends." Gallup. February 15, 2005. http://www.gallup.com/poll/14950/congregational-engagement-ascends.aspx.

World Health Organization. "Life Expectancy." 2013. http://apps.who.int/gho/data/node.main.688?lang=en.

Wright, N. T. *The New Testament and the People of God*. Minneapolis: Fortress, 1992.

Wuthnow, Robert. *After Heaven: Spirituality in America since the 1950s*. New ed. Berkeley: University of California Press, 1998.

———. *Sharing the Journey: Support Groups and America's New Quest for Community*. New York: Free Press, 1994.

Scripture Index

Old Testament

Genesis

1:27 5, 9
2:2 17
2:7 5
2:18 5
3 6
3:7 6, 8
3:8 6
3:8–9 6
3:9–13 8
3:12–13 6
3:17–19 6
3:24 6
4 6
11 6
12:2 82
24 6

Exodus

20 6
31:17 17

Deuteronomy

6:7 135
6:9 135
26:5–9 135

Joshua

24:2–13 135

1 Kings

19 159

2 Kings

3:11 159

Psalms

23 90
25 136
51 136
65:4 xiv
74 136
74:2 136
78:4 135
78:7–8 135
79 136
103:13–14 10
105 135
136 135

Proverbs

15:1 78

Isaiah

42:6 82
54:5 108
60:3 82

Jeremiah

3:20 108

Hosea

1:2 108

Esther

1:10–22 160
2:11 160
2:20 160, 161
4:4 160
4:14 161
4:17 162
8:2 161

New Testament

Matthew

5:14 82
5:48 65
7:9–11 5
16:18 162
18:15–18 19n5
18:20 12
22:37–39 11
25:14–30 106
26:33 163
26:69–75 162

Mark

1:35–37 32
4:7 56
6:52 137
8:17–21 137

8:27–34 137
8:31 137
8:31–10:45 137
9:12 137
9:31 137
10:33–34 137
10:42–44 137
10:45 137
10:46–13:37 137
10:46–52 137
11:1–10 137
12:35–37 137
14:1–15:39 137
15:39 137
16:15 137

Luke

5:16 32
18:15–16 73
24:13–35 110

John

14–16 7
14:15–17 7
14:26 32, 109
14:23 12
15:1–7 108
15:1–11 18
15:12–17 108
17: 21–23 18
21 162

Acts

1:12–26 32, 164
2:42–47 32, 82
2:46–47 82
2:47 82
4:32–37 82
4:34 82
5:1–11 32
6:2–4 164
9:5 57
9:9 57
9:10–19 58
9:26–27 58
11:25–26 58
13:2–3 58
16:1–5 58
17:28 18

Romans

5:6–8 10
8:28 18, 74
12:10 48
12:16 48
13:8 48
15:7 49
15:16 11, 66

1 Corinthians

3:2 106
3:10 32
4:16 183
4:17 58
13:1–2 44
13:12 42
15:28 14

2 Corinthians

3:18 7, 65
5:17–20 12
13:11 49

Galatians

5:13 49
5:22–23 32, 44
6:2 32, 49

Ephesians

4:6 67
4:15 18
4:26 77
4:32 49
5:21 49
5:21–33 108

Philippians

2:19 58
3:17 153

Colossians

1:17 67
3:13 49

2 Thessalonians

3:9 153

James

4:11 49
5:9 49
5:16 49

1 Thessalonians

3:2 58
5:11 33, 49
5:15 49

1 Timothy

2:5 36

Titus

1:5–9 154

Hebrews

2:14–18 11
2:18–19 11
3:13 49
7:25 11
10:24 49
10:25 49

1 Peter

2:5 66
2:9 11
4:8 49
9 66

1 John

3:16 49
4:7 49
4:7–8 10

Revelation

19:7–9 108
21:3–4 6

Subject Index

accountability, 115–17, 119–20
Ammerman, Nancy, 103–5, 116
Anabaptist, 33, 54, 61, 83
Ananias, 57–58
Anglican tradition, 61, 116
Augustine, 9

Barnabas, 58, 93
Baxter, Richard, 61
Bethge, Eberhard, 34–35, 46, 164
Bonhoeffer, Dietrich, xiv, 34–37, 40–46, 164
brokenness, 6–8, 35–36
Brother Lawrence, 43, 103
Bunyan, John, 139–40
burnout, 167–68
busyness, 55–56

Catholic tradition, xvii, 60
character formation, 44–45
confession, 37–45, 60–61, 85, 114–15, 140, 155
congregation
    and building spiritual community, 32–33,
        79–81
    climate of, 39–41
    as "good enough" mother, 30–31, 40–41, 117
consumer-oriented culture, xv, 29
Council of Trent, 82
covenant, 6–7, 64–65, 71, 81–82, 86, 88, 92, 94,
    119–20, 168–70
cultural context, 2–5, 27–31, 54–57, 78–81,
    103–9, 129–34, 152–58
cultural isolation, 2–4, 152–53
culture of spiritual conversation, 41–42

desert fathers and mothers, 47, 59
digital revolution, 80–81, 142–43
discernment, 59–68, 103–21
dwelling-oriented spirituality, xvi, 51

Elijah, 109, 159–60
Emmaus Road, 109–11, 117
empathy, 16, 23,
Erikson, Erik, 128
Esther, 160–62
examen, the practice, 118–19

face-to-face relationships, 6, 80–82
false self, 30–31, 40
fear, 9, 13, 54–55, 110
Fox, George, 61, 164–67
Freudenberger, Herbert, 167–68

history of spiritual direction, 59–61
Hoge, Dean, 152–57, 160
home (as a theological theme), 8–14, 31
"hurry sickness," 56

Ignatius of Loyola, 60, 118
Inner Light, 166
intimacy, 9, 42, 48, 53, 72, 82, 87, 97–98

Jesus Christ
    as healer, 142, 144, 162–63
    as mediator, 11, 32, 36
    as messiah, 57, 111, 136–38
    modeling friendship with god, 108–9
    presence in human relationships, 12–13

as reconciler, 7, 12, 31– 32, 39, 81–82, 88
as savior, 10, 136–38
as Son of God, 136–37
as Son of Man, 137
as spiritual companion, 109–13
as teacher, 57

Kelly, Thomas, 166
kerygmatic, 136–38
koinonia, 81

lectio divina, 43, 48, 90–91, 120–21, 122–24
Lewis, C. S., 83–85
life course theory, 127–34
life cycle theory, 128–30
listening, 14–17, 65–66, 88, 149
love
    as the church's mission, 89
    of God, 10–14
    in Scripture, 48–49, 163
Luther, Martin, 33, 60, 83–84, 120–21

metaphors for God, 166
Methodist tradition, 33, 84–85, 138
ministers,
    and life on a pedestal, 153–56, 162, 166–67
    need for community, 155–57
    self-care, 157, 164, 168
Mordecai, 160–61
Moses, 103, 109

narrative of Scripture, 6, 134–38

one-anothering, 32, 48–49

Palmer, Parker, 157
paraclete or Holy Spirit, 7–8, 13–14, 32, 81,
    109, 112, 116, 144
pastoral care, 17, 21, 174–75
pastoral counseling, 21–22
Paul the Apostle, 32–33, 44, 57–58, 92–93, 106,
    153
personal narrative, 138–142
Peterson, Eugene, xv
Peter the Apostle, 57, 162–64, 92–93, 136–37,
    162–64
practice-oriented spirituality, xvii
prayerful listening, 15–16, 24

preaching, 22, 78
presence, xx
    of God in our lives, 67–68, 103– 9, 118–19,
        166
    of God in Scripture, 12, 31–32, 109–13
    of the spiritual director, 14–18, 23–24
Protestant tradition, 8–11, 33–34, 59–62, 78,
    82–85, 113–21, 138–40, 164–67
Putnam, Robert, 3–4

Quaker, 61, 164–67
questions in spiritual companioning, 17–18,
    67–68, 72, 96–97, 99–100, 110

reconciliation, 7, 10, 12
reflection, 17–18, 148–49
restoration, 38–39
Rule of Saint Benedict, 59

Sabbath, 17–18, 99, 170
sacramental relationship, 13
seeker-oriented spirituality, xv–xvii, 29–30, 165
shame, 2, 6, 8–9
sleep deprivation, 55–56
social isolation, 3–5, 61, 152–53, 157
sola scriptura, xviii, 121
speaking the truth in love, 18–19, 45, 61
spiritual autobiography, 140, 148
spirituality language, definitions of, xix–xx
spiritual practices, xv–xvii, 20, 43–44
studying Christian spirituality, 43, 140
support groups, 22–23, 85, 89

teaching, 22, 94–95, 174
Timothy, 58
training in spiritual direction, 71, 74
transformation, 5–8, 81–82
trinitarian theology, 14, 31
true self, 41, 170

welcoming, 40, 63– 64, 71
Wenger, Jacqueline, 152–57, 160
Wesley, Charles, 113–14
Wesley, John, 33, 84–85, 89, 113–17, 119–20
Wesley, Susanna, 113–15
Winnicott, D. W., 30, 40, 62
worship, 22, 26, 29, 47, 105, 135
Wuthnow, Robert, xv–xvii, 79–81

Made in the USA
Middletown, DE
21 August 2019